IMAGES of America
AUBURN CORRECTIONAL FACILITY

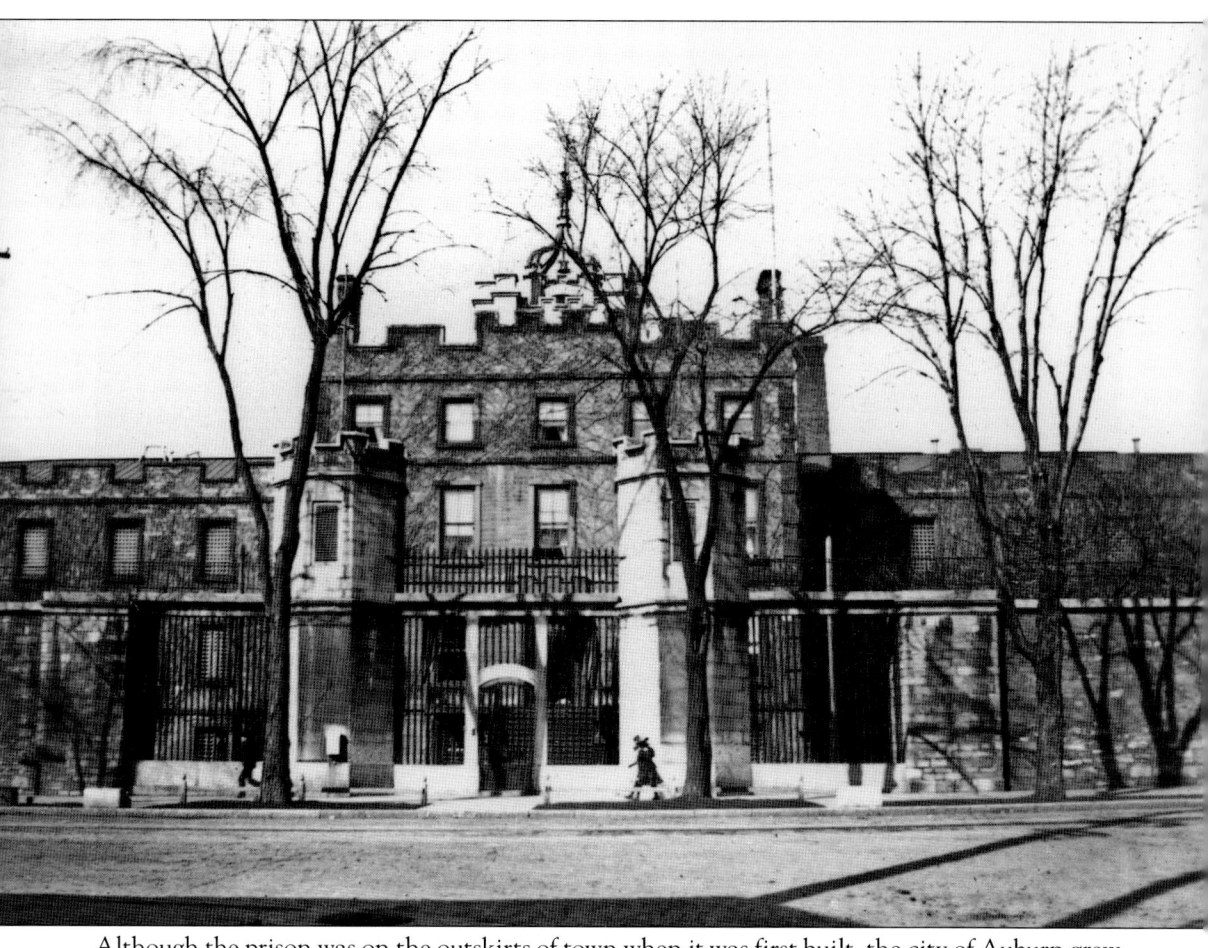

Although the prison was on the outskirts of town when it was first built, the city of Auburn grew up around the prison. Generations of Auburn residents walked past the prison daily on their way to school, work, or church. This photograph from a glass-plate negative was taken from the railroad depot across the street from the prison, around 1905. (Courtesy of the Cayuga Museum of History and Art.)

ON THE COVER: Lockstep marching was a key component of the Auburn System. Every step an inmate took outside of his cell was regulated. Men marched in formation, each man's hands under the arms of the man in front of him, all stepping at the same time. The keepers, or the guards who dealt directly with prisoners, carried canes to signal to the inmates without speaking. Here principal keeper John Martin supervises a line of inmates in their iconic striped uniforms, around 1880. (Courtesy of the Cayuga Museum of History and Art.)

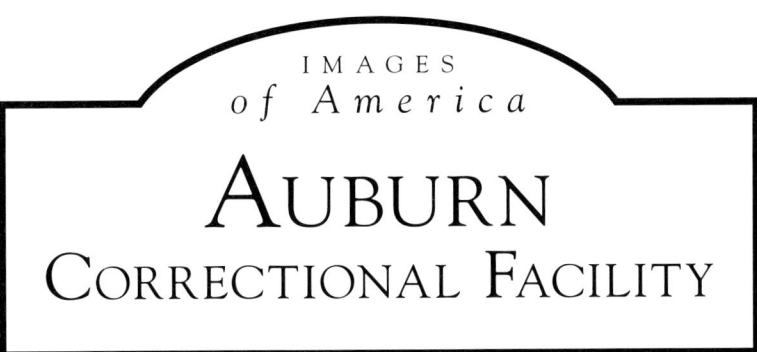

AUBURN CORRECTIONAL FACILITY

Eileen McHugh for the Cayuga Museum
Foreword by Michael Pettigrass

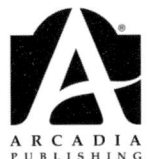

Copyright © 2010 by Eileen McHugh for the Cayuga Museum
ISBN 978-0-7385-7252-9

Published by Arcadia Publishing
Charleston SC, Chicago IL, Portsmouth NH, San Francisco CA

Printed in the United States of America

Library of Congress Control Number: 2009936092

For all general information contact Arcadia Publishing at:
Telephone 843-853-2070
Fax 843-853-0044
E-mail sales@arcadiapublishing.com
For customer service and orders:
Toll-Free 1-888-313-2665

Visit us on the Internet at www.arcadiapublishing.com

*This book is dedicated to the people
of the New York State Department of Corrections,
who dedicate their careers to keeping the rest of us safe.*

Contents

Acknowledgments		6
Foreword		7
Introduction		8
1.	Auburn Becomes a Prison Town	11
2.	The Auburn System	17
3.	Working for Copper John	23
4.	Early 20th Century	31
5.	The Asylum and Women's Prison	61
6.	The Electric Chair	69
7.	Thomas Mott Osborne and Prison Reform	73
8.	Deadly Riots in 1929	93
9.	The Modern Prison	103
10.	Auburn Correctional Facility Today	121

ACKNOWLEDGMENTS

This book is a product of the work of a great number of people over a great deal of time, people who recognized the importance of Auburn Prison's history and made an effort to preserve it. Those of us who want to see what the prison was like under the Auburn System owe a debt of gratitude to the unnamed warden who allowed a stereoscopic publisher to document the prison story in the new medium of photography in the 1850s. The history of the prison owes much to Walter Long, the founding director of the Cayuga Museum of History and Art, who began collecting the material history of the prison in 1936. It was Professor Long who convinced Charles Rattigan, who kept albums of photographs from his tenure as warden, that those albums belonged in the museum's collection. Principal keeper John Martin was an amateur photographer, and his grandson, Fred Kerr, has graciously shared those photographs with the museum. Capt. Richard Rourke and counselor Michael Pettigrass have both worked for several years to collect and document the stories of the prison. Both generously shared their work with the Cayuga Museum.

No history of Auburn Prison can be discussed without acknowledging the work of John Miskell. An employee of Auburn Prison from 1947 through 1980, Miskell held numerous positions throughout his career and retired as deputy superintendent of programs. Miskell's abiding interest in the history of the prison led him to be known to scholars and prison buffs alike as the prison historian. Miskell worked for decades researching and recording the history of the prison, and he provided a living link to the old-timers who were still on the job when he started just after World War II. John Miskell's extensive writings on the history of Auburn Prison can be read on the extraordinary New York Corrections History Web site, maintained by Thomas McCarthy, www.correctionhistory.org. John Miskell passed on in 2006, but his tireless attention to preserving the history of Auburn Prison made this book possible.

Unless otherwise noted, all images appear courtesy of the Cayuga Museum of History and Art.

Foreword

As the facility historian for what is now Auburn Correctional Facility, I can proudly say that our prison has truly stood the test of time. Since its first days in 1817, when Auburn Prison accepted its first prisoners, to our current days and forward, Auburn Prison has maintained inmates for 192 consecutive years. This is no small feat. One would likely have a hard time finding any business, let alone a prison, that can boast keeping its doors open 24 hours a day, 365 days a year for 192 years and counting. That being said, for better or worse, Auburn Prison has seen many changes, some obvious and some that took decades to evolve. As a physical structure, not much remains from the earliest days of construction. However, upon entering the facility, the first steps off of the sidewalk still take people between two "castle-like" stone turrets, reminding them of a bygone era. Should one glance up from street level, they would still be greeted by Copper John, the copper statue of a sentinel continental soldier atop the administration building that has stood guard since 1848.

Positive public perception is not usually synonymous with running a prison. Due to the nature of the business of maintaining maximum-security inmates, it is likely that media attention would only be drawn when something unpleasant has happened. Yet, for the most part, Auburn Prison has done well in maintaining business without much hoopla in its 192 years. However, it would be difficult to operate any prison for so long without drawing some attention once in a while.

Who would have foreseen that Thomas Edison himself would have taken an interest in the method of execution of an Auburn inmate? Or that the assassin of a president of the United States (William McKinley) would end up executed in the Auburn electric chair? For fun, Buffalo Bill Cody brought his entire Wild West show right smack dab into the middle of Auburn Prison's main recreation yard 100 years ago.

I was very pleased to be a part of the making of this book. Compiling photographs to represent 192 years of history turned out to be the easy part. Deciding which photographs to omit was much harder. It would seem impossible to cover every relevant event in one book; however, author Eileen McHugh has done a tremendous job of providing a great overview of our rich history. I am sure you will enjoy her efforts.

—Michael Pettigrass

INTRODUCTION

Auburn Correctional Facility has been open at the same spot in Auburn, New York, since 1817. It is now the oldest continually operating prison in the country. At the forefront of both the American and international penal systems since the day it opened, Auburn was the first prison in the world to house inmates in individual cells. Auburn was where the widely duplicated Auburn System of inmate management was developed. Auburn was the first prison to have a chaplain on staff, and it was the first prison to separate the mentally ill from the general prison population. On August 6, 1890, Auburn was the first prison in the world to execute an inmate in the electric chair.

The act authorizing the erection of a new state prison was passed in April 1816. Auburn boosters lobbied the state legislature for the placement of the proposed prison in Auburn. Four men—Samuel Dill, David Hyde, Ebenezer Beach, and John Beach—donated land to the state as a site for the new prison. Work started on the main building and the prison wall in 1816. The state granted the authority to use convict labor in building the prison in April 1817, both to relieve the crowded jails and to save the wages of free workmen. The first 53 inmates arrived in 1817 and were immediately put to work on the building.

The construction of the prison went on for several years under the direction of William Brittin. The state inspectors appointed Brittin as the first agent and warden of Auburn Prison in 1818. It was Brittin who designed the north wing at Auburn Prison, completed in 1821, which was made up entirely of solitary cells. It became the model for most American prisons.

The Auburn System was designed to prevent the corruption of one prisoner by another. The goal was to totally isolate each prisoner while forcing him to work for the prison's profit. The Auburn System was based on complete silence, strictly enforced with the threat of the whip. Prisoners were forbidden to communicate with each other in any way. Such a system, which violated the most basic human nature, could not be maintained without extreme physical cruelty. One goal of the Auburn System was to have the prisoners defray the costs of their incarceration through their own labor. For decades, the prison shops at Auburn produced shoes, coverlets, clocks, clothing, agricultural implements, furniture, and more, with much of it sold in downtown Auburn. The contract labor system was discontinued at Auburn Prison in 1890. It was replaced by the state use system in which inmates were "to manufacture articles solely for the use of all state departments, institutions, and political subdivisions."

Auburn prison shops are still on the state use system. Under this system, the shops at Auburn Prison have made brooms and furniture, metal bed frames, baskets, clothing for inmates, and blankets. In 1920, the license plate shop opened. Every license plate in the State of New York is still made behind the walls of Auburn Prison.

In 1855, a growing reform movement opposed housing the mentally ill with common criminals. The New York State Legislature approved an expenditure of $20,000 to build a separate asylum for the mentally ill at Auburn Prison in 1857. The asylum opened in February 1859. It was immediately adjacent to Auburn Prison but surrounded by its own 12-foot wall. In 1879, the state asylum for insane criminals held 121 inmates, 109 men and 12 women, less than its maximum capacity of 160. With rising costs, facilities available elsewhere, and a growing need for a women's prison, the state asylum in Auburn closed in 1893. The buildings were converted to the state prison for women, which opened the following year.

Women were received at Auburn Prison starting in 1825 and were confined in a large room in the attic of the south wing. The first matron ever employed in any New York State prison was Lucinda Foot, who was hired by the warden of Auburn Prison for $16 a month in 1832. With 125 rooms and accommodations for as many as 250 women, the women's prison served the entire state until 1934.

Auburn Prison again made corrections history when it became the site of the world's first use of the electric chair in the late 1800s. On August 7, 1881, a man in Buffalo, New York, accidentally killed himself by touching a generator. A local dentist, Alfred P. Southwick, became fascinated with the man's death. Southwick became a vocal advocate for the use of electricity when instant death is warranted. In 1886, New York governor David Hill established a commission to investigate and report the most humane and practical method of carrying into effect the sentence of death in capital cases—the Gerry Commission was also known as the Death Commission. Alfred Southwick was appointed to the three-member commission. The commission's final report recommended electrocution as the official method of capital punishment. In June 1888, the bill making death by electricity New York State's official method of execution was signed into law.

In March 1889, William Kemmler killed his lover, Tillie Ziegler, with a hatchet. He went to trial in Buffalo in May 1889 and was convicted of murder in the first degree. On May 13, Judge Henry Childs sentenced Kemmler to die by electricity. Kemmler was executed in the wooden electric chair on August 6, 1890, while a crowd of hundreds of reporters and onlookers waited outside the prison. Between 1890 and 1916, when New York concentrated all capital punishment at Sing Sing, 55 people were electrocuted in Auburn Prison. In all, 686 men and nine women died in the electric chair in New York between 1890 and 1963, the date of the last execution in New York State.

Auburn Prison was the birthplace of the Mutual Welfare League, an organization designed to better the lives of inmates and facilitate rehabilitation. Thomas Mott Osborne was appointed chairman of a commission on prison reform in 1913 and arranged to go into Auburn Prison undercover to get a glimpse at prison life. Entering the prison on September 29, 1913, under the name Tom Brown, he stayed for one week and lived as a regular inmate. His incarceration turned Osborne into a lifelong advocate of prison reform. He believed that the prison should be treated as a community and that the prisoners should have some say in governing that community. He was the driving force behind the creation of the Mutual Welfare League, which was established at Auburn Prison in December 1913. The league was successful in improving the lives of inmates, but there was no organized training program to develop leaders among the prisoners. Eventually, abuse crept into the system. When the Mutual Welfare League was blamed by many for the deadly 1929 riots, the league was abolished.

The worst troubles at Auburn Prison occurred on July 28 and December 11, 1929. In July, the prison was overcrowded. Although cell capacity was 1,285, there were 1,768 inmates. This overcrowding was due to longer sentences and the decrease in early release for good conduct. With longer sentences and the hope of parole slim, inmates had little to lose by rioting. On July 28, 1929, the hottest day of the year, inmates gained access to the arsenal. Four prisoners escaped over the wall. A riot spread, and the prison shops were set on fire, causing six buildings to be destroyed. After several hours, the rioters were subdued and locked in their cells. Two inmates were killed and one wounded. Five officers and three Auburn firemen were injured.

On December 11, the coldest day of the year, warden Edgar Jennings, six guards, and a foreman were taken hostage by a group of convicts. Some of the inmates were armed with guns that had been concealed since the July riot. Principal keeper George A. Durnford was shot and killed. Eventually, the rioters were subdued with the use of gas. Eight prisoners were killed, and nine people, including two inmates, were wounded. Three convicts were later executed at Sing Sing for their roles in the riots.

A third, less deadly riot took place at Auburn Prison in 1970. Responding in part to the civil rights movement, African American inmates at Auburn Prison demanded a Black Solidarity Day observance. When their request was denied, a number of inmates refused to go to work or school on November 4. They took over the main yard and gained control of three cell blocks, the kitchen, and mess hall areas. Protestors controlled the public address system in the main yard and made speeches all day. No attempt at escape was made. When inmates were told by deputy commissioner Harold Butler that state troopers were ready to retake the facility using force, they gave up.

In 1970, the facility's name was changed from Auburn Prison to Auburn Correctional Facility, to reflect a change in the philosophy of the penal system in New York State. The facility continues to be a walled, maximum security prison for male convicts. With more than 840 full-time employees, the state prison at Auburn is the largest employer in Cayuga County and Auburn's longest lasting business.

One
AUBURN BECOMES A PRISON TOWN

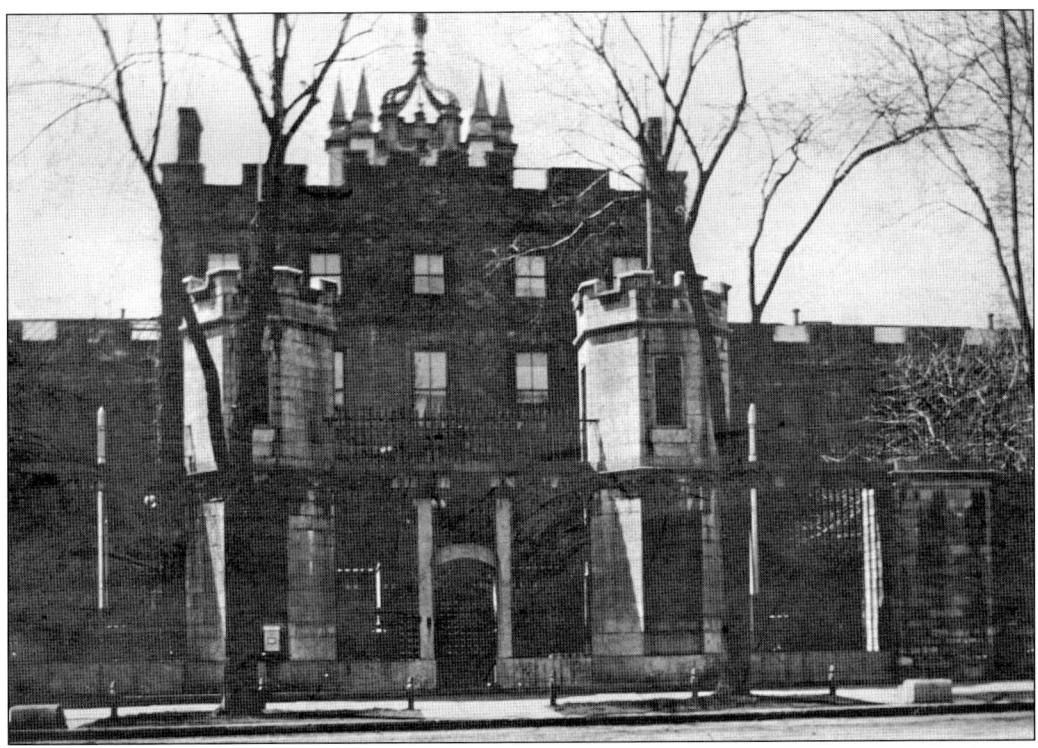

The leaders of the village of Auburn actively sought the location of the newly planned state prison in their community. The cornerstone for the stone wall of Auburn Prison was laid in 1816. At that time, the prison site was at the edge of the village. The construction work went on for several years, employing skilled tradesmen as well as convicts, and brought an unprecedented level of prosperity to Auburn.

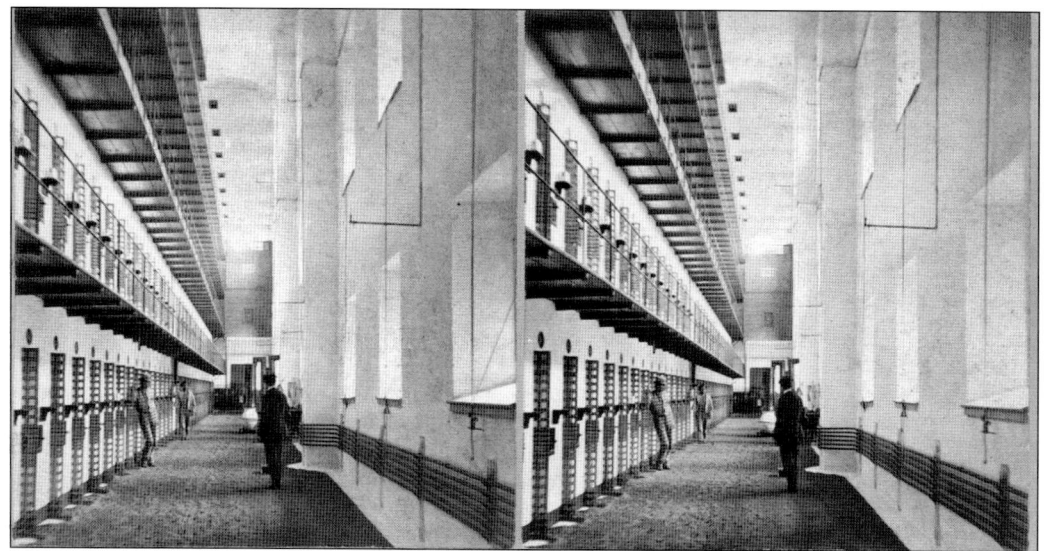

The new cell blocks at Auburn Prison, completed in 1821, were the first in the world to house the inmates in individual cells. The cells were 7 feet long, 7 feet high, and 3.5 feet wide. There were 40 cells in a row, two rows back-to-back, stacked five tiers high. Note the wooden plank walkways and the open railings.

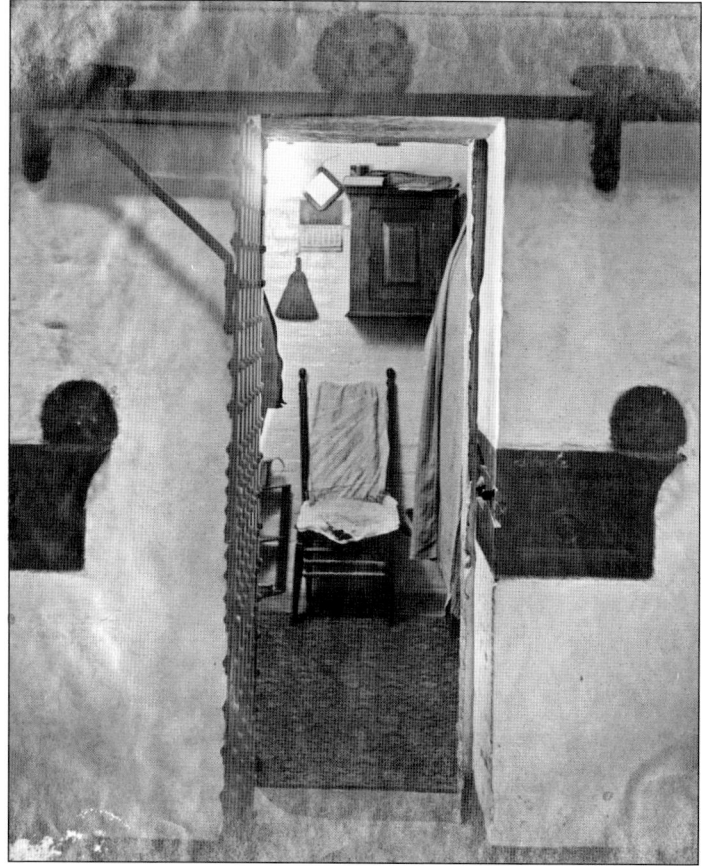

This cell appears to have been staged for the photograph. There was no light, heat, or running water in the cells, and a chair and carpet were not standard furnishings.

The doors were not vertical bars, but a lattice of iron and rivets. Each door was opened individually by key.

There was a small shelf above the lock plate outside each cell on which a metal cup was kept.

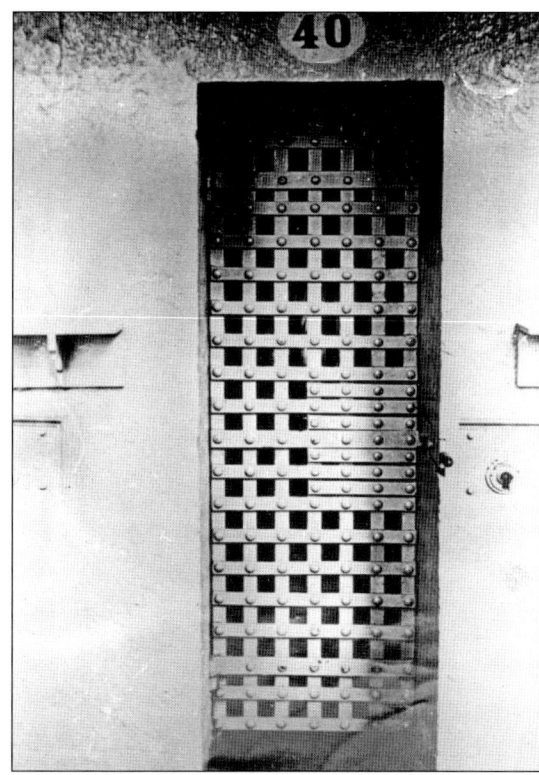

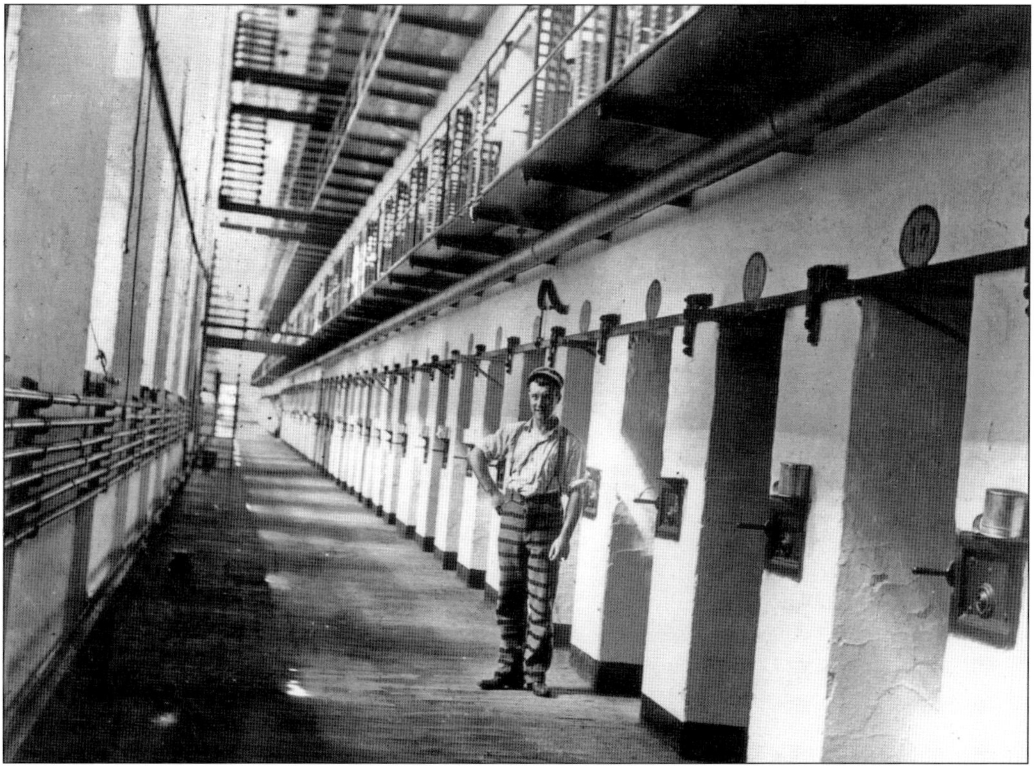

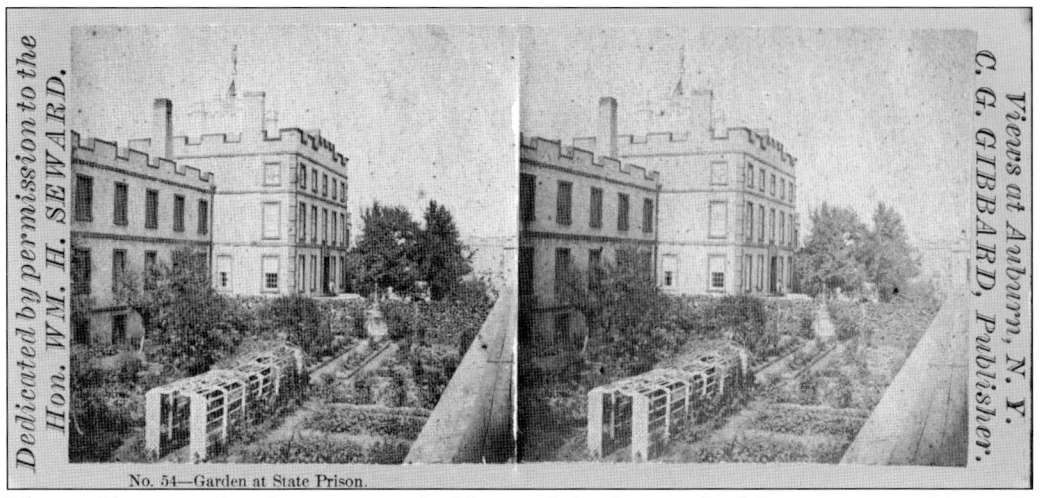

The yard between the administration building and the front wall of the prison was elaborately landscaped from the beginning. This image, from a stereo card published by C. G. Gibbard in the 1850s, shows the front of the administration building before the front porch and second floor landing were added. The arbor and bushes do not appear in later photographs.

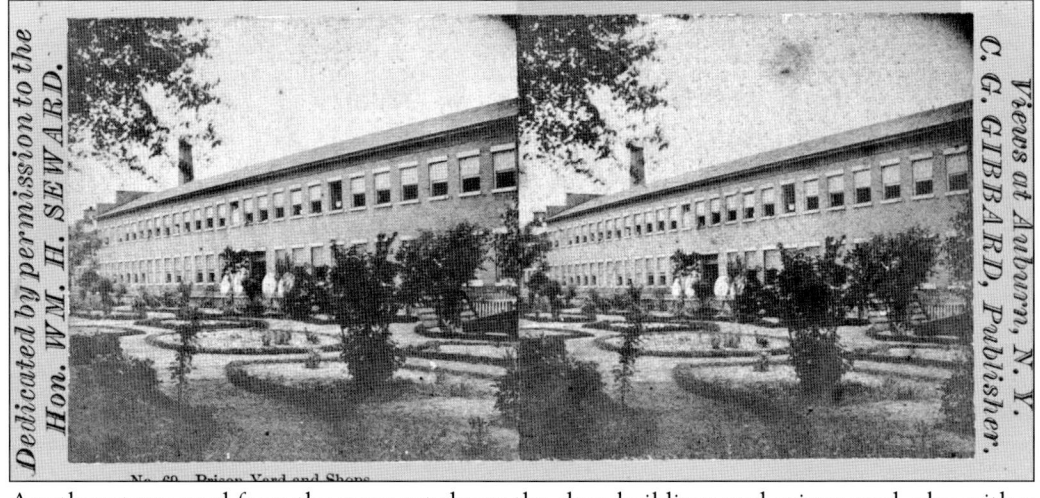

Another stereo card from the same set shows the shop buildings and prison yard, also with a number of bushes and landscape designs that do not appear in later photographs.

This image from the same set of stereo cards, taken from atop the prison wall, shows the bucket yard. There were no toilets in the cells; each man had a covered bucket, a crude and inexpensive chamber pot. Every morning the prisoners lined up and carried their buckets to the yard. They marched back through the bucket yard after a day at work in the shops and picked up the buckets to take back to their cells for the night.

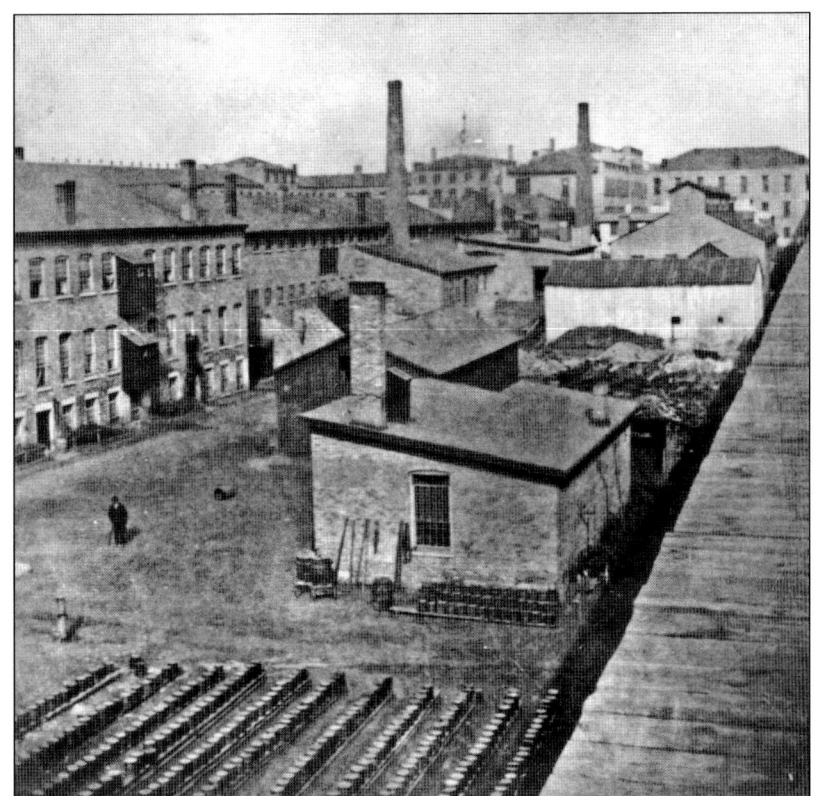

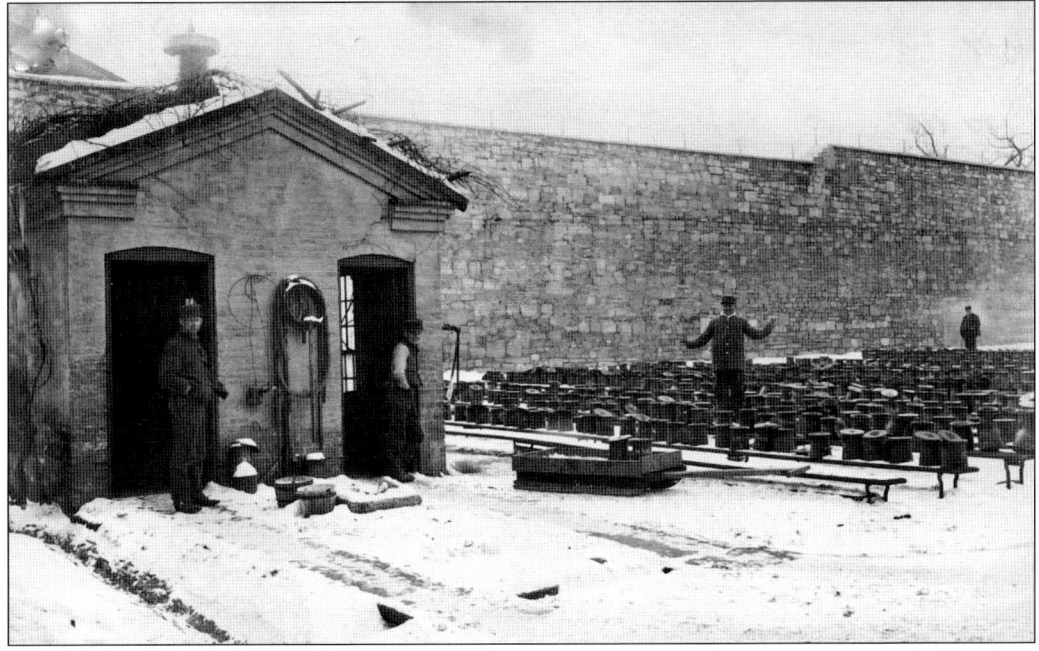

This is another view of the bucket house and buckets, or slop jars, lined up in the yard. The slops were emptied into the Owasco River right on the other side of the wall. Note the sled in the center of the photograph, used for hauling heavy items over snow.

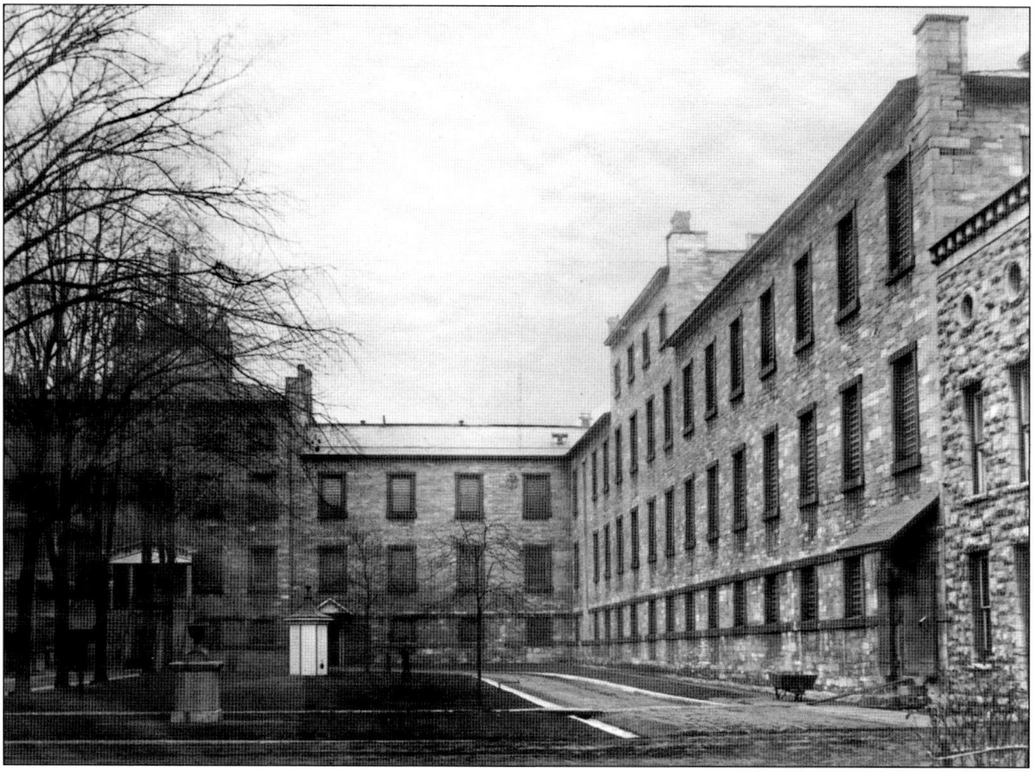

The original design of the prison was in a giant U-shape, with the administration building across the bottom of the U, facing State Street, and the cell blocks and workshops forming the sides of the U. There was a front yard, between the administration building and the street, and the main yard, inside the U formed by the buildings.

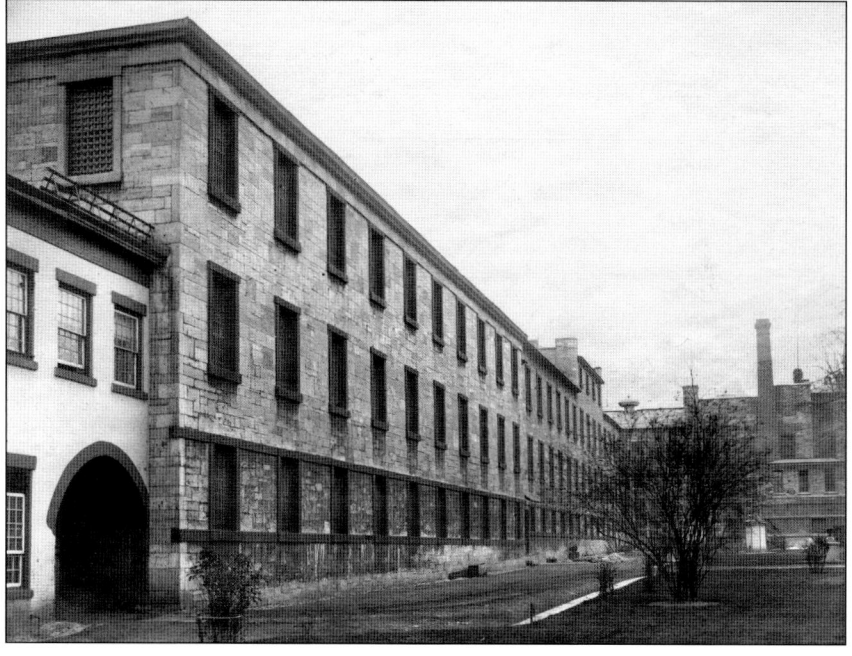

Two

THE AUBURN SYSTEM

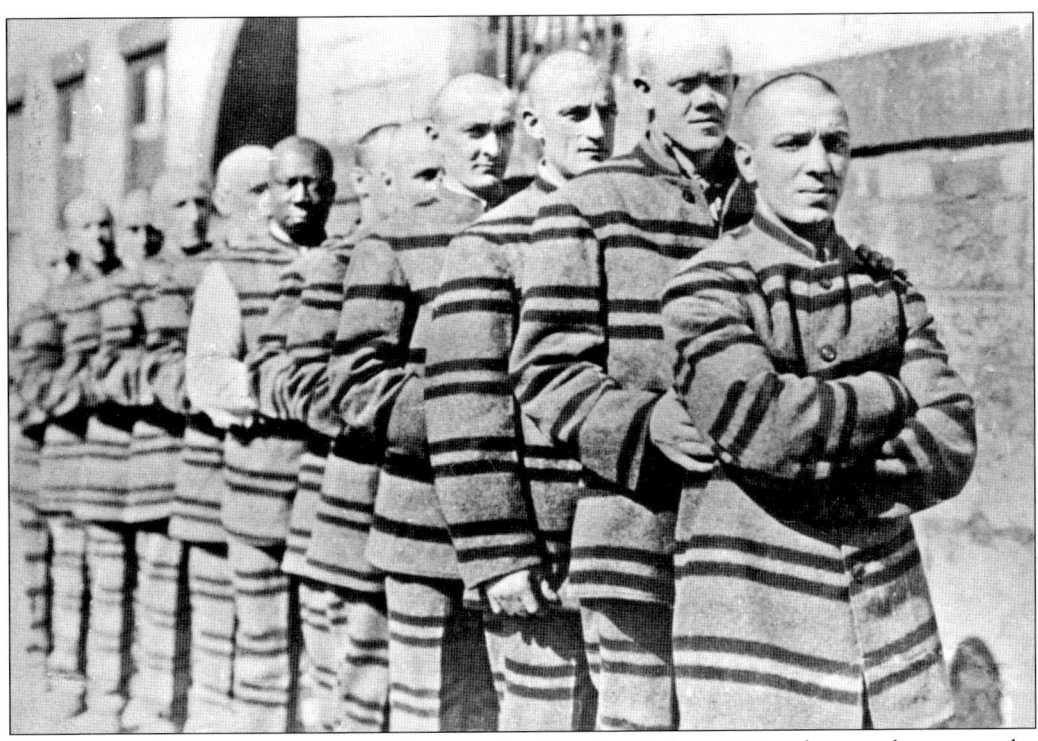

The system of inmate management that was developed at Auburn Prison became known as the Auburn System and was copied all over the world. In the mid-1800s, the Auburn System was viewed as a progressive way to keep the inmates from corrupting one another and to teach them the value of hard work. The Auburn System included total silence, lockstep marching, forced labor, and the humiliating striped uniforms that have become iconic for inmates. Prisoners' heads were shaved as another way of breaking down individuality.

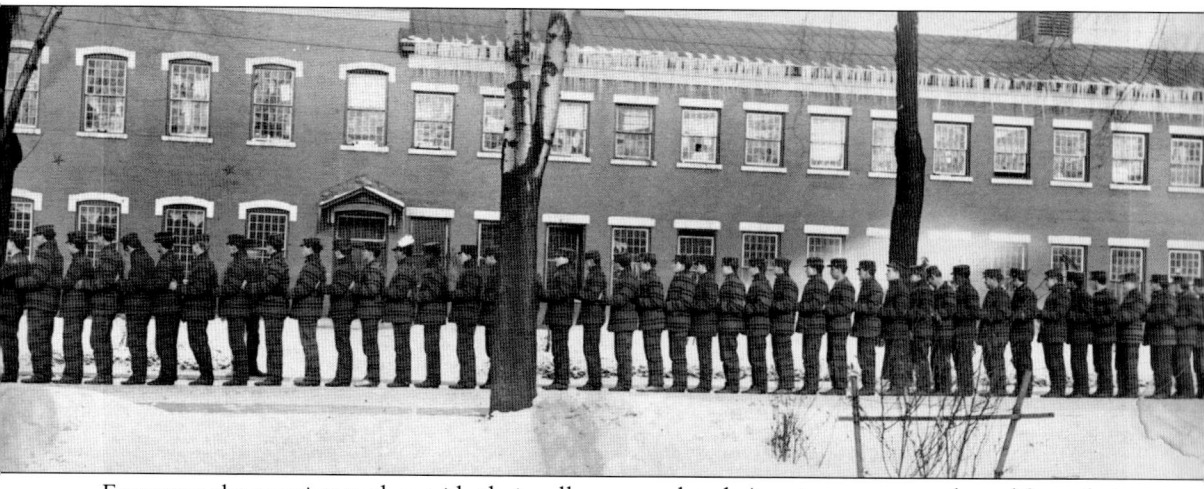

Every step the convicts took outside their cells was regulated. As prisoners were released from their cells, they lined up in the order of their cells and marched in what became known as lockstep. Each man's hands were under the arms of the man in front of him, marching in unison, all looking to the side. They were marched first to the bucket yard, then to the shops, then to breakfast (mush and molasses) in the mess hall, back to the shops, to dinner, and back through the bucket yard on their way to the cell blocks in the evening. The prisoners' uniforms consisted of a jacket, vest, and pants, all striped, as well as a shirt and hat. The keepers wore dark suits, with vests and jackets, and distinctive hats that resembled top hats. A key component of the Auburn System was complete silence. Even the keepers, the men who supervised the convicts, did not speak to them. The keepers signaled directions by tapping their metal-tipped canes on the ground.

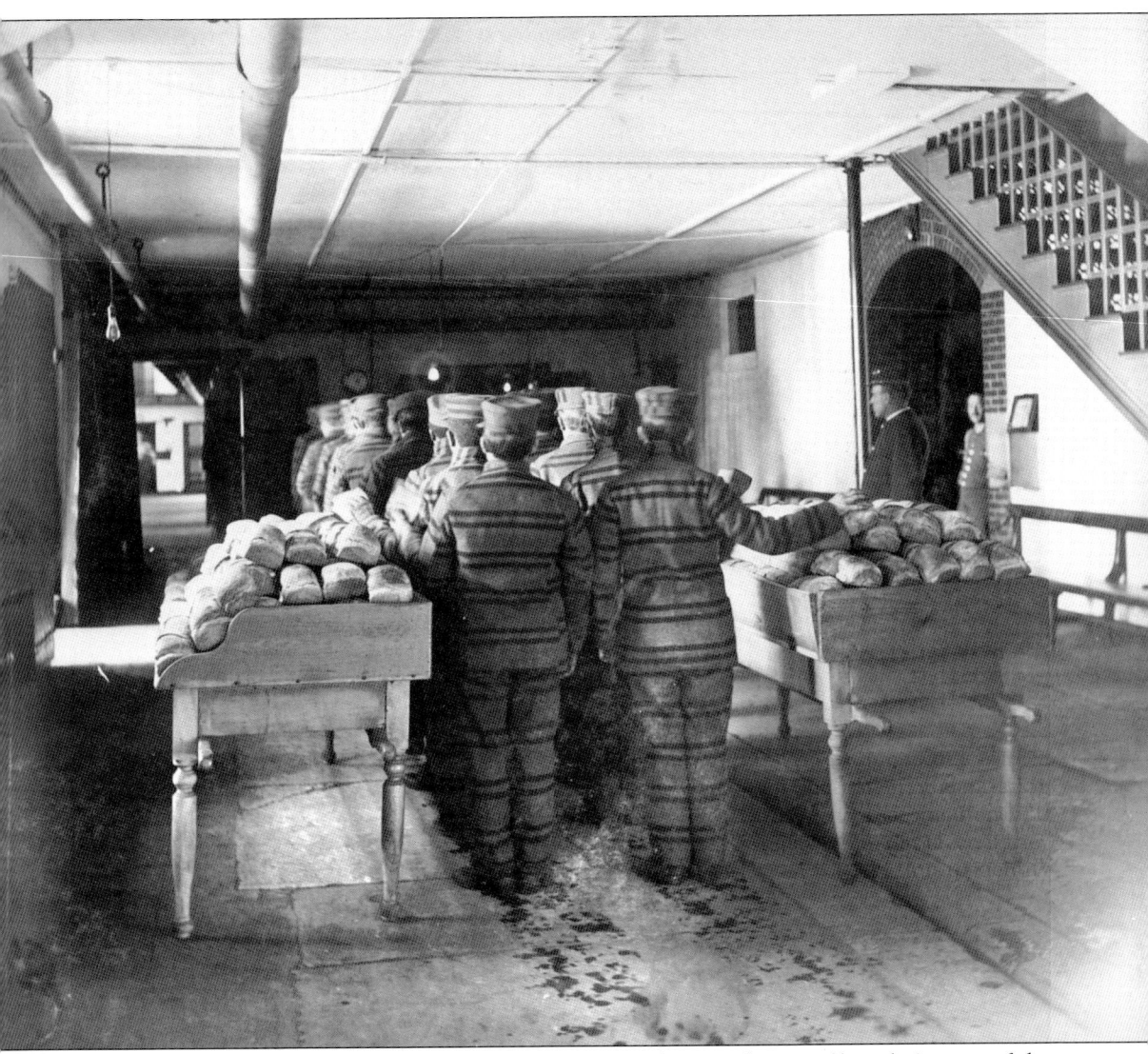

These prisoners were on their way into the mess hall, picking up loaves of bread. As part of the Auburn System's goal of isolating the inmates from each other, seating was arranged in the mess hall so that all the prisoners faced outward. They were never allowed to be face-to-face.

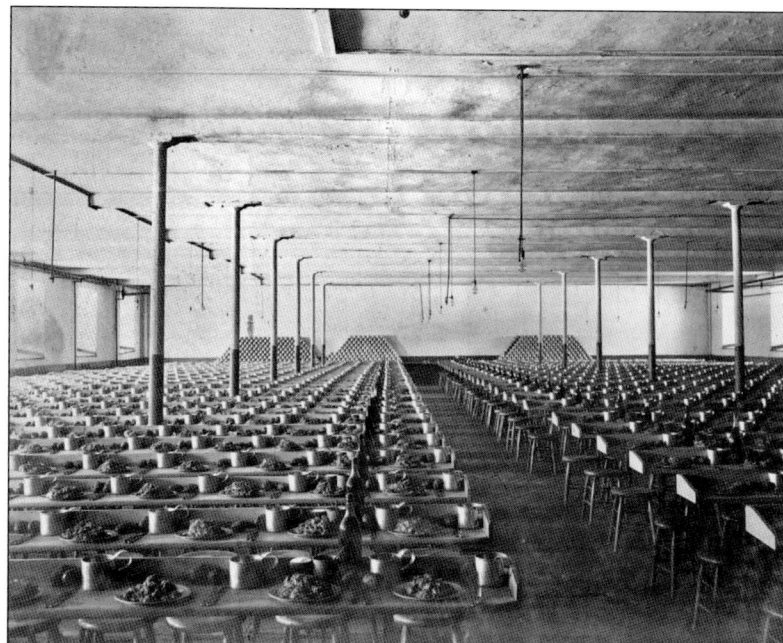

This late-1800s mess hall scene was almost certainly staged for the photograph. (Note the electric lights.) The meals were not waiting on the prisoners' plates before they entered the mess hall.

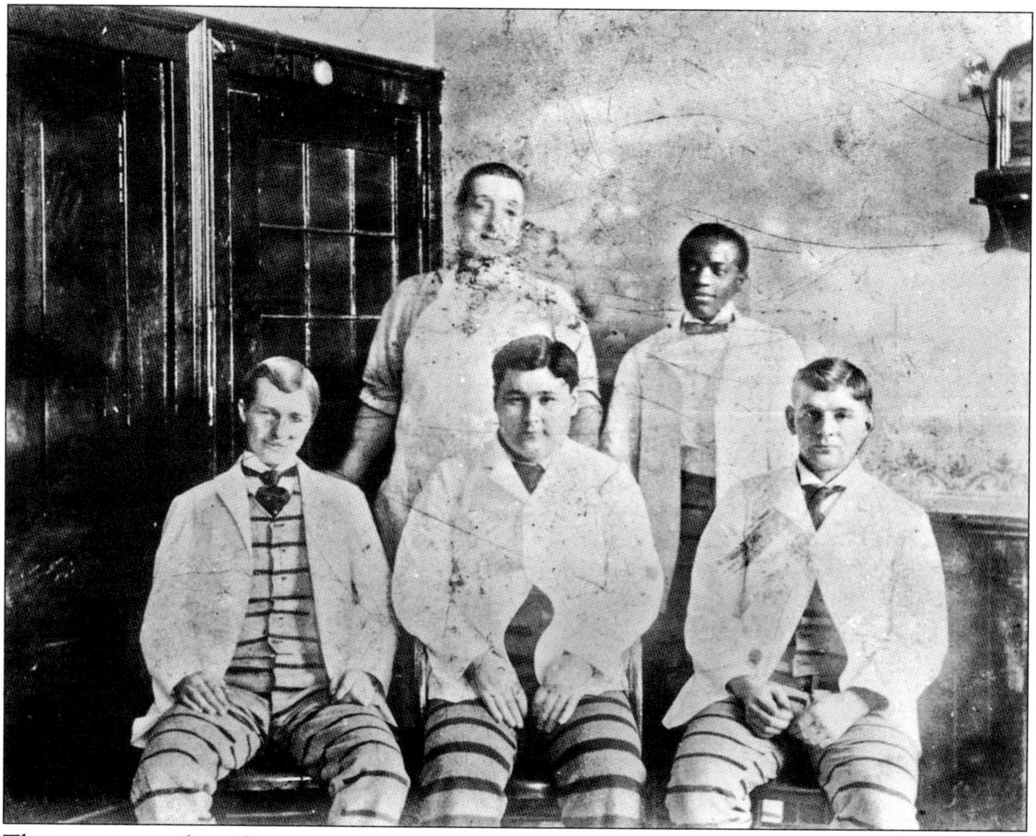

These men must have been trusted prisoners. The white coats over their striped uniforms place them as either waiters in the staff mess hall or workers in the hospital.

Convict workers staffed the kitchen. It was no easy task feeding more than 1,000 men every day.

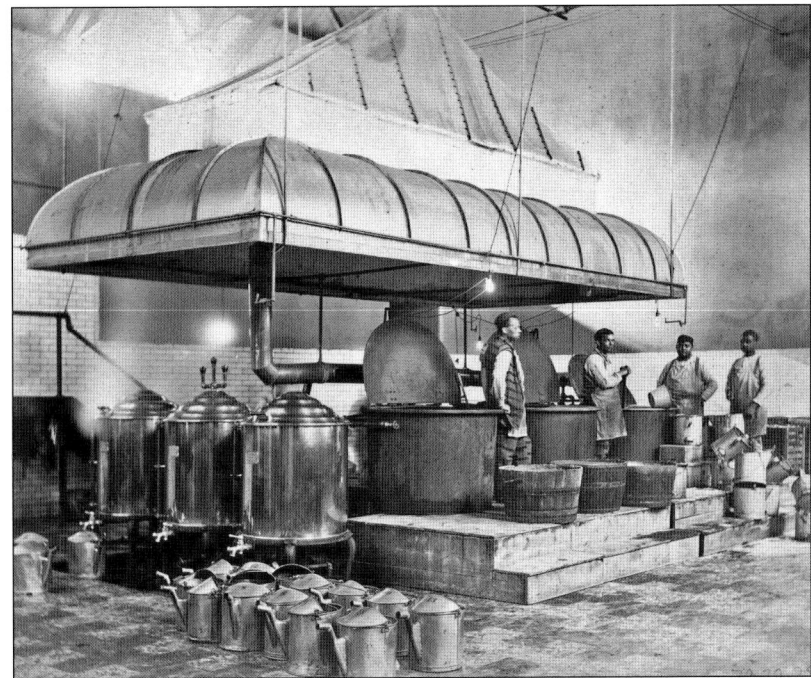

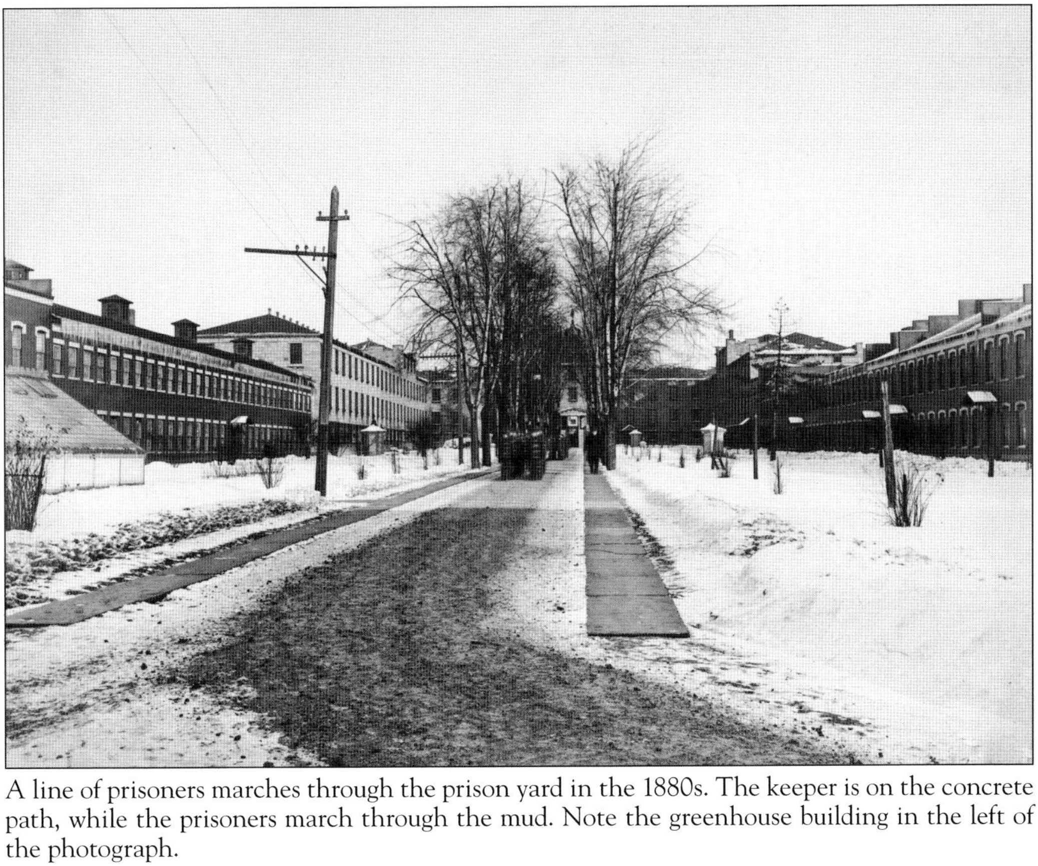

A line of prisoners marches through the prison yard in the 1880s. The keeper is on the concrete path, while the prisoners march through the mud. Note the greenhouse building in the left of the photograph.

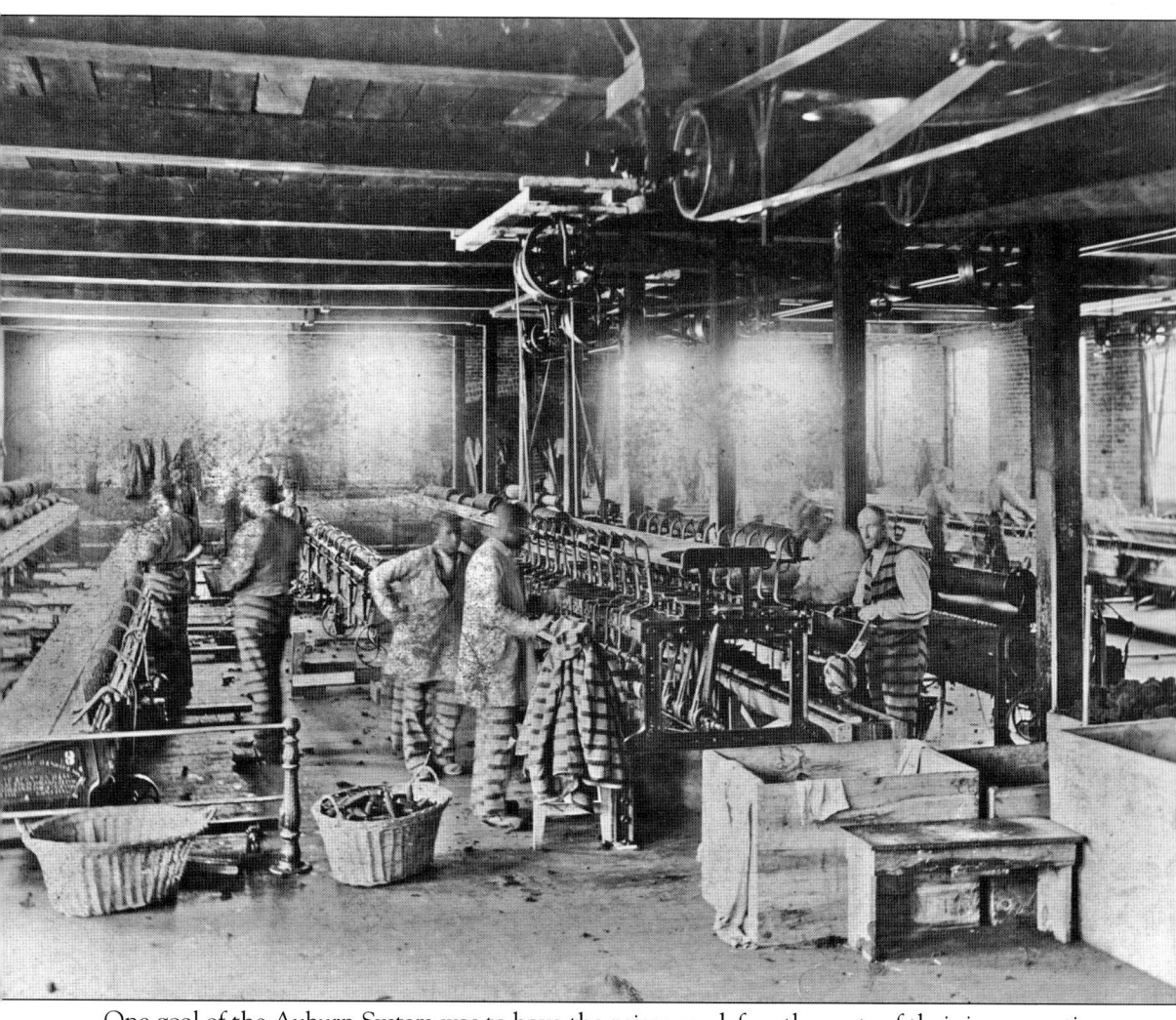

One goal of the Auburn System was to have the prisoners defray the costs of their incarceration through their own labor. A key factor in locating the state prison in Auburn was the availability of water power from the Owasco River. Workshops using the water power were built as early as 1819. Manufacturing began in Auburn Prison that year. The forced labor of the inmates, while benefiting the state with revenue from manpower, was also seen as redemptive, a means of teaching criminals the value of hard work. Spinning was one of the first industries to be started inside the prison, but the convicts also made shoes, hames, clocks, tools, and more. In the 1830s, there was a silk industry in the prison, in which inmates raised silk worms and wove the fabric.

Three
WORKING FOR COPPER JOHN

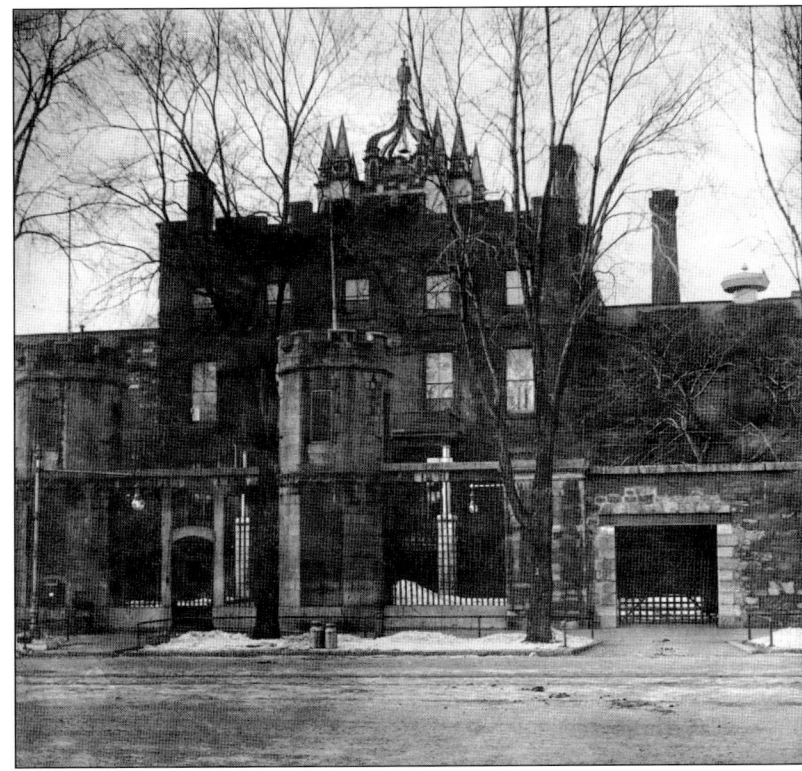

This ever-vigilant soldier in the uniform of the Revolutionary War has stood on the peak of the administration building since 1821. Originally made of wood, he was taken down in 1848 because he was so badly decayed. A replica was hammered out of sheet copper in the prison foundry, and he has been known ever since as Copper John.

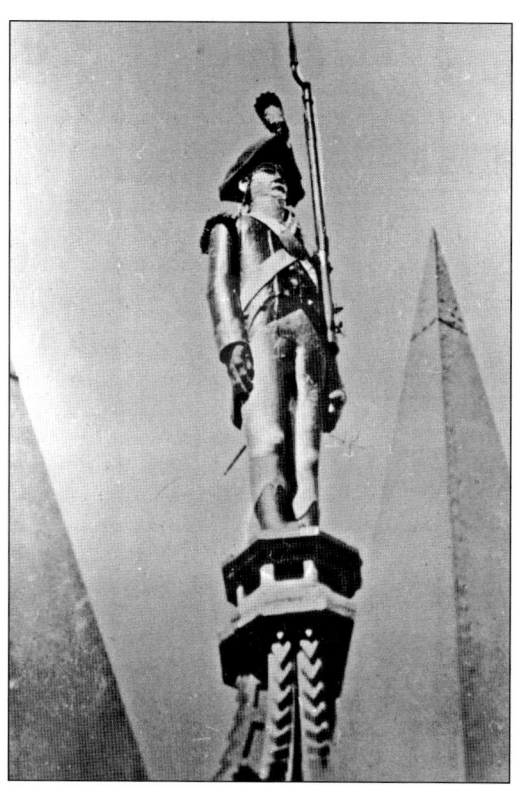

One of the most recognizable sights of the Auburn skyline, Copper John stands 11 feet, 5 inches tall from his boots to the tassel on his hat. His boots are 14 inches long.

His original post was on the peak of the administration building, shown in this 1900 photograph, where he stood atop the giant prison belfry, circled by a series of dramatic points. The bell was used to signal shift changes at the prison and could also be rung in case of emergency. Prisoners referred to being incarcerated at Auburn Prison as "working for Copper John." Copper John faces outward. To be released meant a man could look Copper John in the face.

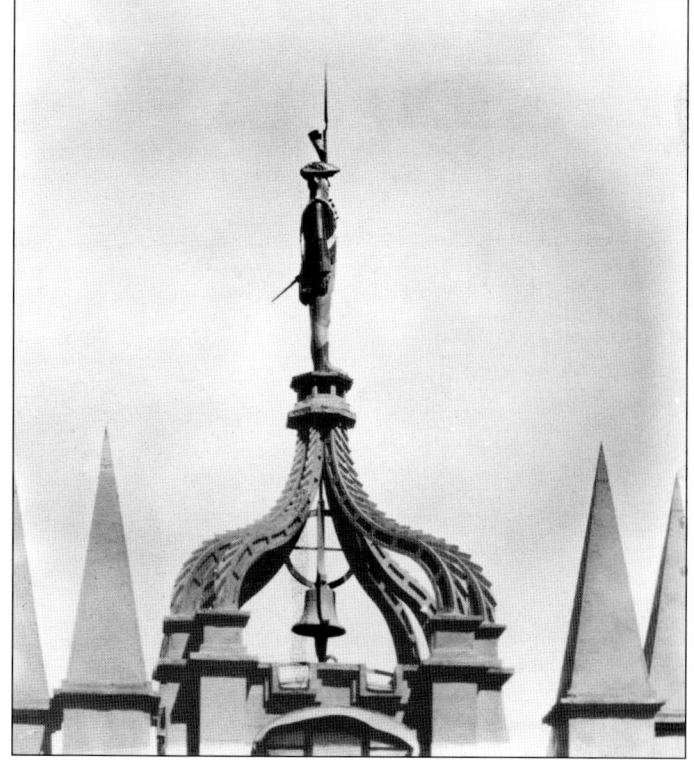

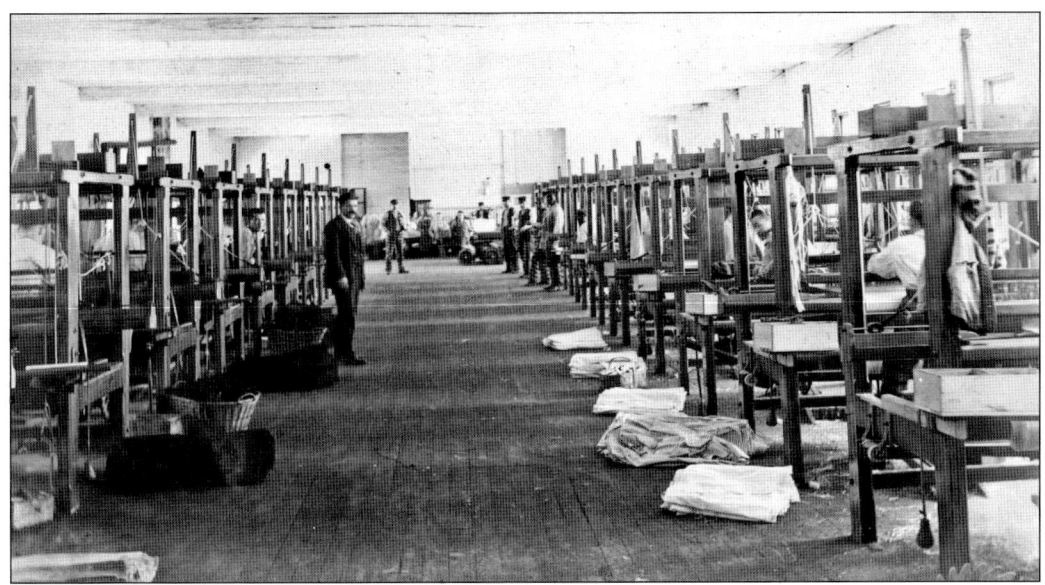

Weaving was one of the earliest industries to be installed at Auburn Prison. Weaving was considered a skilled trade, and the hope was that the convicts could find honest work as weavers after their release. In the photograph above, the convicts are weaving mattress ticking. In the photograph below, the larger looms may have been used for weaving carpets. Auburn businessman Joseph Barber signed prison contracts year after year for the weaving of carpets and other cloth inside the prison. The prison weaving shops produced coverlets, mattress ticking, the cloth for the prisoners' striped uniforms, carpets, and more.

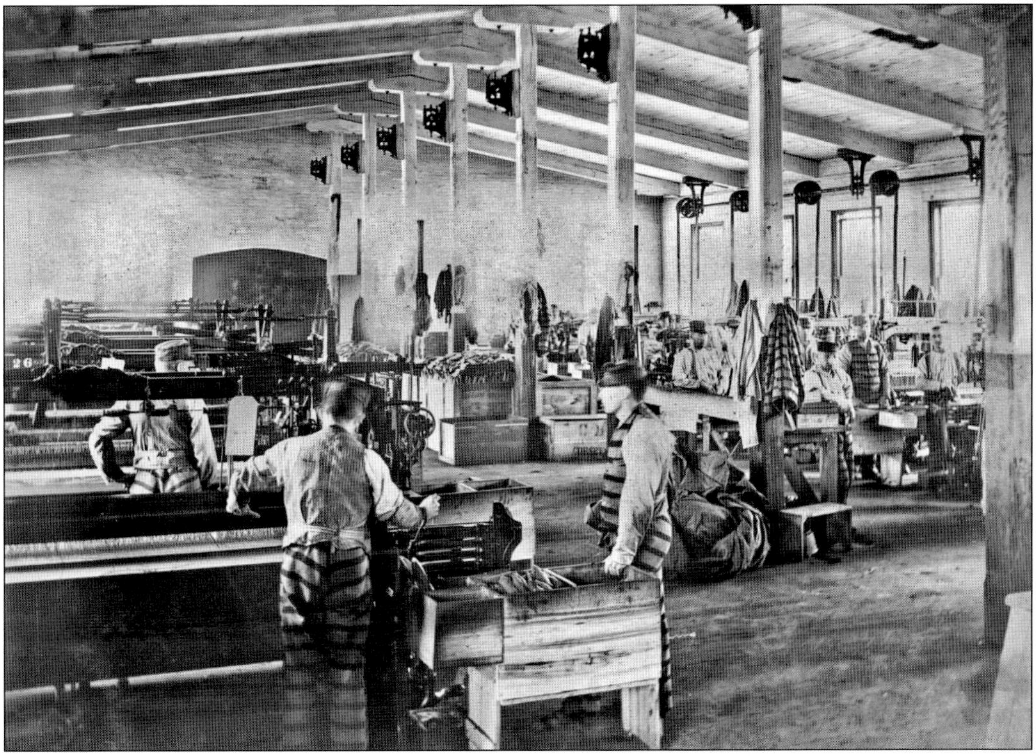

In the 1800s, many of the products made in the prison shops were sold in downtown Auburn. When the Smith and Pearson building was demolished in 1953, it revealed the painted sign on the next building, which had been protected from the elements by the closeness of the walls. Barber's Prison Warehouse was just one of the stores that sold the goods produced in the prison shops, including carpets, coverlets, coats, shoes, tools and more.

Spinning was done at Auburn Prison as early as 1819. These complex machines were labeled "spinning mules" in 1910.

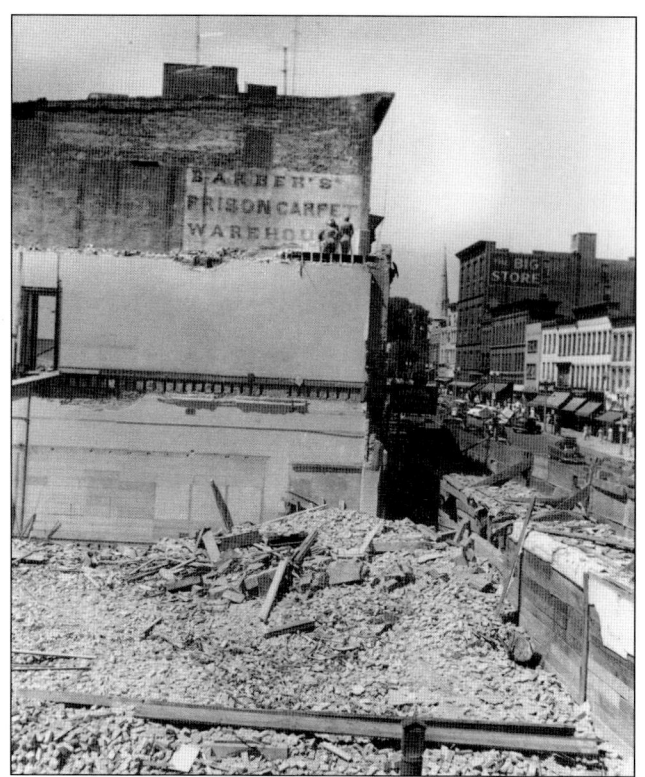

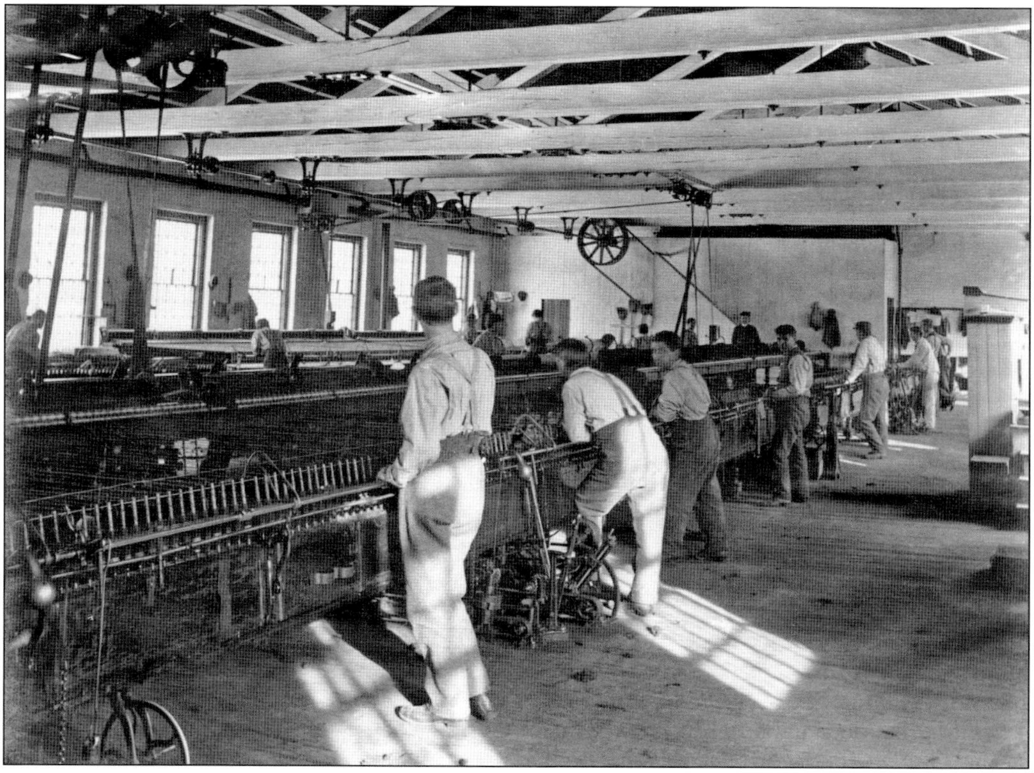

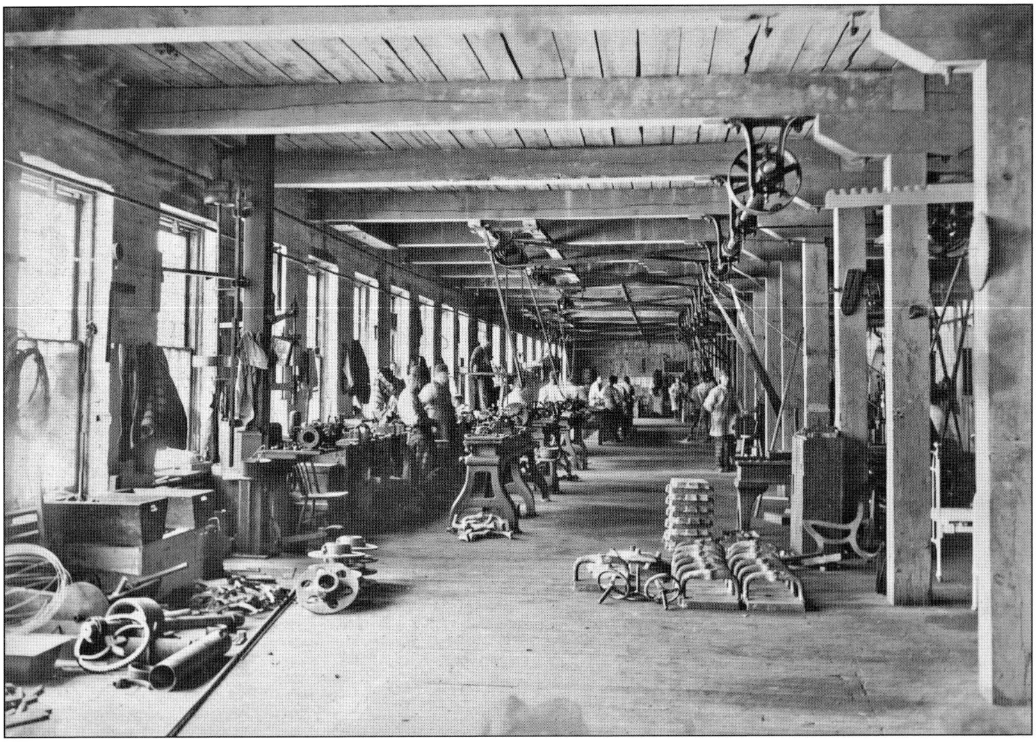

This 1880s photograph, from warden Charles Rattigan's personal album, does not indicate what the products of this shop were. The date can be inferred from the workers' striped uniforms, which were discontinued around 1890. Note the keeper on the platform on the left side of the shop, raised above the floor to provide a better view of the prisoners at work. The current shops inside Auburn Correctional Facility still feature the same kind of raised platforms, used for the same purpose.

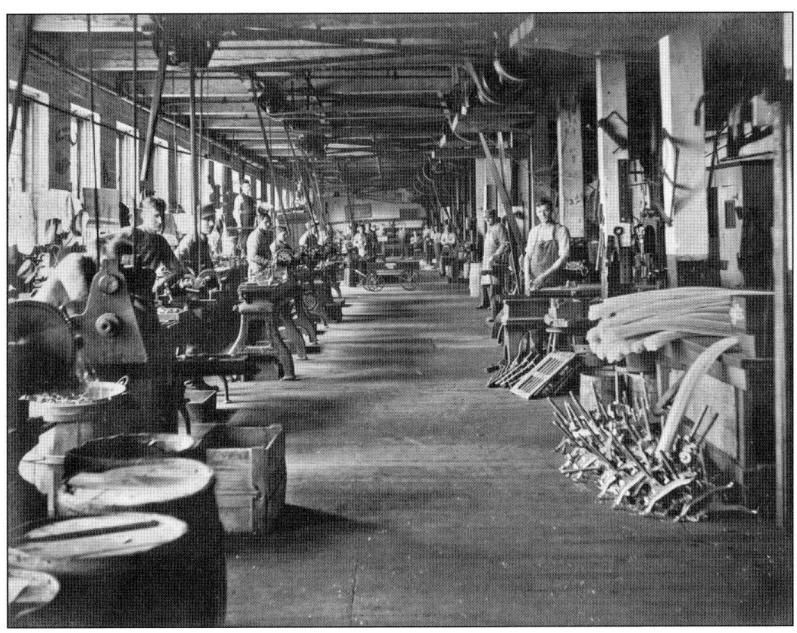

These products, too, are unidentified. From the same album, this photograph can be dated to after 1890; the men are not wearing stripes.

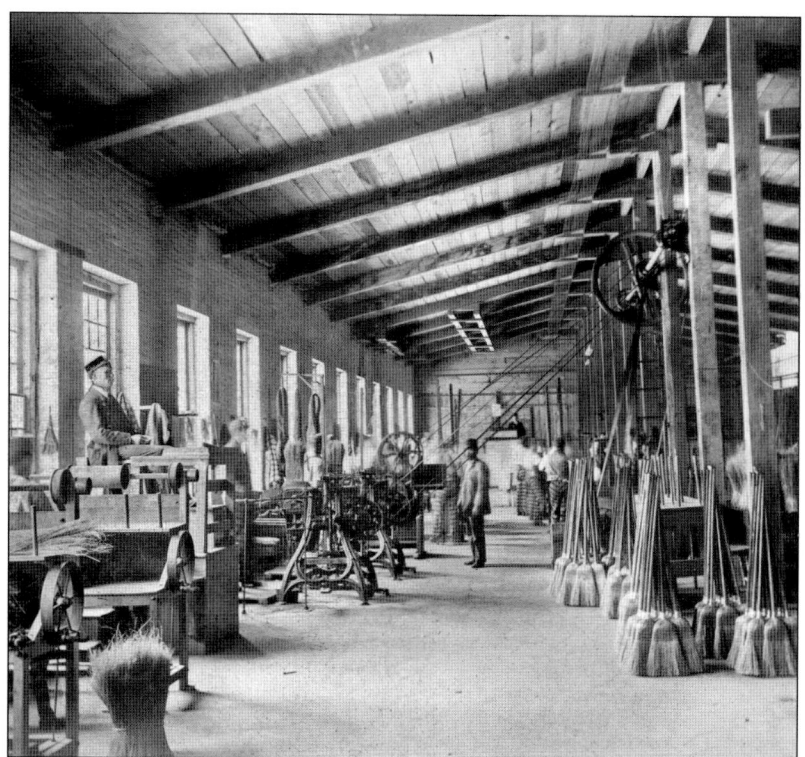

New York State ended the prison contract labor system in 1890. All the prison shops went on the state use system, meaning they could only produce goods for the use of the state. These brooms were destined to sweep the floors of state offices, classrooms, or other prisons. The back of this photograph is inscribed "Presented by Johnnie Goodsom to his mother, January 10, 1899."

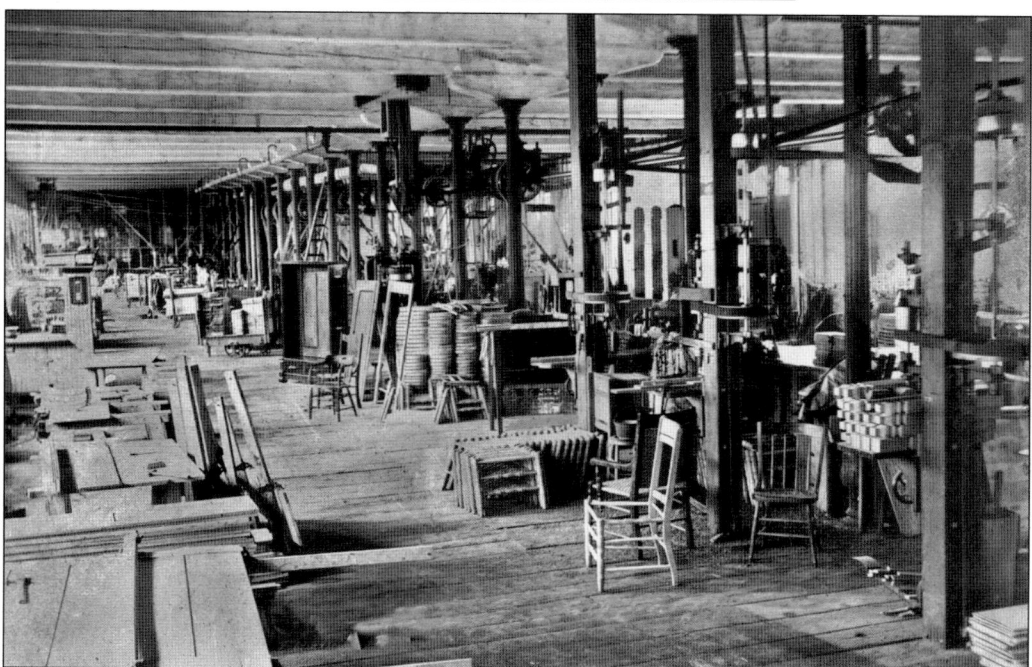

There was a large furniture-making industry at Auburn Prison throughout the 1800s. This photograph, used for a popular Auburn postcard, shows the chair shop in the 1890s. The color notes for the postcard state that the pillars were dark green. Gustav Stickley, the famous American furniture designer, was the foreman of the Auburn Prison chair shop in 1889 and 1890.

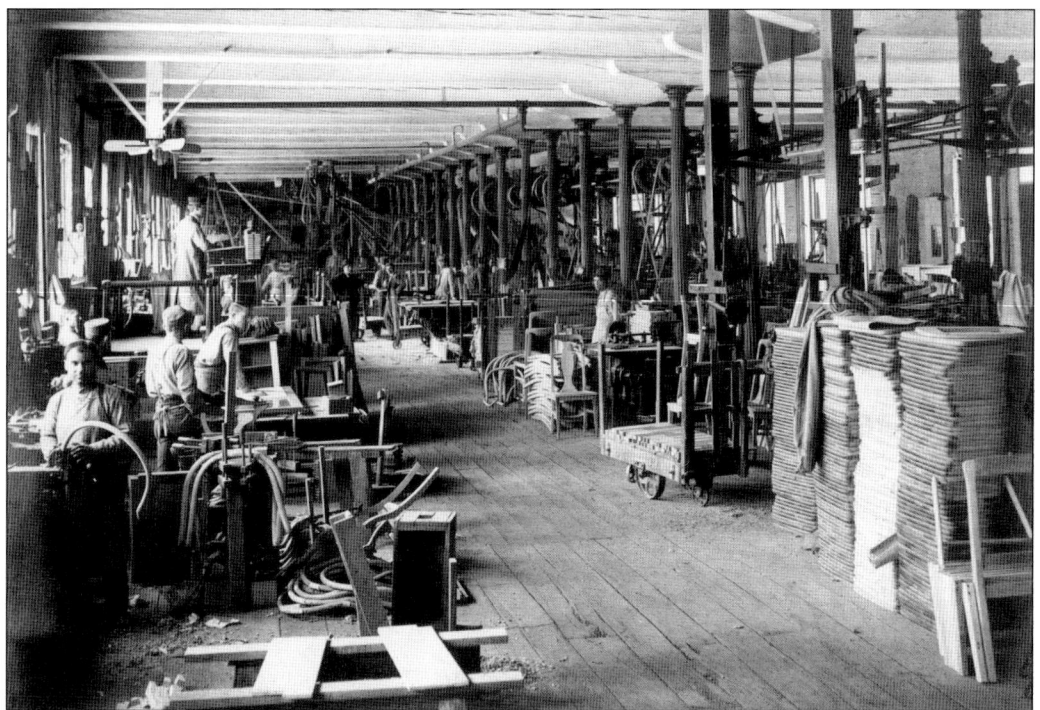

This is another view of one of the furniture shops, taken around 1890. Note the fan above the keeper's platform on the left.

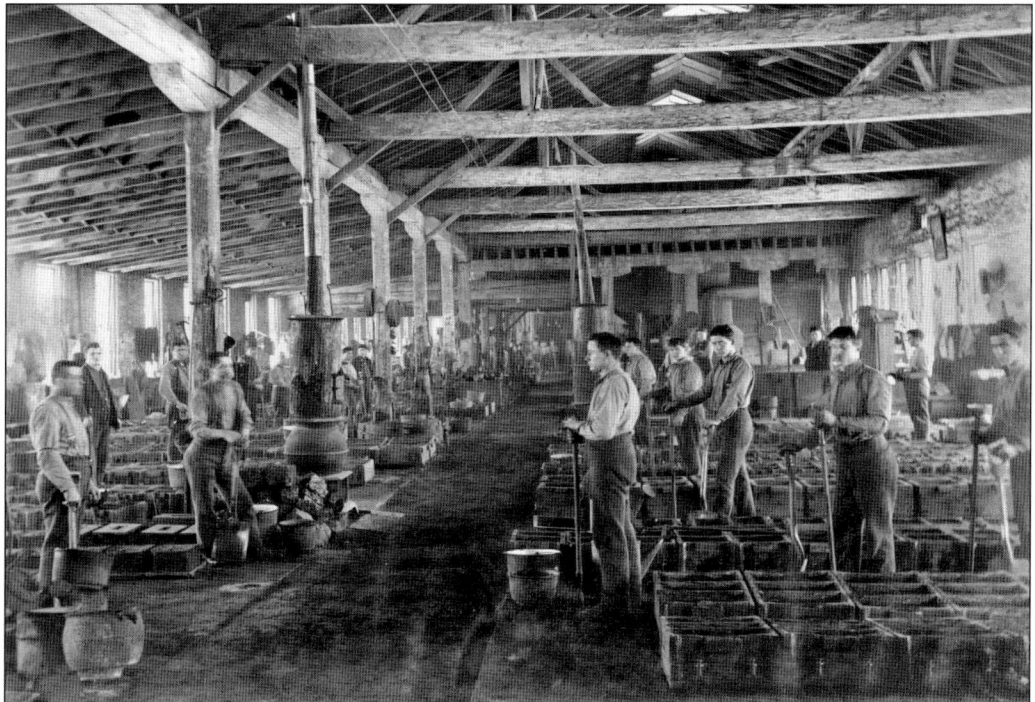

This photograph of the brick shop, taken around 1910, shows just how large the workshops were and why they burned so easily in 1929.

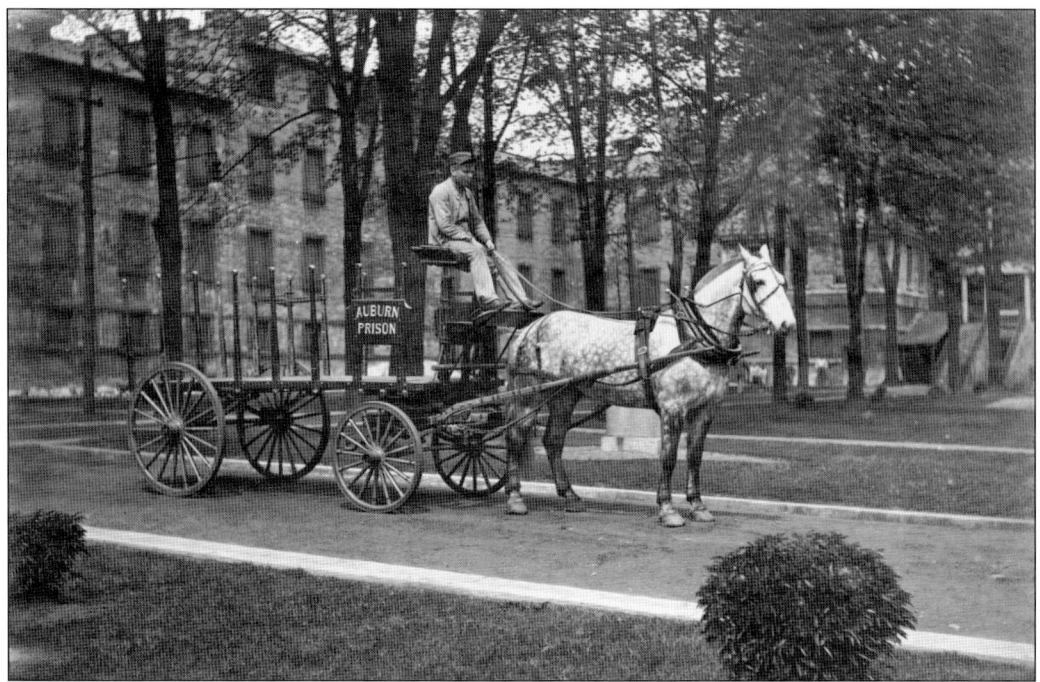

Men were not the only workers inside the prison. The prison kept a well-equipped stable on the grounds, and several horses served life sentences in the service of Copper John. Even after the advent of the automobile, the prison kept horses for hauling freight.

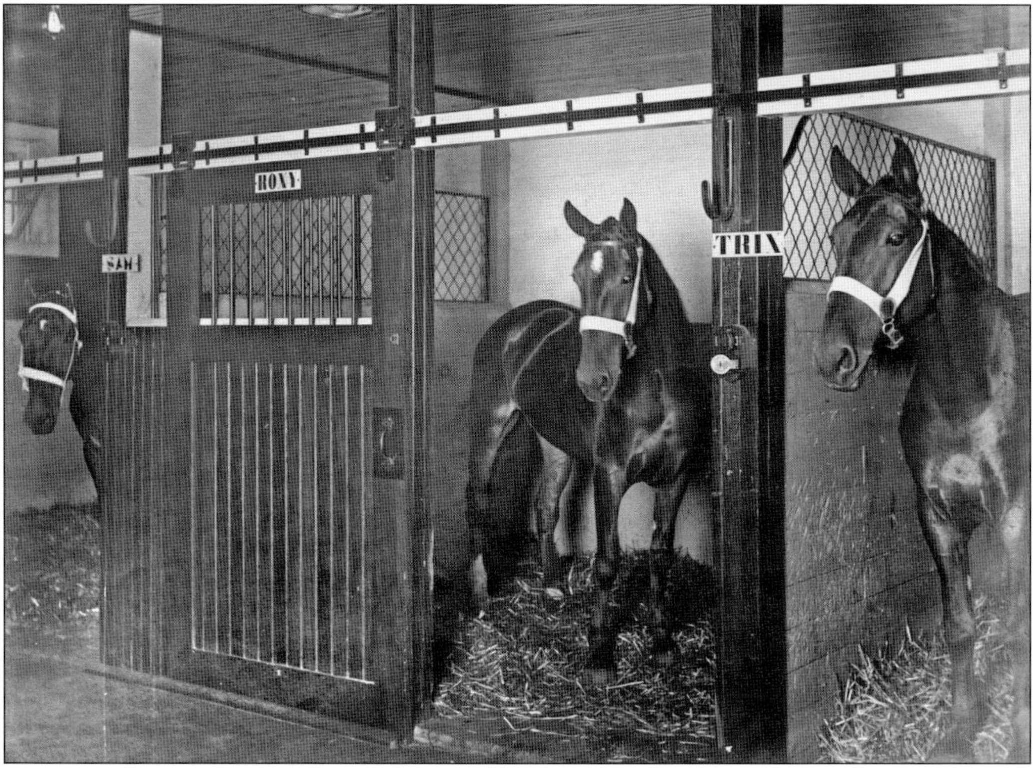

Four
EARLY 20TH CENTURY

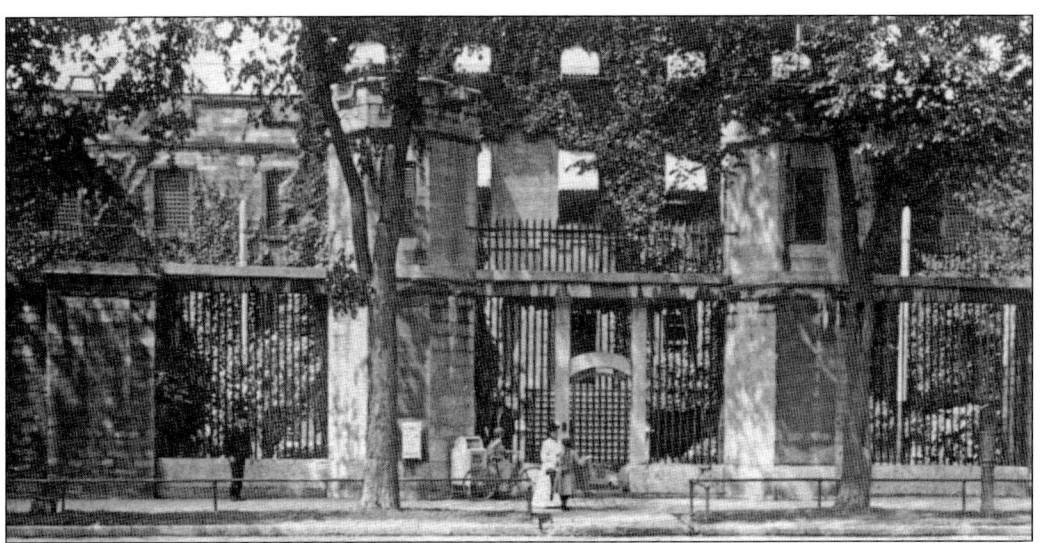

By the early 1900s, the barred gates and stone towers right on the sidewalk of State Street were a point of pride for Auburn residents. Many of the most popular postcards sold in Auburn featured images of the prison. Today the stone towers are all that remain of the original 1816 prison structures.

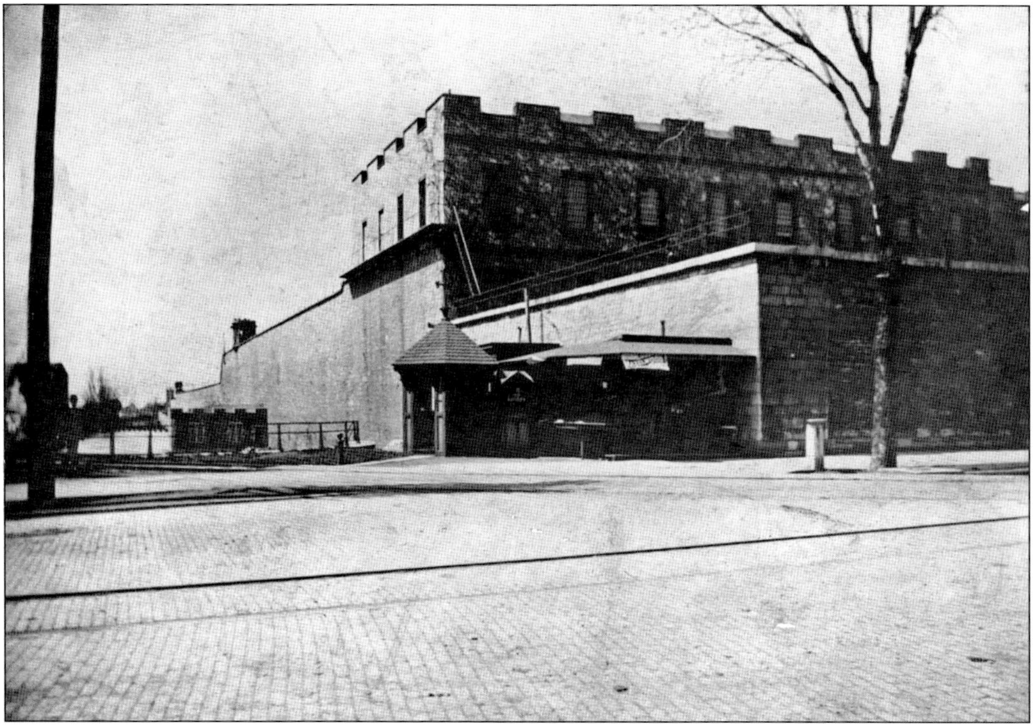

Although the outer walls and buildings remained, changes did come to the prison. Here is the southeast corner of the prison site, fronting State Street and the Owasco River in April 1900. The tiny building adjacent to the wall is a cigar shop. The back of this photograph is inscribed "Auburn State Prison. Located in 1816. First convicts received 1817. Number of cells—about 1,400. Number of prisoners April 1900—about 1,300."

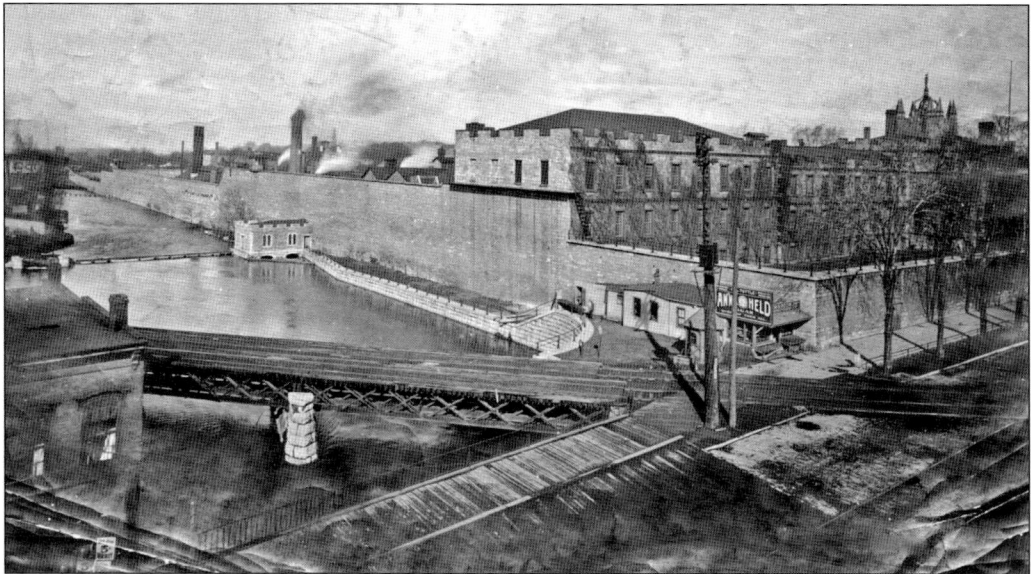

This larger view of the same corner is from a postcard. This is where the New York Central Railroad tracks crossed the Owasco River and State Street to head into the depot, across the street from the prison.

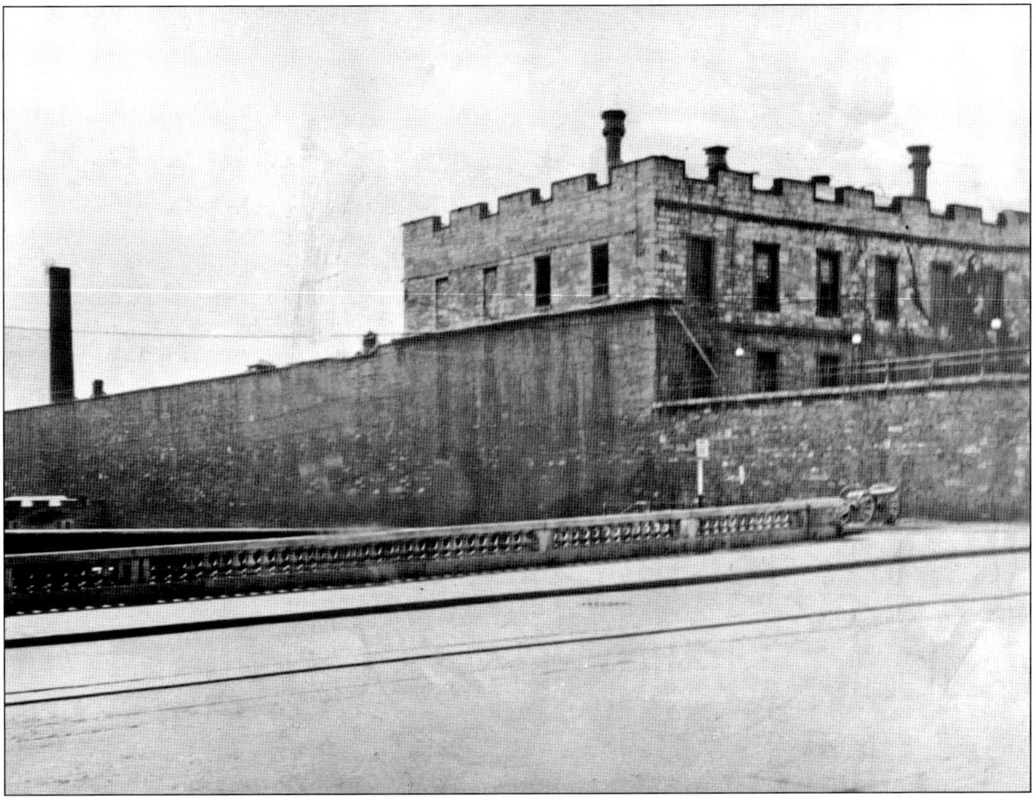

Here is the same corner in a photograph from a glass-plate negative. Note that electric lights have been added to the top of the wall, and there are chimneys on top of the building. A Civil War cannon from one of Auburn's volunteer regiments was displayed in place of the cigar store (as seen on the top of page 32). (Courtesy of Michael Pettigrass.)

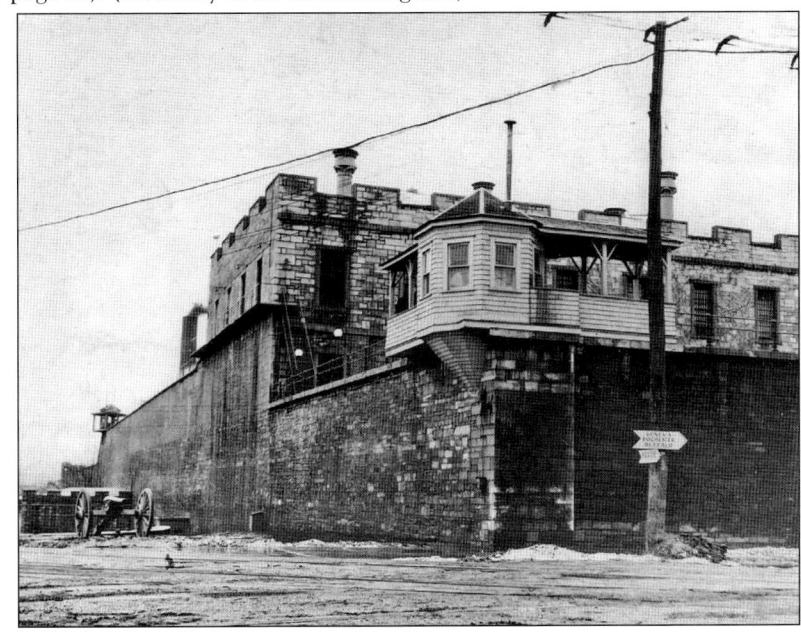

This is the same corner, with the addition of a wooden guard station on top of the wall, around 1912. The cannon is still there, complete with a stack of cannon balls.

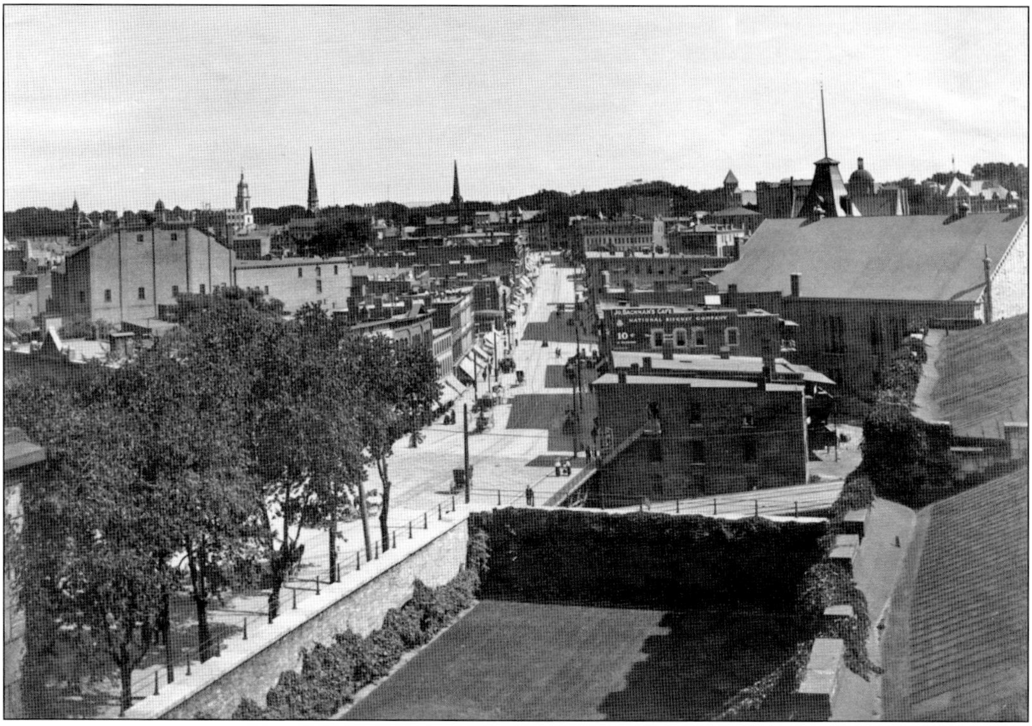

When it first opened in 1817, the prison was on the outskirts of the village of Auburn. By 1900, the prison was at the center of a thriving commercial and residential area. Taken from the top of the administration building in 1905, this photograph looks down on the same southeast corner of the front yard and up State Street to downtown Auburn.

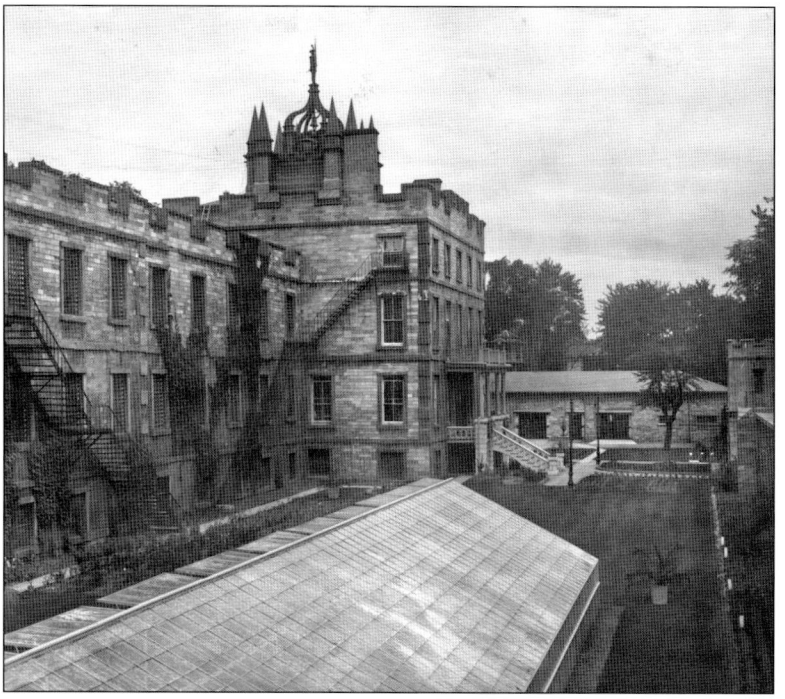

There are many images of the front yard of the prison taken from this same vantage point atop the State Street wall. Here a glass greenhouse replaces the elaborate landscaping shown in the early photographs. Fire escapes snake up the building's facade, and a second floor has been added to the front porch of the administration building. Ivy is just starting to grow up the wall. (Courtesy of Michael Pettigrass.)

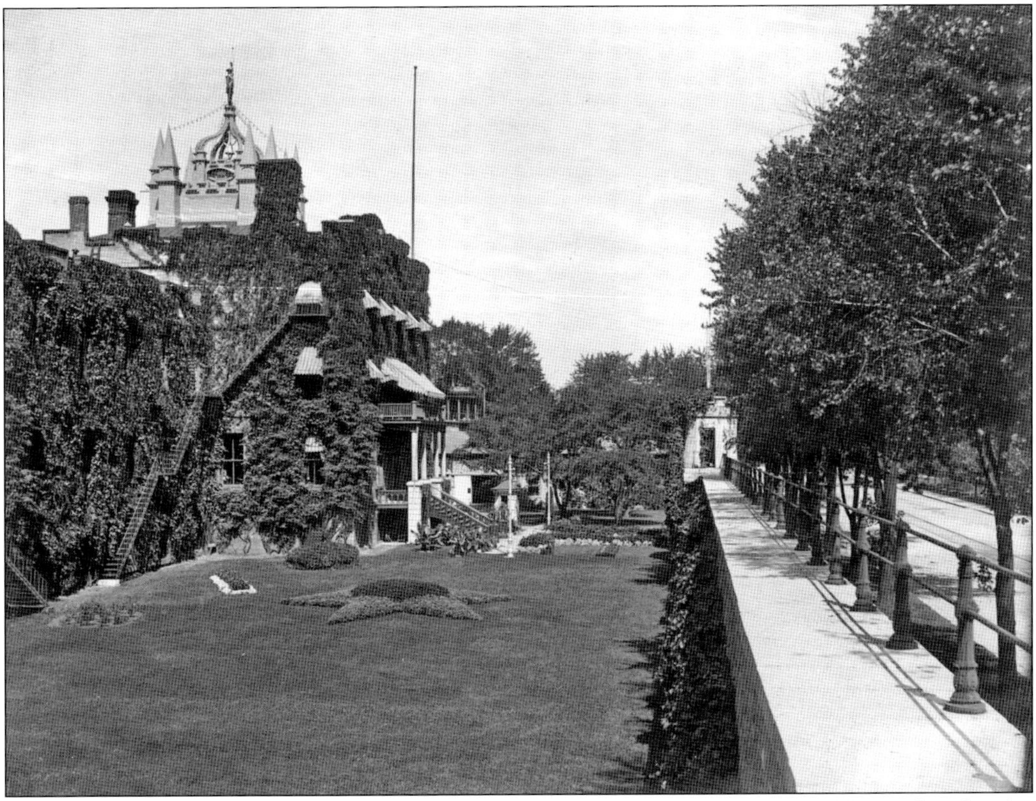

Here is the same view several years later, around 1912. Ivy covers the building's facade, the greenhouse is gone, and a star design has been added to the landscaping. Note the pennants gracing Copper John's pinnacle.

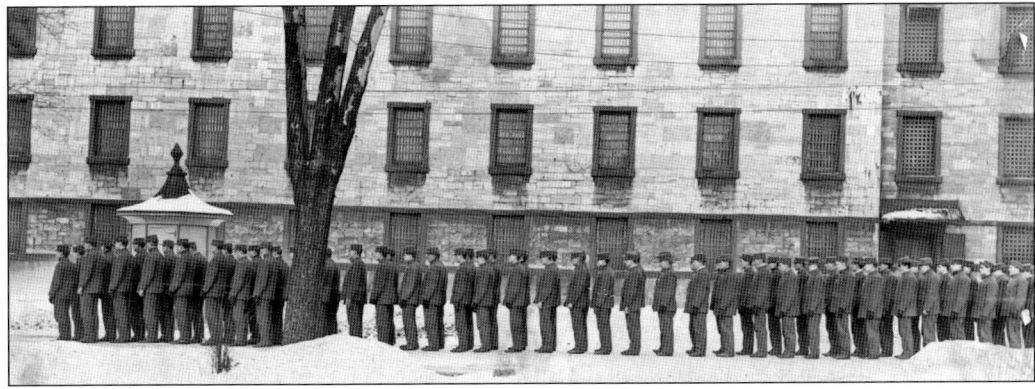

By 1900, the Auburn System had been discontinued. The striped uniforms were eliminated, as was lockstep marching. Prisoners marched back and forth to the mess hall and the shops in military formation.

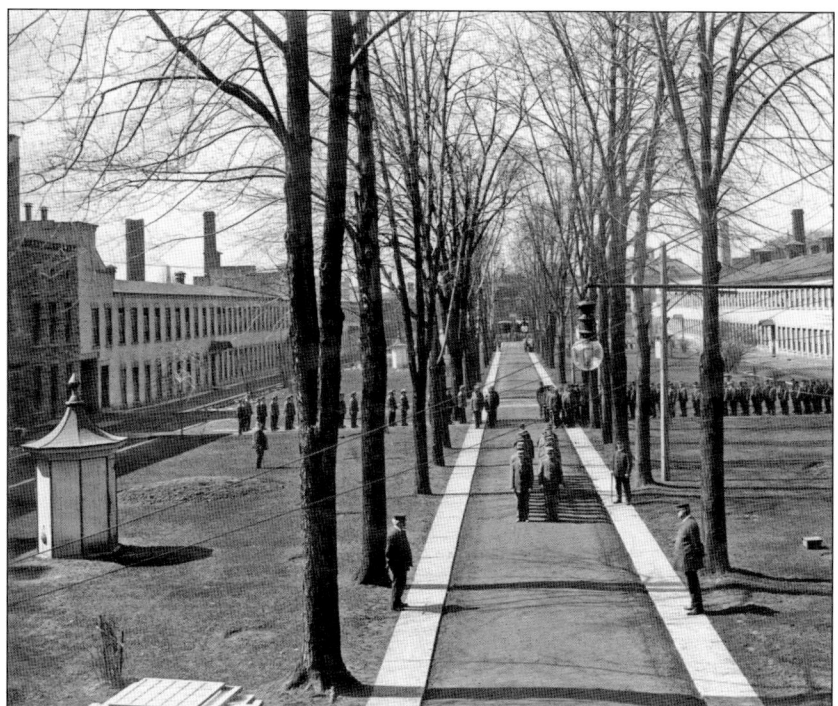

In place of their stripes, the prisoners wore gray military-style uniforms. The staff wore dark blue uniforms. There is no record of what the little white structures in the four corners of the yard were. They may have been decorative sheds.

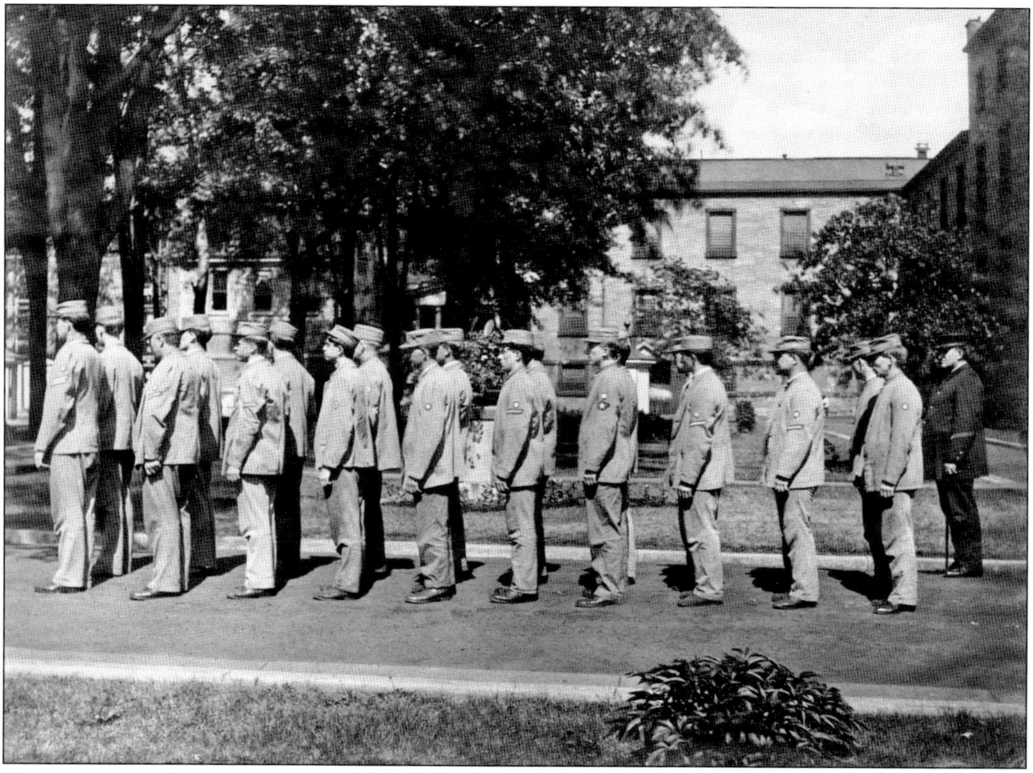

The winter uniforms were wool; the summer uniforms were a lighter weight but still included jackets, vests, and hats.

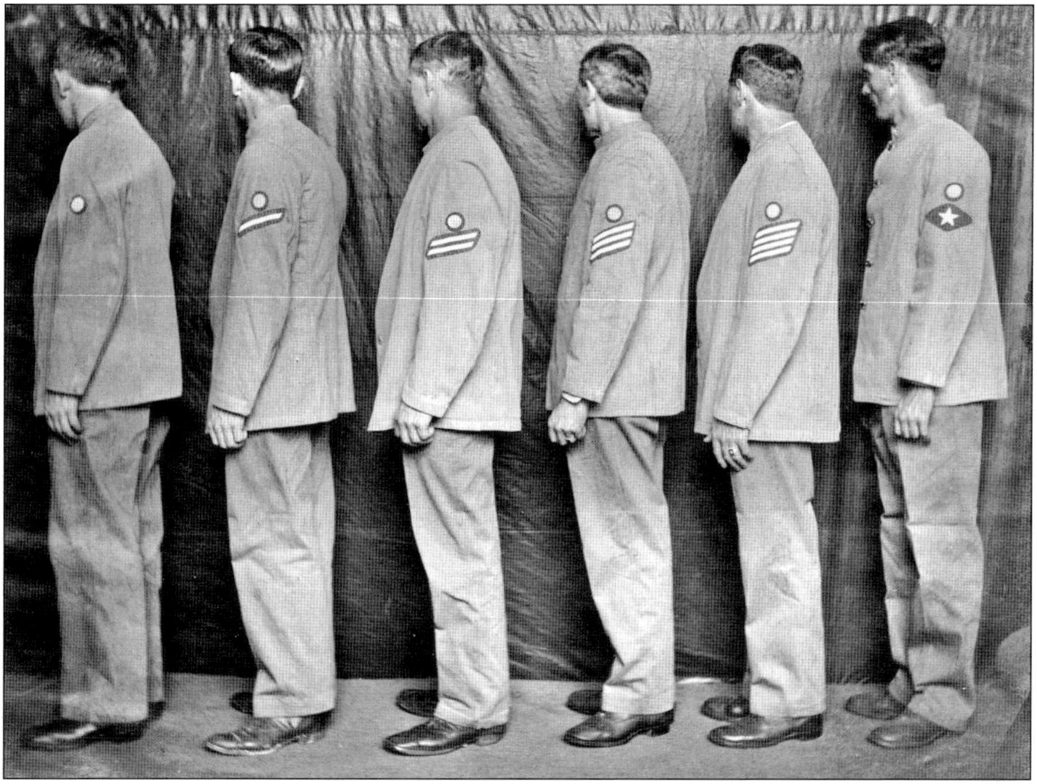

Well-behaved convicts wore emblems on their sleeves, called honor bars, to denote their status. Here the first man wears a circle showing he has served less than one year's time. The second man has served a full year with perfect conduct. The third man has served two full years with perfect conduct, the fourth three years, the fifth four full years with perfect conduct, and the star on the sixth man shows he has served five full years with no blots on his record.

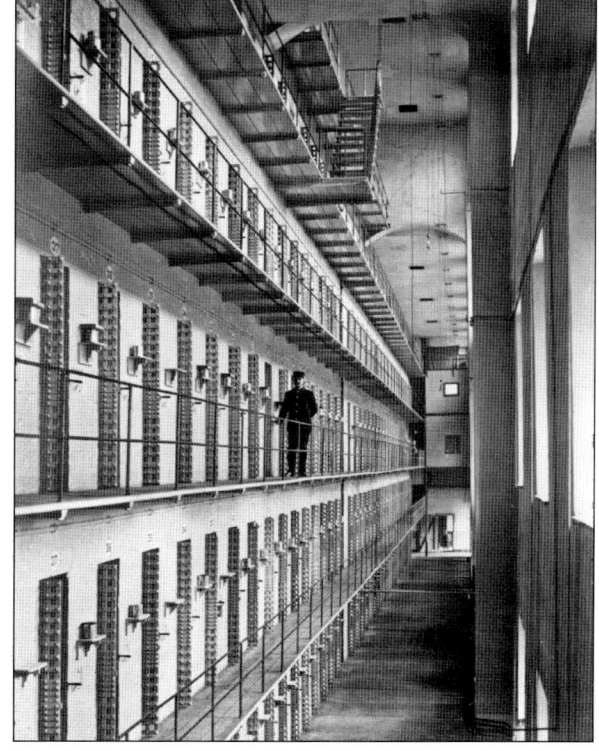

Changes may have come to the prison, but the cell blocks remained much the same as they had been when first built in 1821. The image at right, which became a popular Auburn postcard, provides a good view of the five tiers of cells.

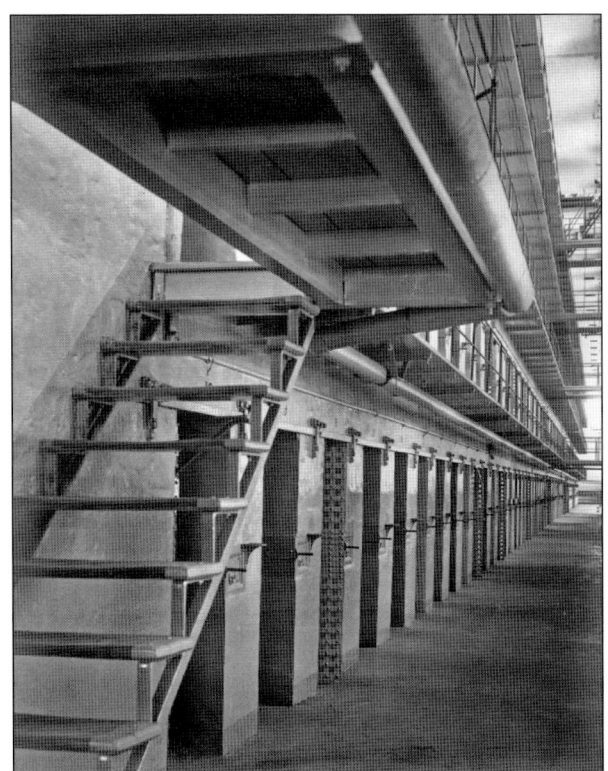

This photograph shows the north side of the south wing of cells, around 1912. The lock plate outside each cell was bolted to a heavy angle casting embedded in the masonry. The bolt held the hand lever up until the key was turned in the lock. The lever could then be pushed down, releasing the barred door.

The prison was not completely electrified until after the first electrocution in 1890. Eventually, there was a light bulb in each cell. A bucket was still necessary because there was no running water in the cells.

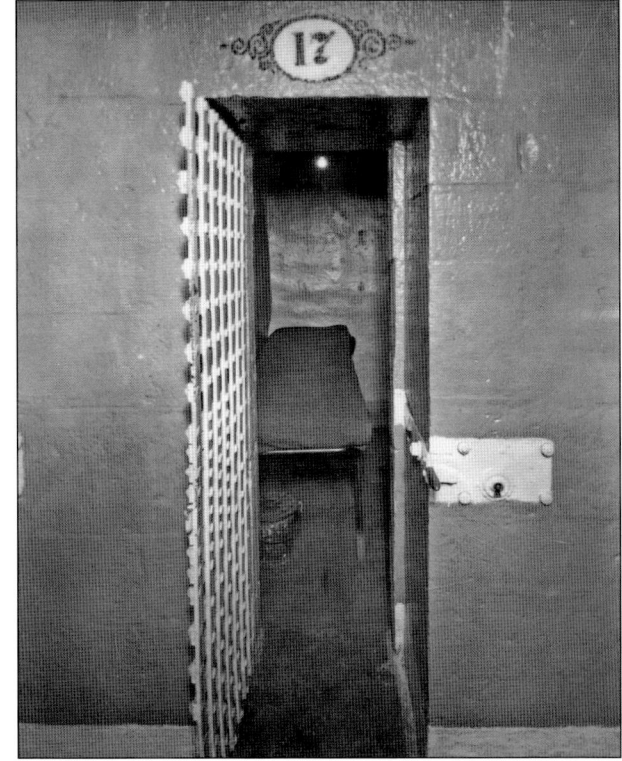

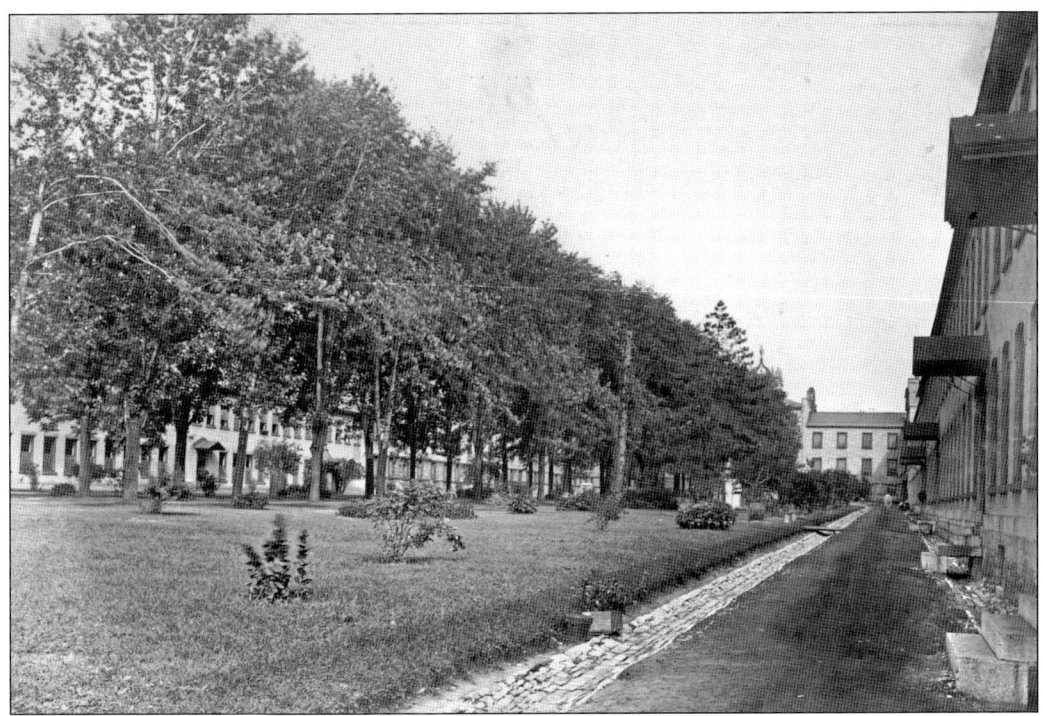

This photograph shows the main yard and shop buildings around 1910, looking west down the inside north side from the back of the administration building.

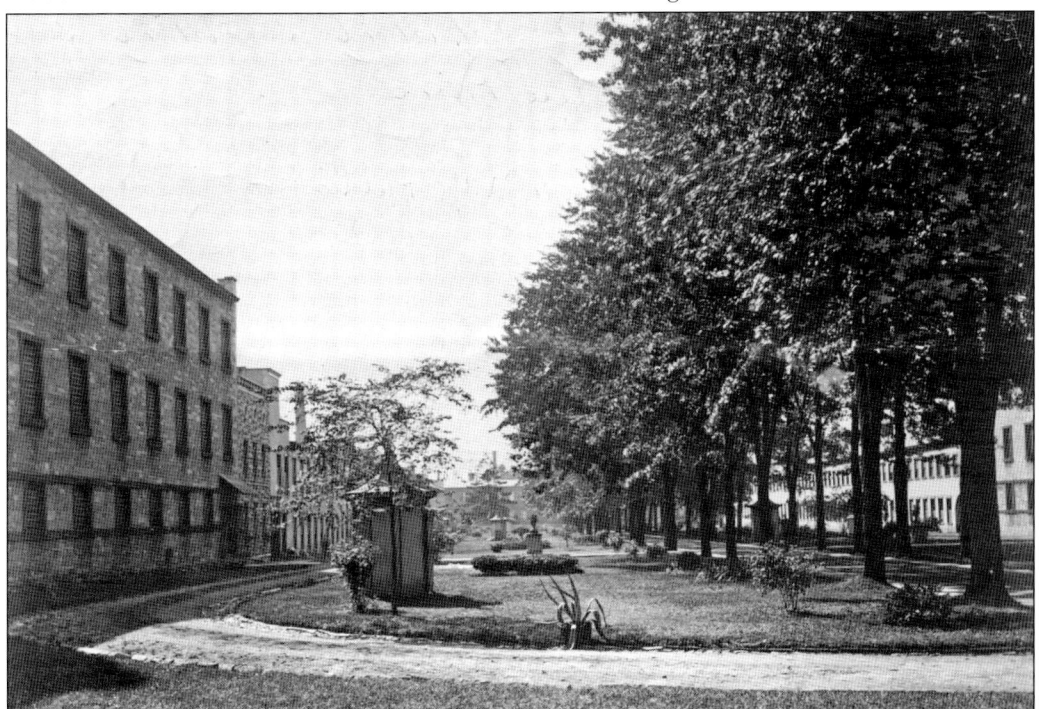

This image, probably taken the same day as the above photograph, shows the same side of the yard looking east. The back of Copper John is just visible standing above the trees.

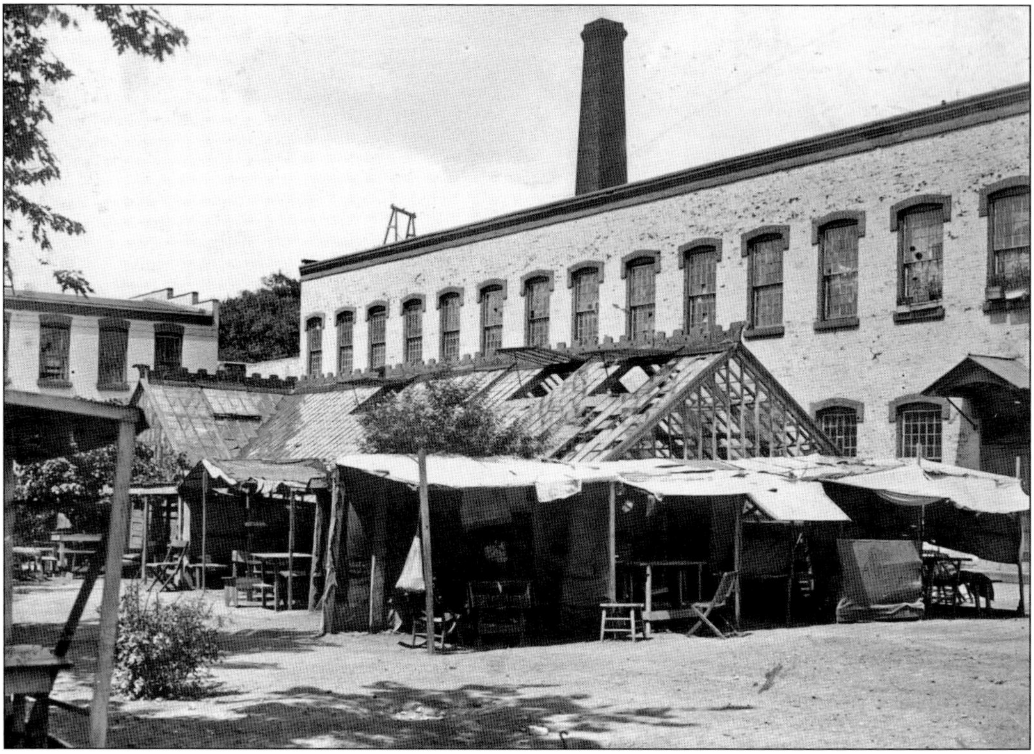

In the early 1900s, there were often events held in the prison yard that were open to the public. These photographs, taken around 1915, appear to show the yard being set up for some kind of event featuring a number of booths and chairs for visitors. (Both, courtesy of Michael Pettigrass.)

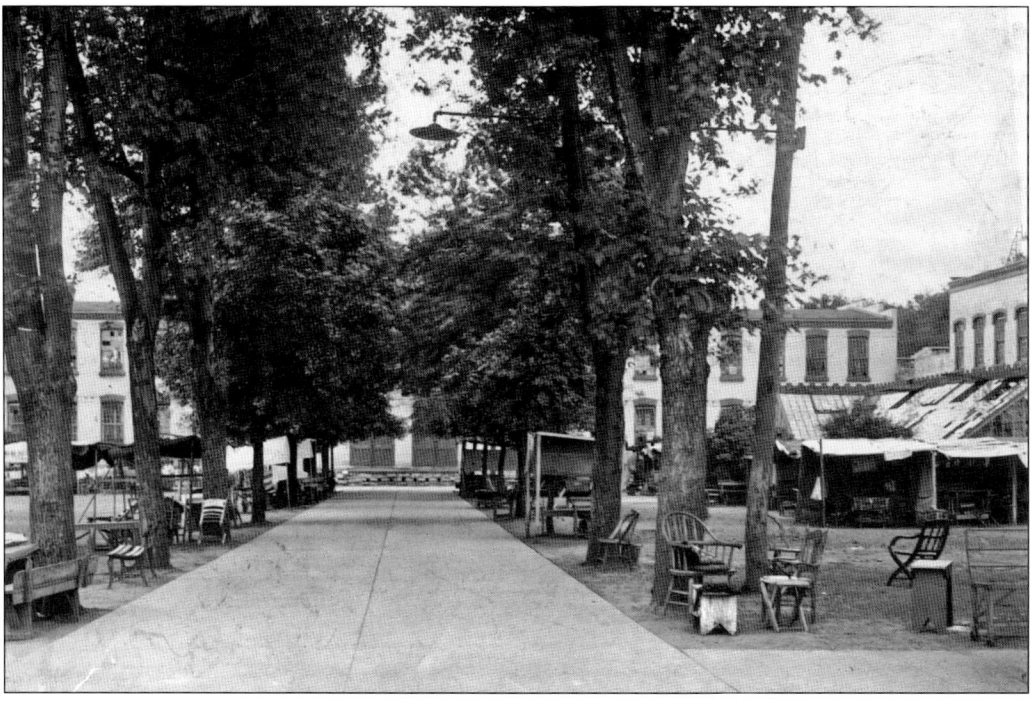

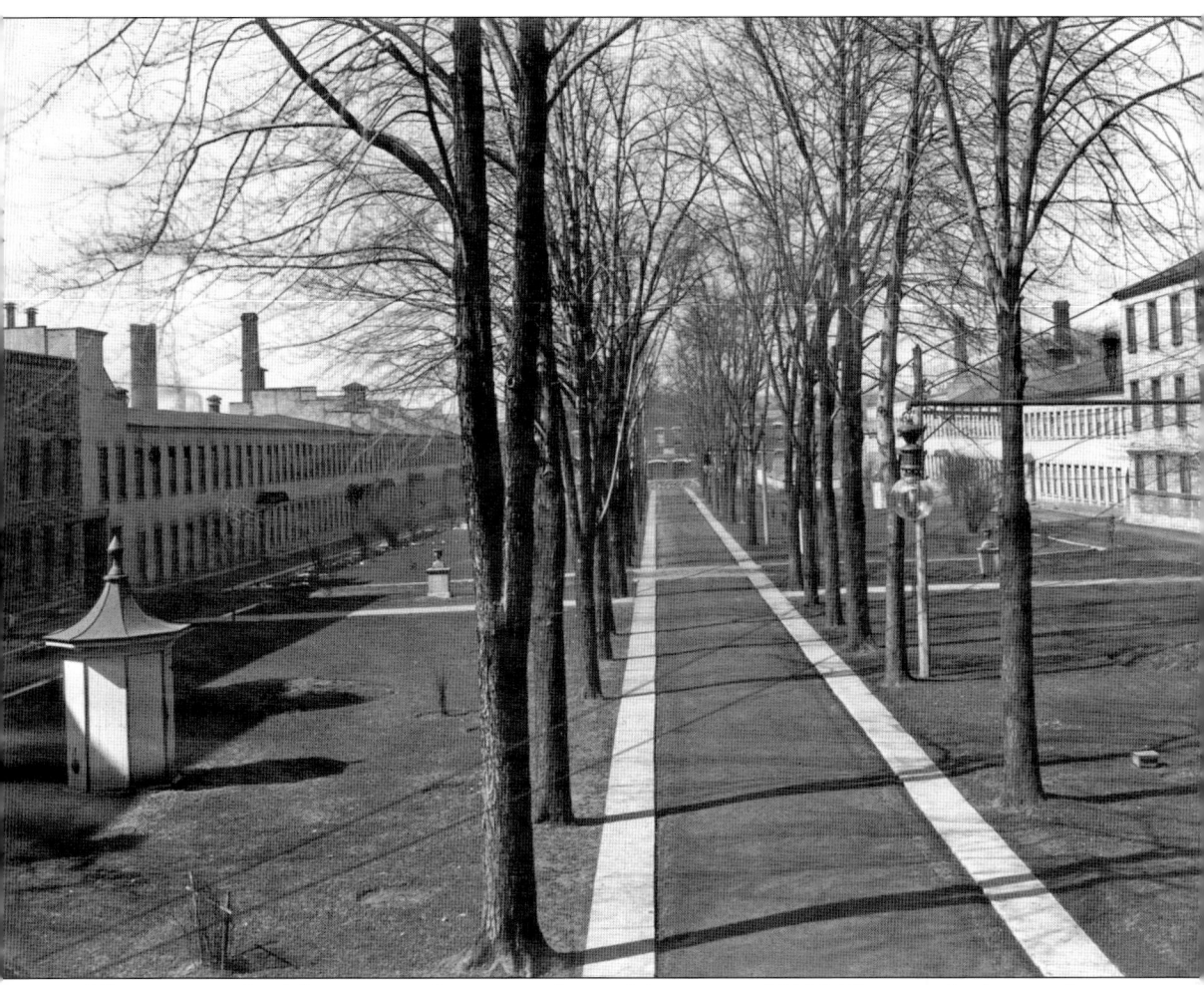
The center path of the main yard appears to be mud free, around 1900. This view looks west from the back of the administration building.

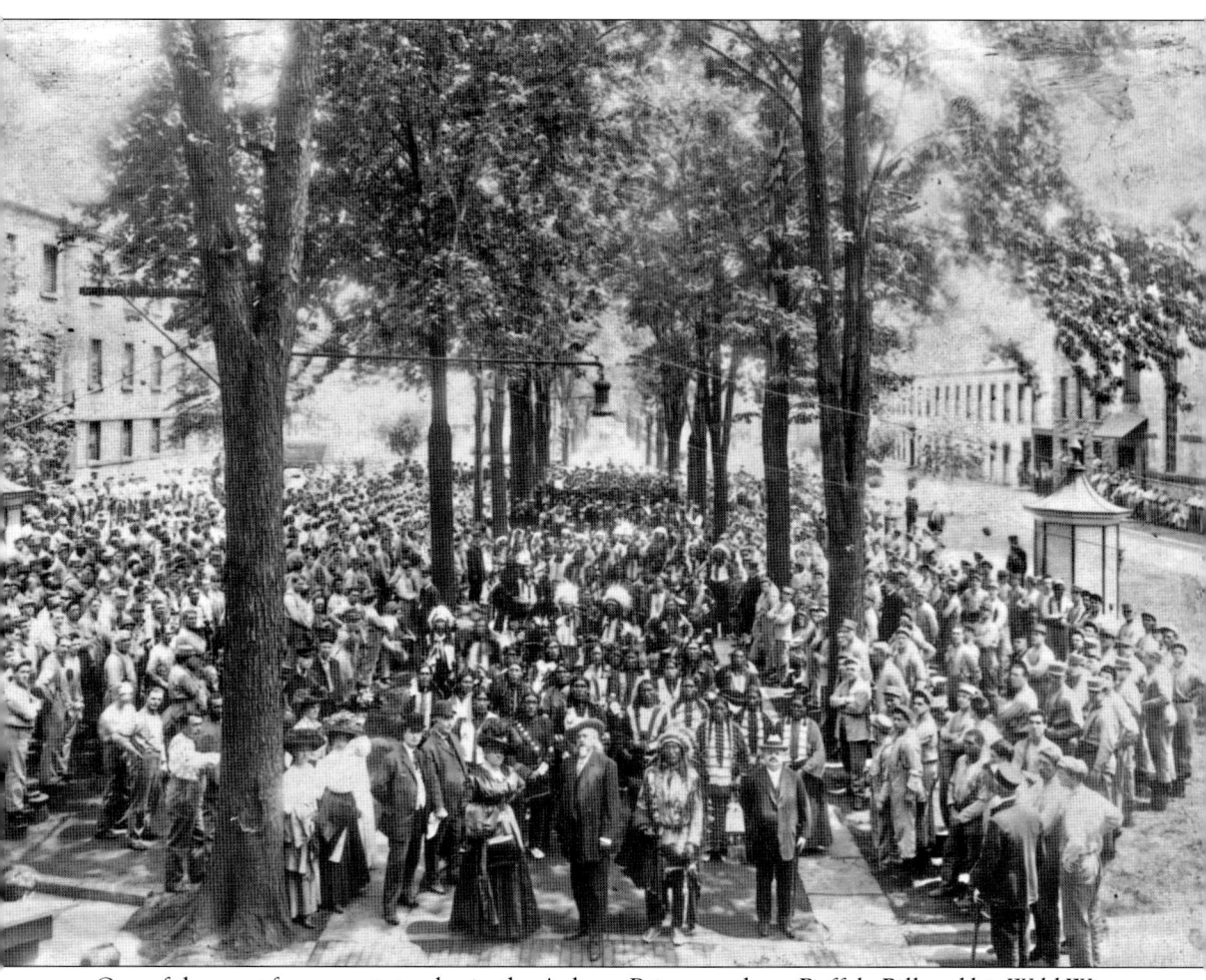

One of the most famous acts to play in the Auburn Prison yard was Buffalo Bill and his Wild West show, which appeared on July 30, 1908. Buffalo Bill himself, William F. Cody, is in the center with his wife, Louisa, to his right. Warden George Benham is to her right. Chief Black Hawk stands to Cody's left, and next to him is deputy warden Allen Tupper.

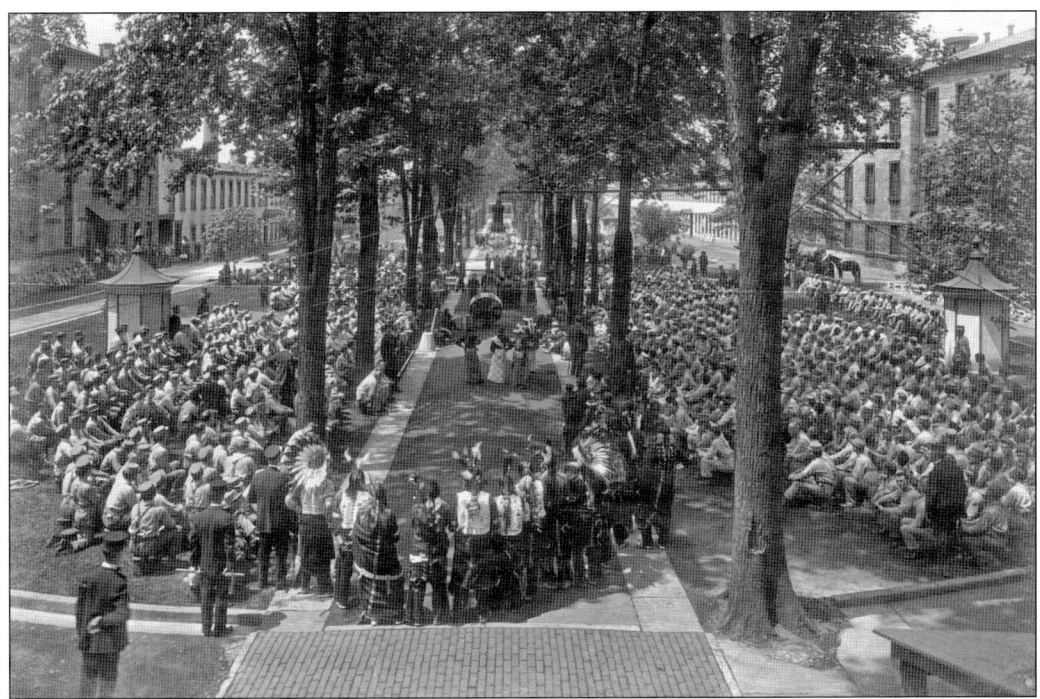

Here are two more photographs taken at the Wild West show in the Auburn Prison yard in 1908. The Wild West show was in town to perform two shows at Wait's Field on Franklin and Elm Streets, at 2:00 and 8:00 p.m. on July 30. General admission tickets were 50¢ each, "including seat." The Wild West show performers and their animals arrived by train to the New York Central Railroad station across the street from the prison.

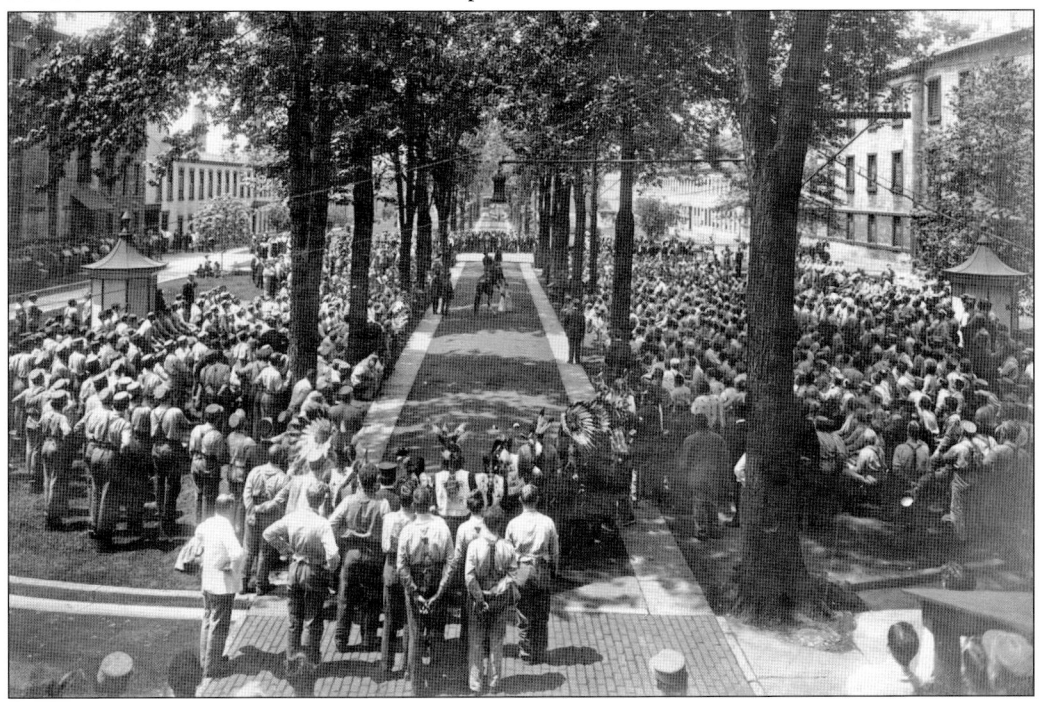

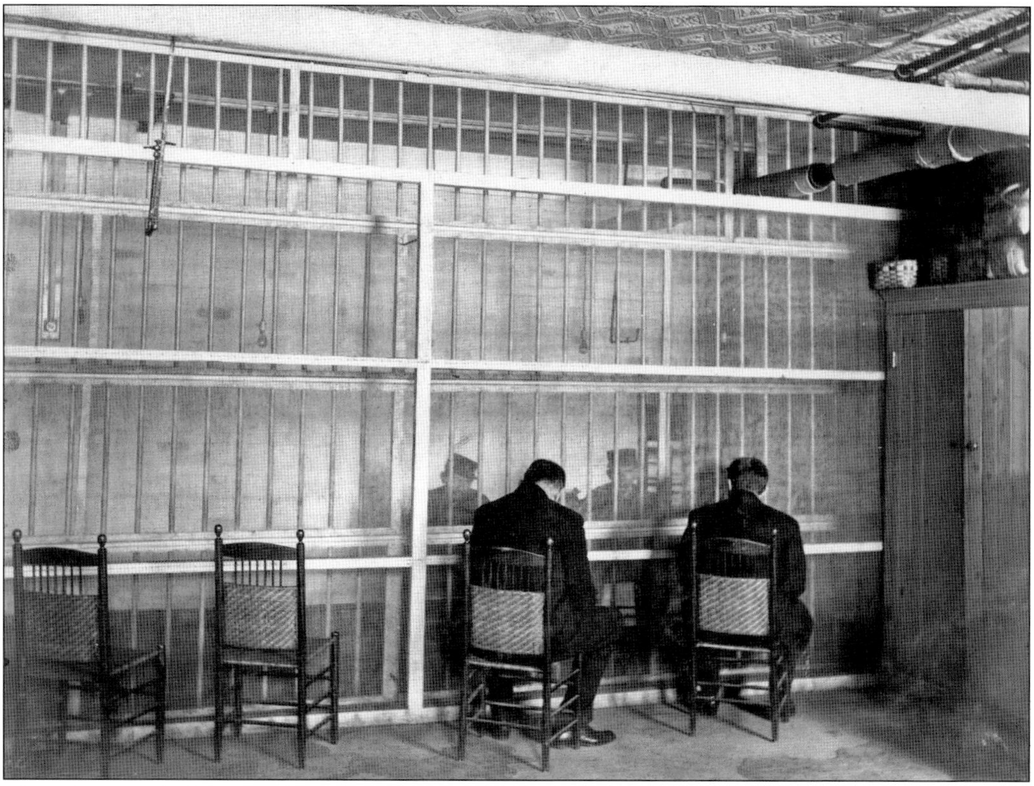

This photograph from warden Charles Rattigan's personal album seems to show a visiting room at the prison around 1912. The men on the far side of the bars appear to be wearing convict hats.

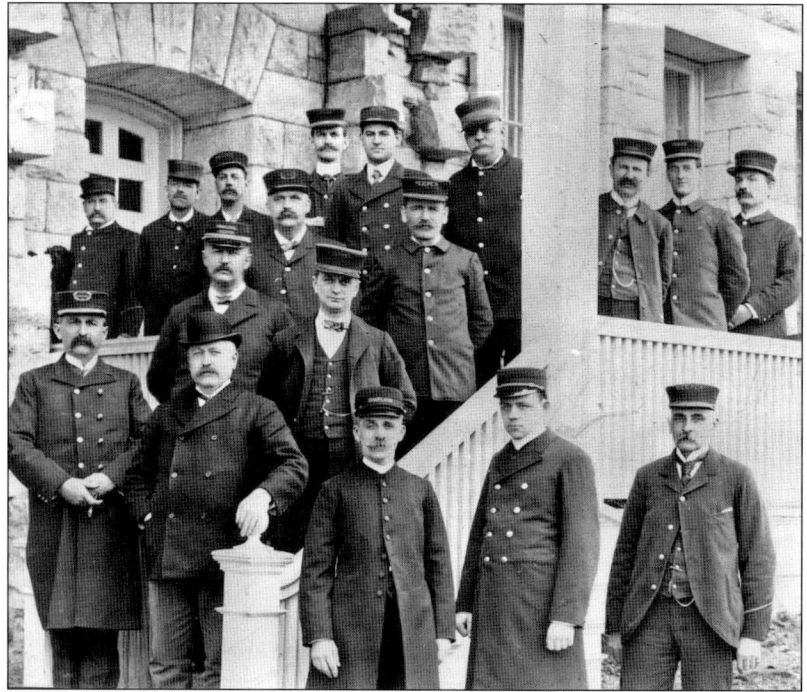

Posing for a photograph around 1890, these unidentified staff members of Auburn Prison wear their titles on their hats. Keepers supervised convicts, and guards patrolled the outer walls. The principal keeper was in charge of both the keepers and guards.

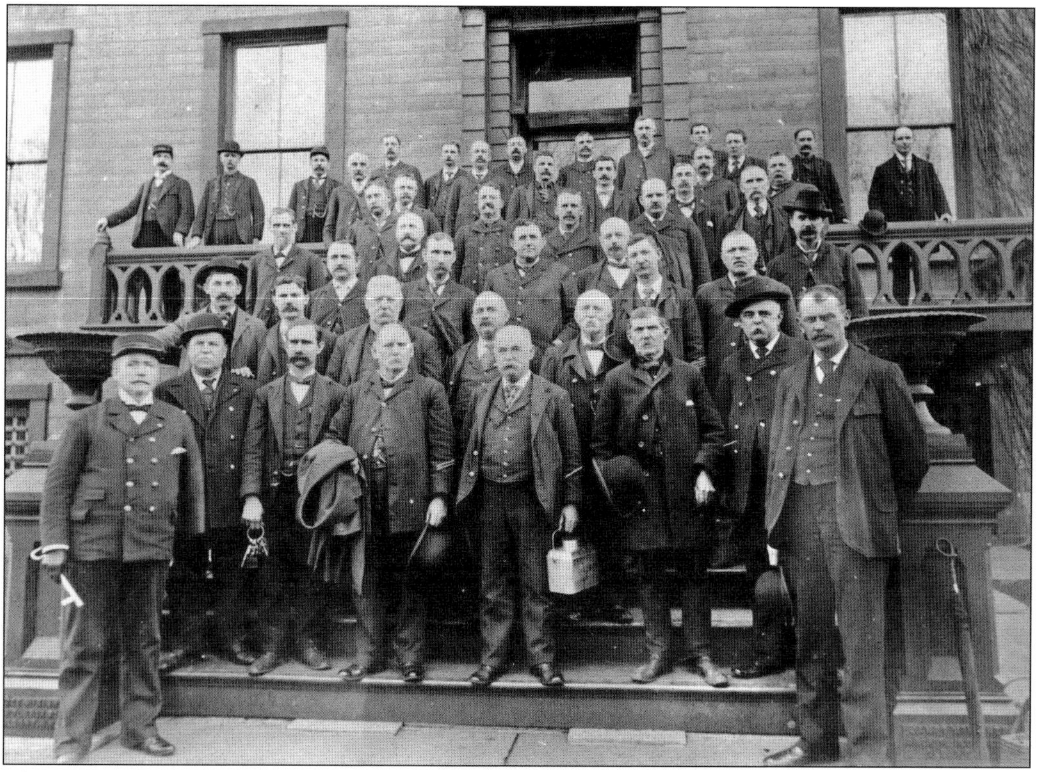

This is another group of unidentified Auburn Prison employees, photographed around 1910. The man in the front left is holding the giant key to the front gate of the prison.

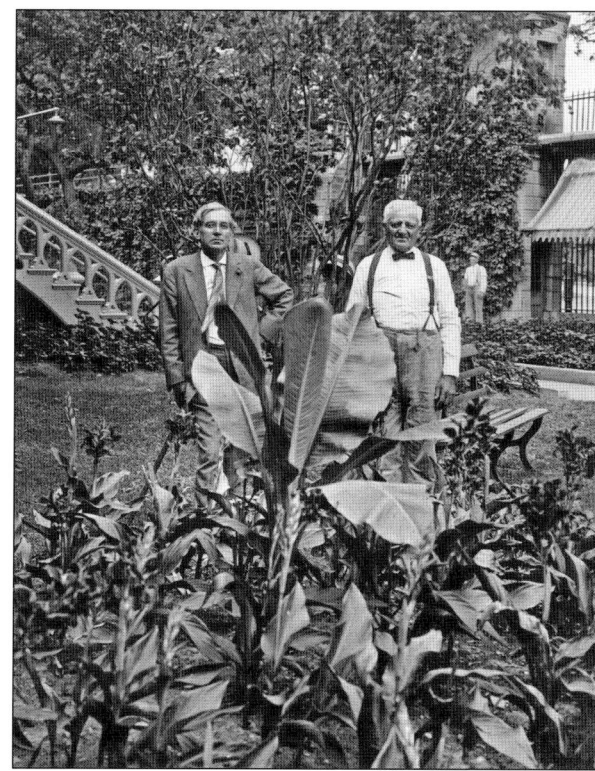

Warden Charles Rattigan (left) and an unidentified man, perhaps a convict gardener, stand amid the lush foliage of the prison's front yard around 1912.

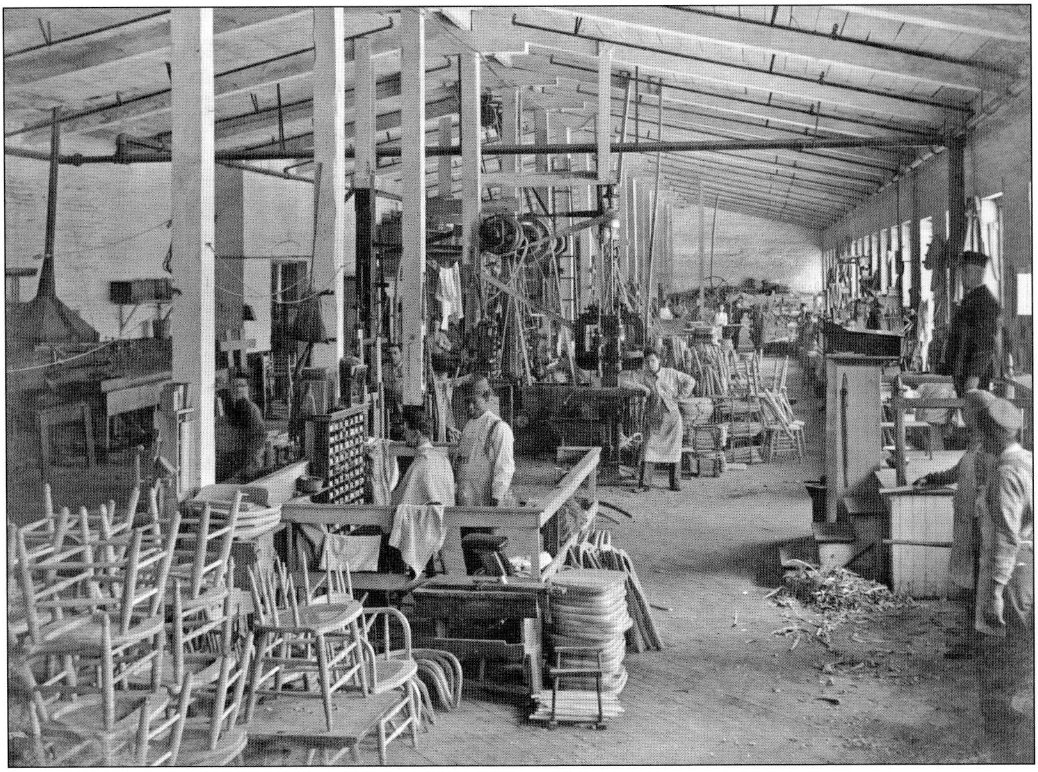

Furniture production continued on a large scale even after the prison went on the state use system in 1890. This photograph of the chair shop, taken around 1910, shows both the raised keeper's platform on the right and the barber's corral in the center. With more than 1,000 men needing haircuts, barbering is still done inside the shops at Auburn Correctional Facility.

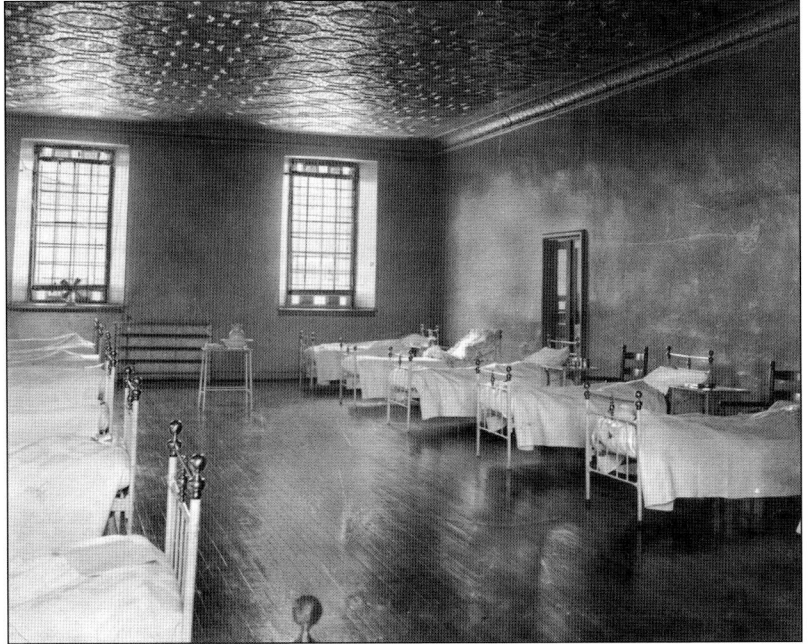

This photograph of one of the wards in the Auburn Prison hospital was used for a postcard. There is no sign of electrical service in this image. There is a fan on the windowsill, but no cords can be seen.

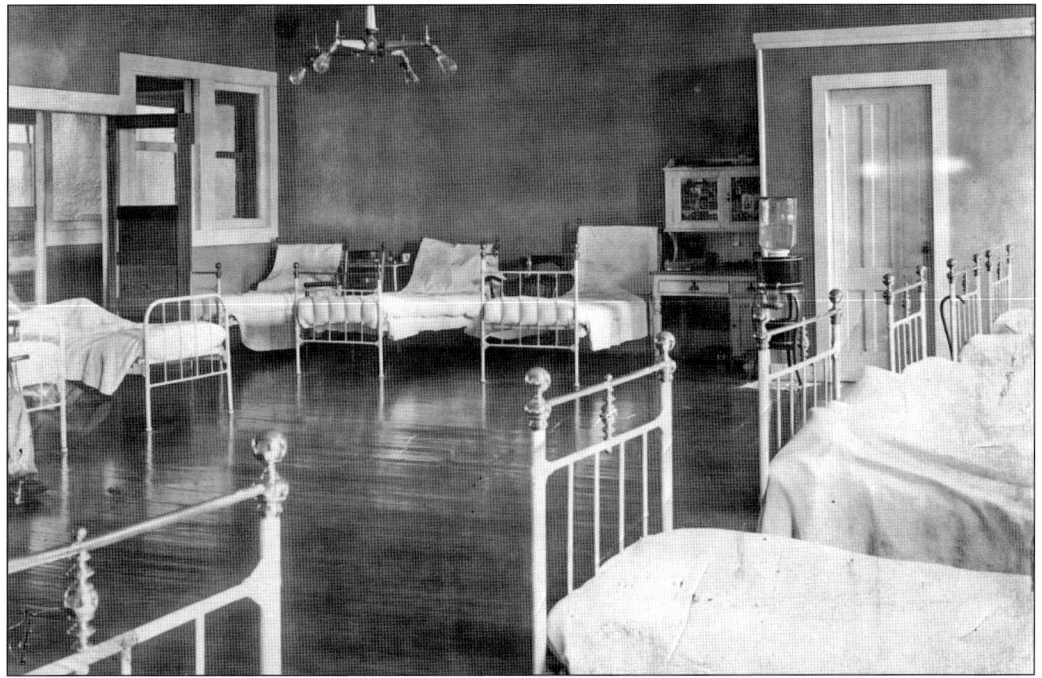

Here is another view of a ward in the prison hospital, taken around 1910, clearly showing a ceiling light fixture that has been converted from gas to electricity. Eight inmates died in Auburn Prison in 1910, in addition to the two who were executed.

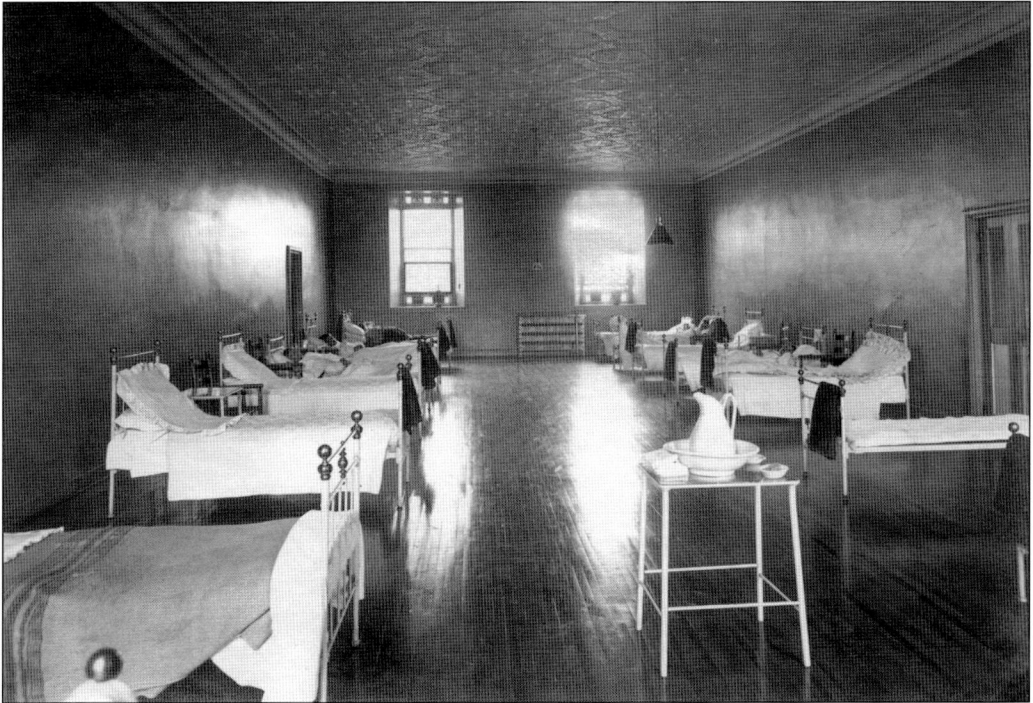

This later view of a ward in the Auburn Prison hospital shows new electric light fixtures. Five of the beds are occupied by sick inmates.

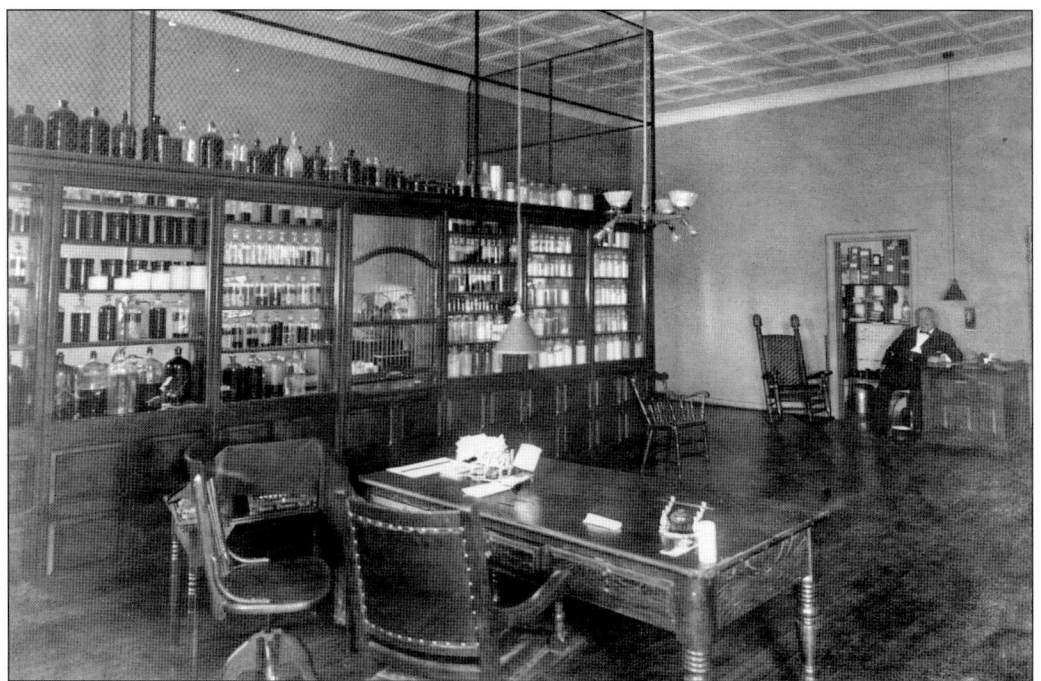

Here is the prison hospital dispensary around 1910. Hospital steward William Patterson is seated to the right. This room features both the four-armed ceiling light fixture converted from gas and the newer electric ceiling lights.

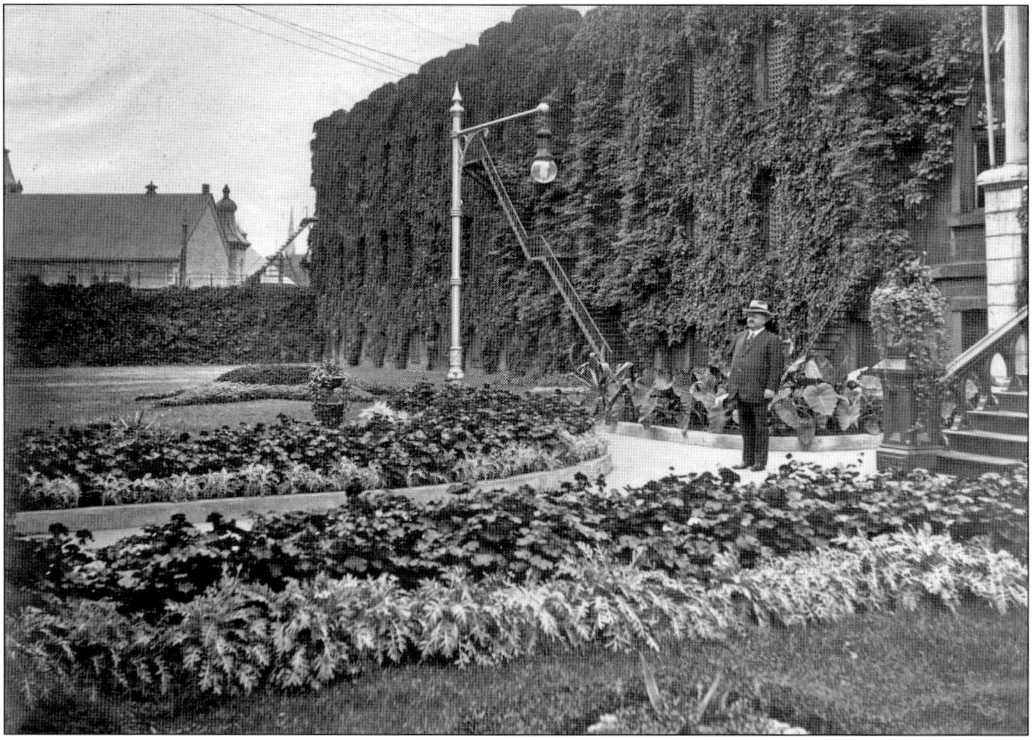

This is deputy warden Allen Tupper in front of the administration building, around 1910.

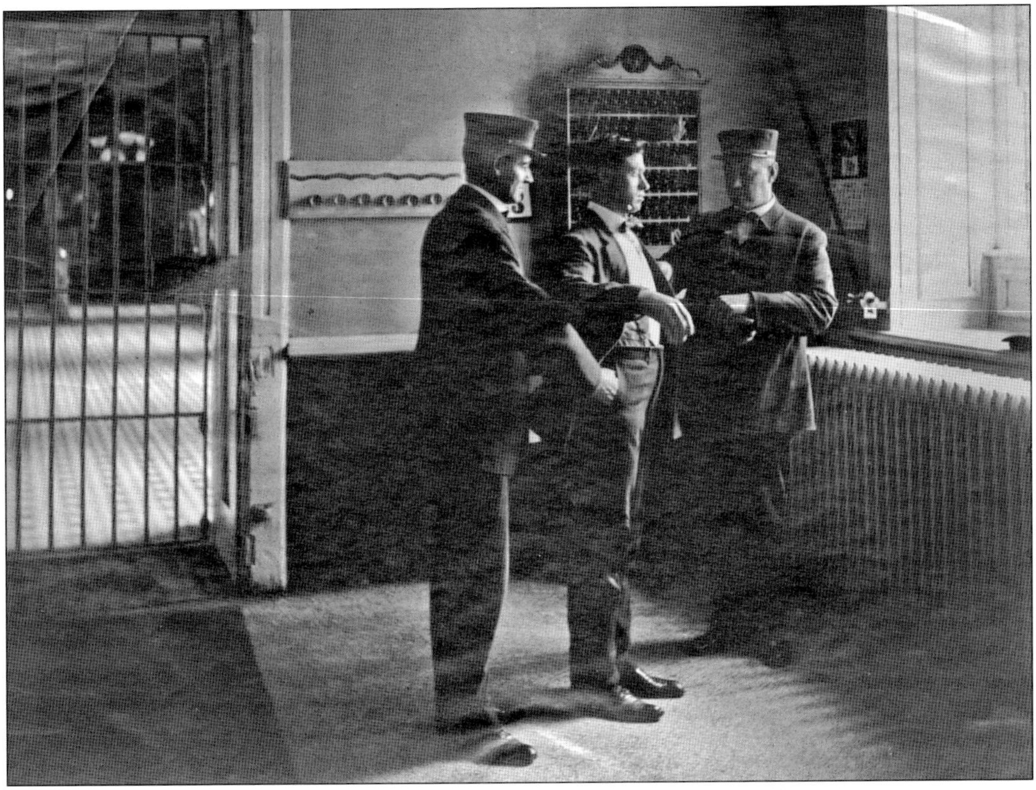

The record does not indicate the purpose of this photographic essay, depicting a new convict from his arrival at Auburn Prison until his eventual release from incarceration. Taken in August 1909, the 12 photographs feature real keepers and staff at the prison, but the supposed convict is unidentified and may have been a volunteer model. In this first photograph, the new convict arrives at the prison and is searched by staff.

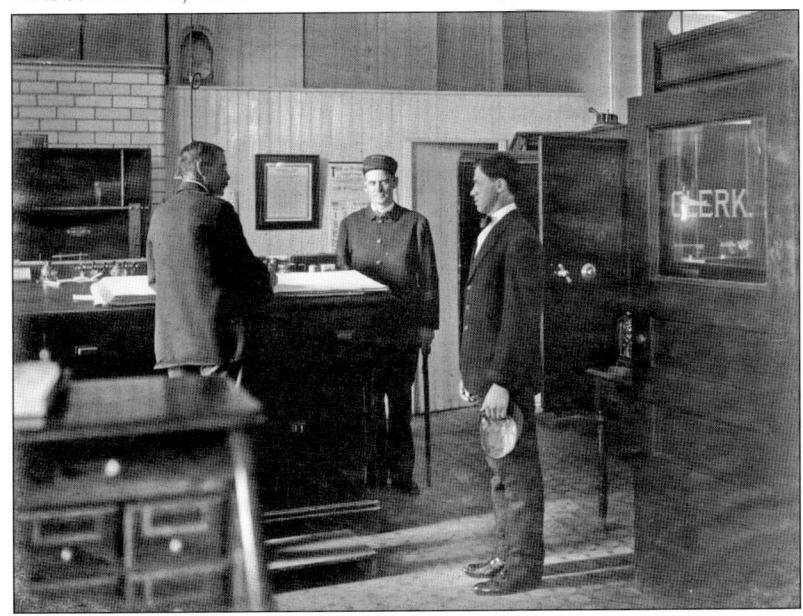

In the second step, the new convict's arrival is recorded in the clerk's office. The record included the inmate's crime and sentence, his country of origin, whether he could read and write, and his drinking habits (temperate or intemperate).

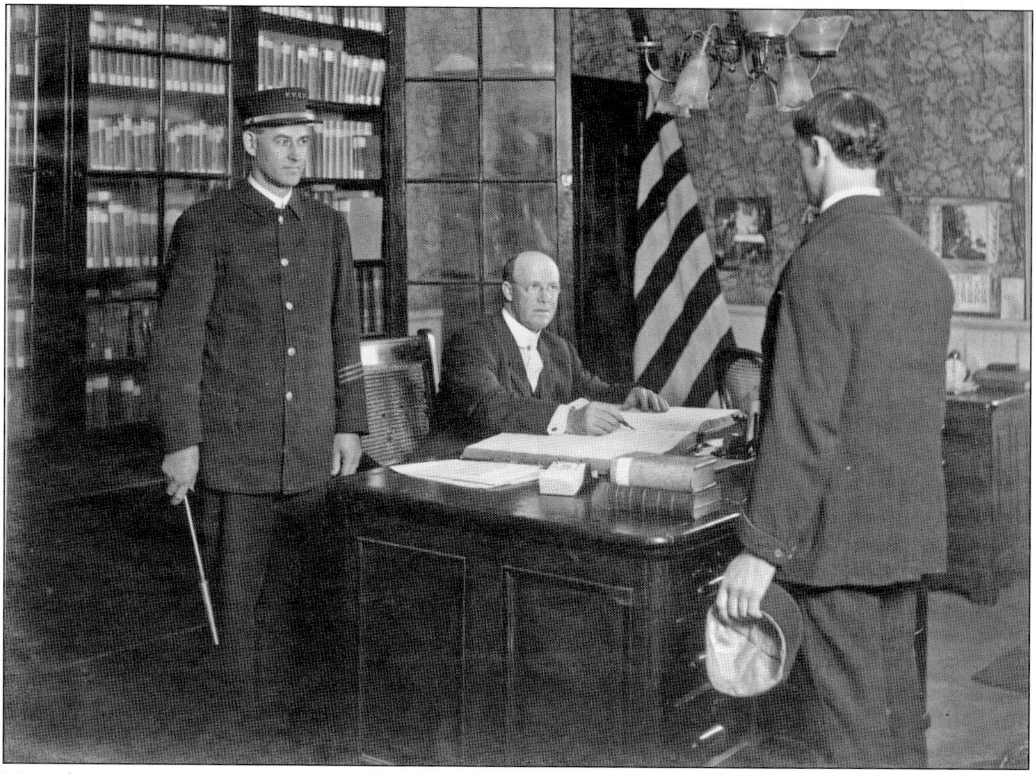

Here the new convict receives instruction from the warden. Despite the evidence of this photographic essay, it is doubtful that the warden met each new prisoner individually.

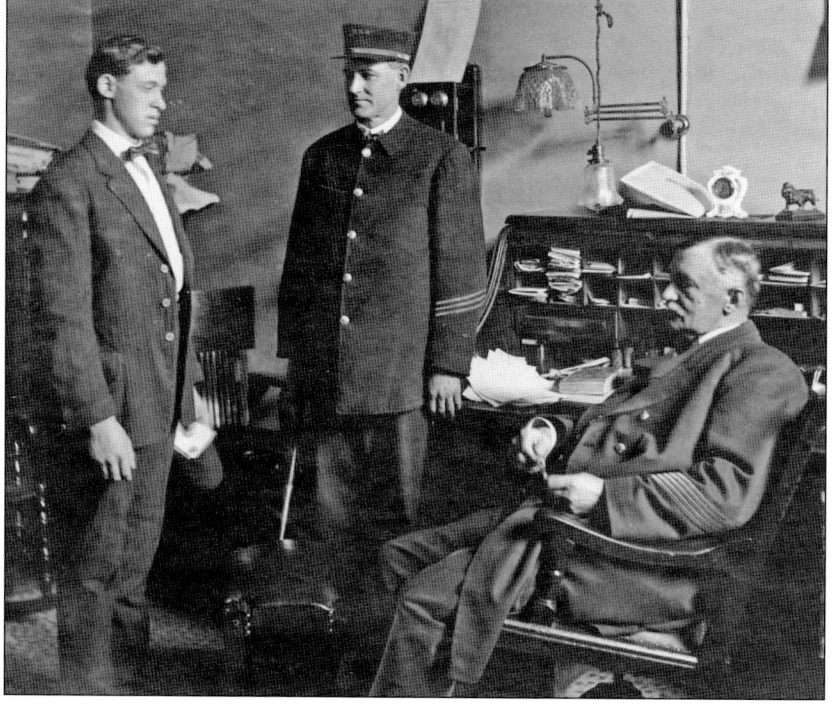

The new prisoner gives his record to the principal keeper and receives instructions.

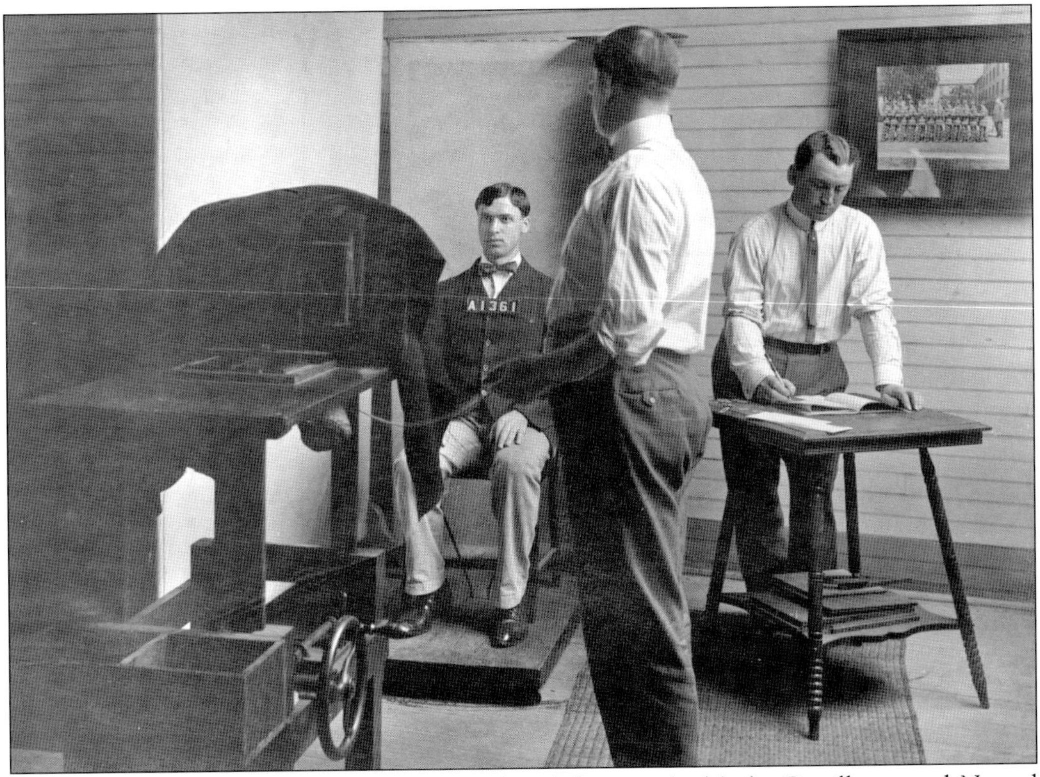

The new convict is precisely weighed, measured, and photographed for his Bertillon record. Named after French criminologist Alphonse Bertillon, the Bertillon record was a system of identifying individual people by means of a detailed record of body measurements, physical description, and photographs. These precise measurements could be used to identify repeat offenders, even if they changed their names. The Bertillon record was made obsolete by the use of fingerprints to identify criminals, although everyone arrested is still photographed for a mug shot.

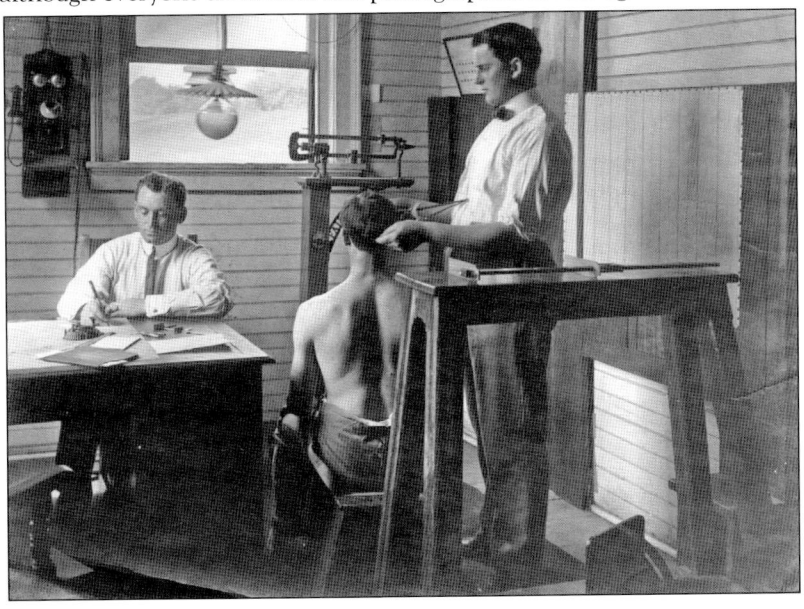

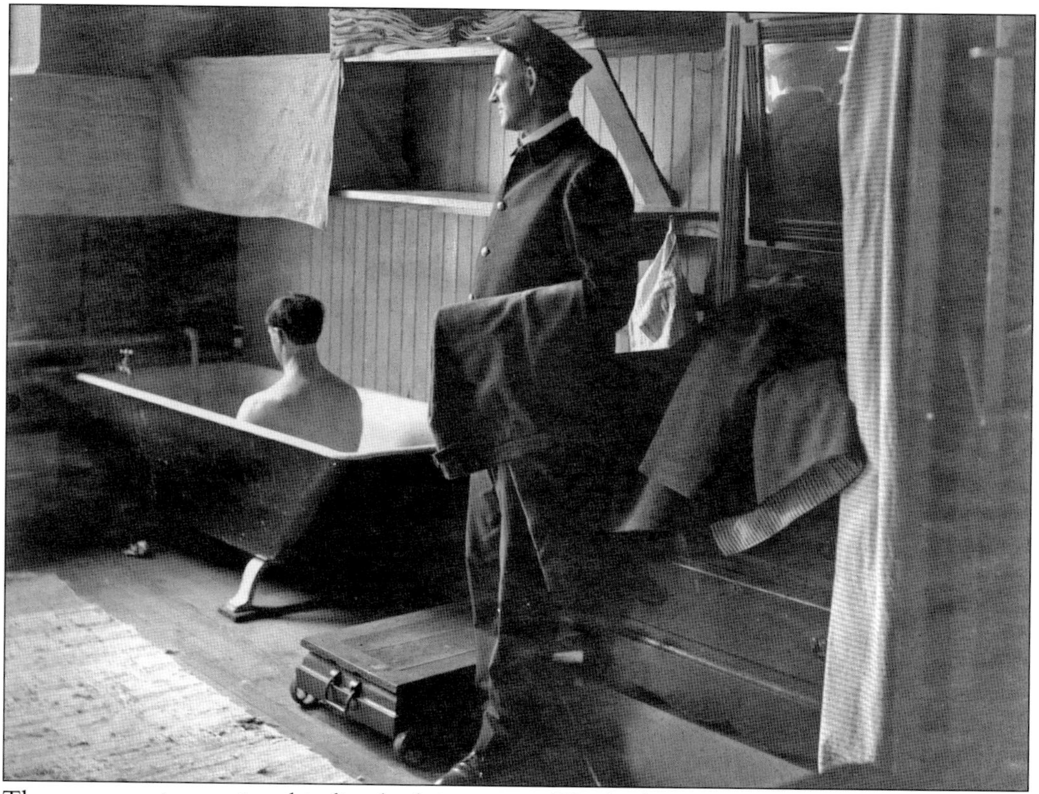

The new convict receives his first bath in prison. The bathroom for newly received convicts, located in the basement of the administration building, was used for the first electrocution because it had a sink.

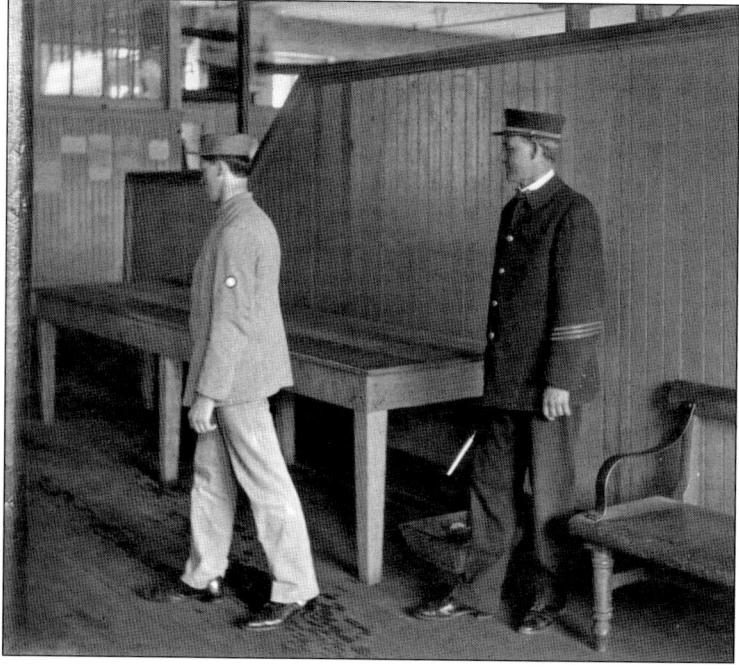

Measured, photographed, and clean, the new prisoner heads off to the cell block in his fresh convict uniform.

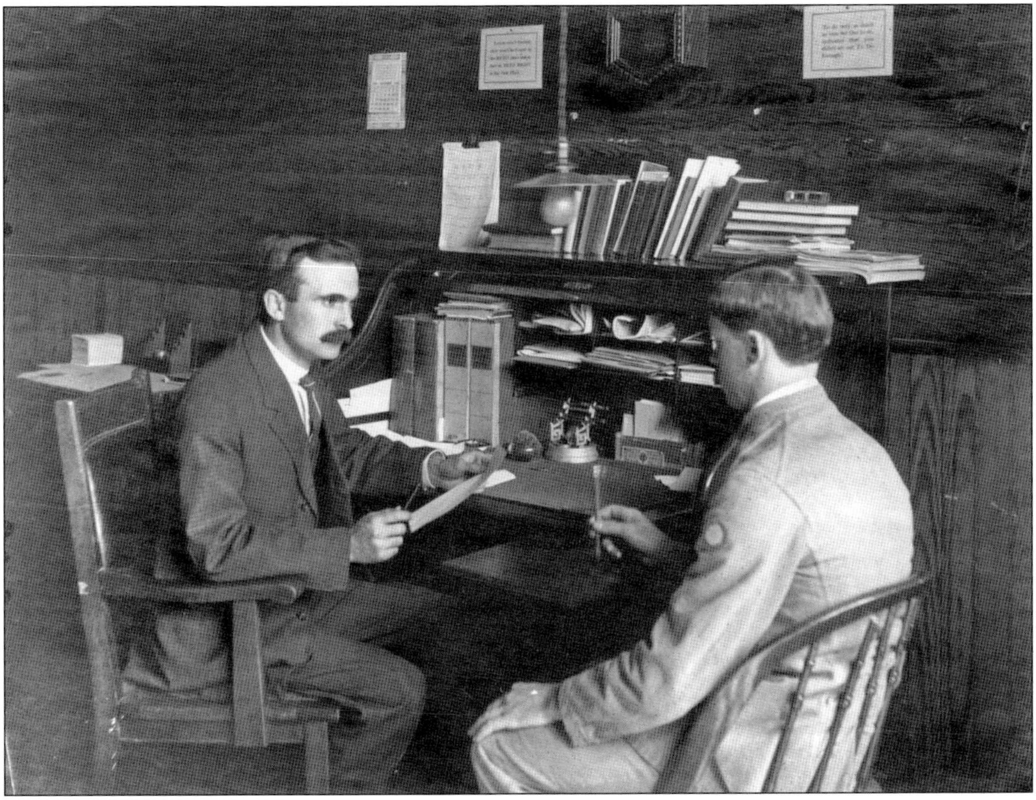

The prisoner meets with the head teacher. The teachers worked under the direction of the chaplain. The chaplain was responsible for both religious and educational services. In 1827, Auburn Prison became the first prison to have a chaplain on staff when Rev. Jared Curtis went on the New York State payroll as full-time chaplain at Auburn. His salary was $200 a year.

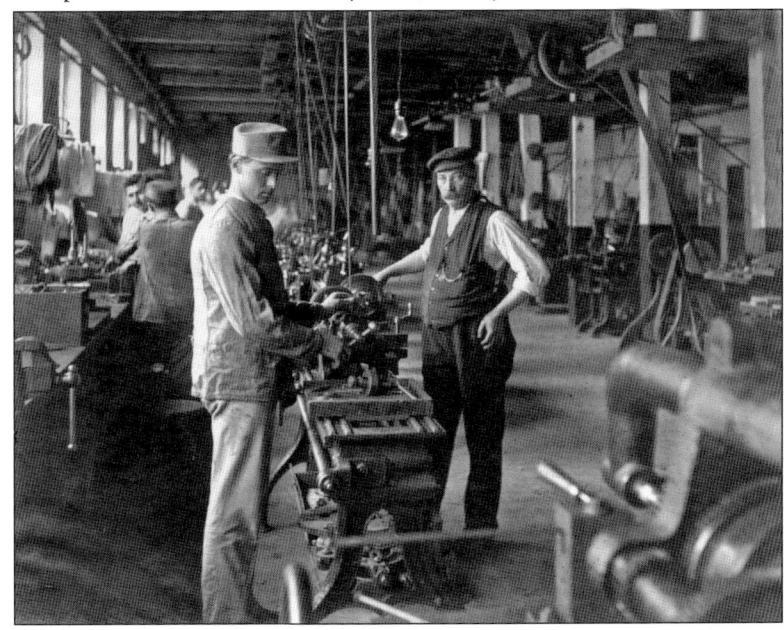

Like all prisoners, this one is put to work. Here he receives instruction from the foreman in the machine shop, Anders Magnusson (right). Magnusson was an immigrant from Sweden who started working at Auburn Prison in 1895. Even in 1909, prisoners still worked six days a week in the prison shops.

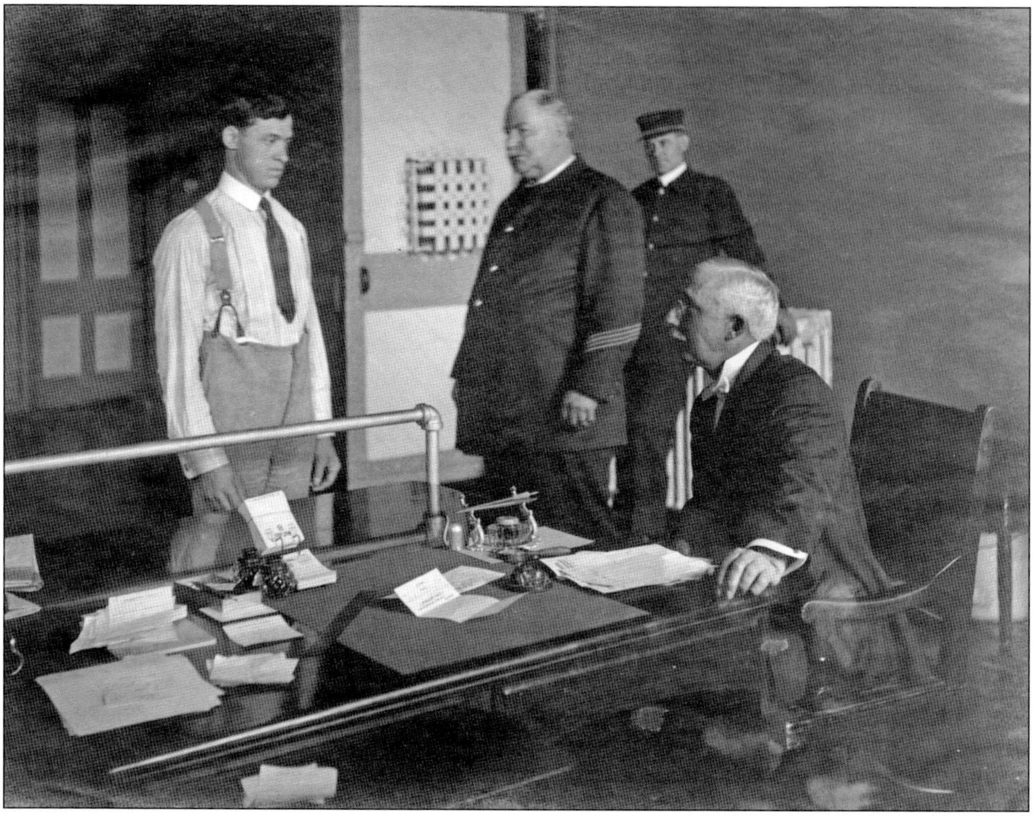

The prisoner meets with the prison doctor (seated). Hospital steward Billy Patterson (without the hat) and an unidentified keeper listen as well. Note the barred window in the sliding door behind them.

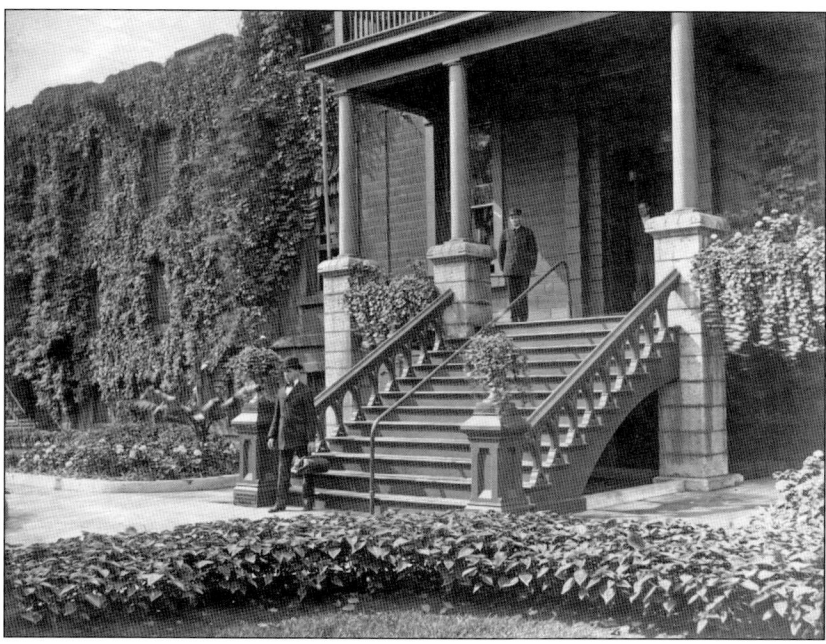

Having served his time, the rehabilitated prisoner leaves Auburn Prison behind him.

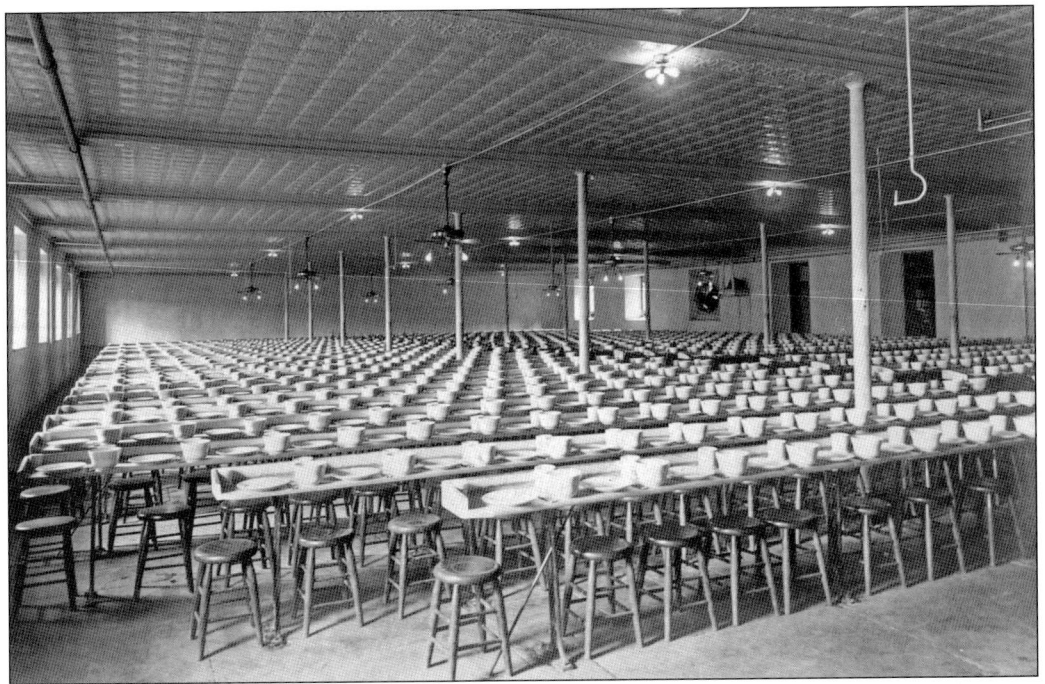

Like most of the larger rooms in the prison, the mess hall featured a decorative tin ceiling. By 1910, ceramic cups and bowls had replaced the metal cups of the 1800s. The men sat on wooden stools and ate at narrow counters.

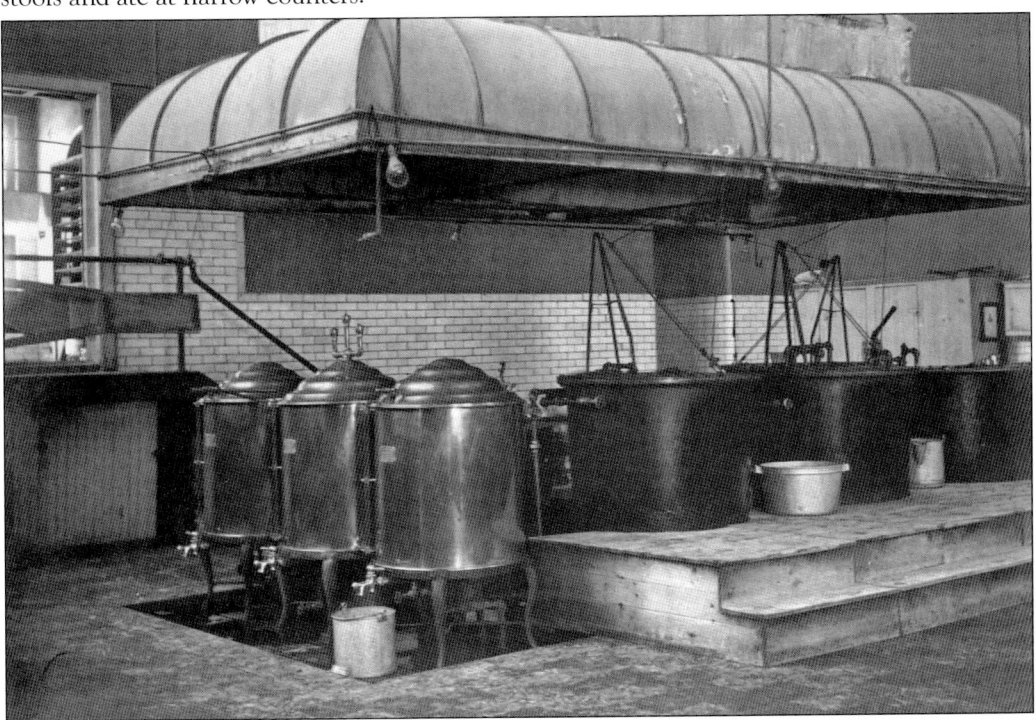

In this photograph, few changes, besides the addition of electric lighting, have been made in the prison kitchen.

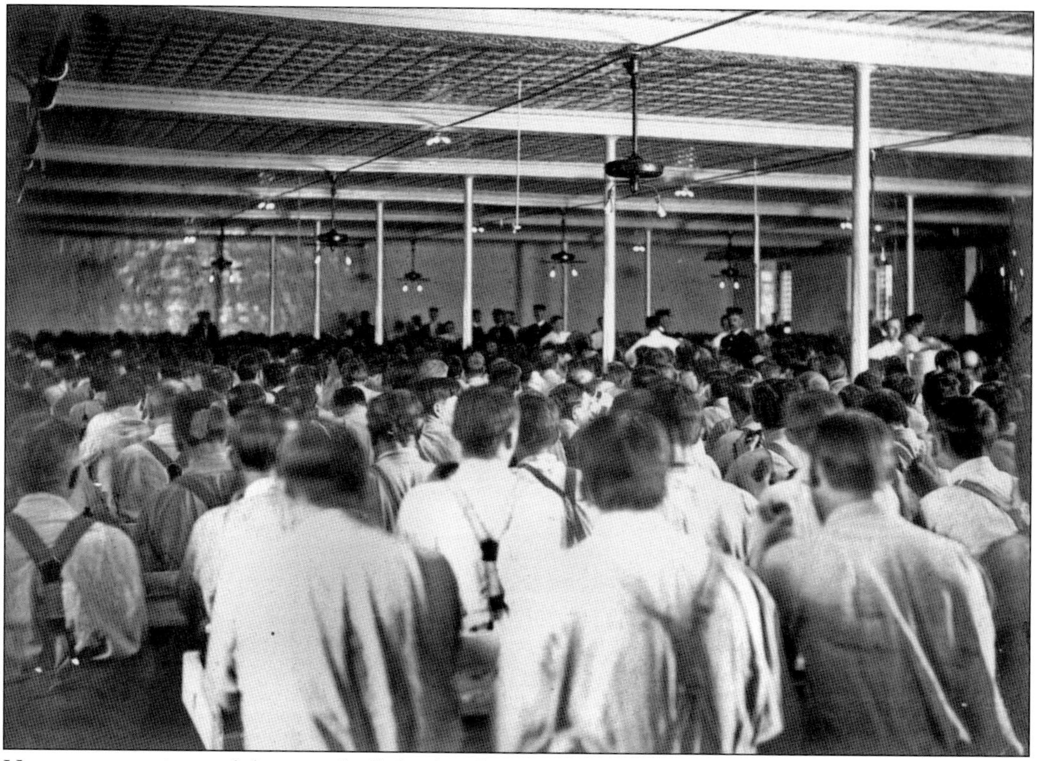

Here are two views of the mess hall, both taken around 1912. The prisoners pictured above are in their summer uniforms, and those shown below are in their woolen winter suits. The silent Auburn System has ended, but all the seats in the mess hall still face in the same direction.

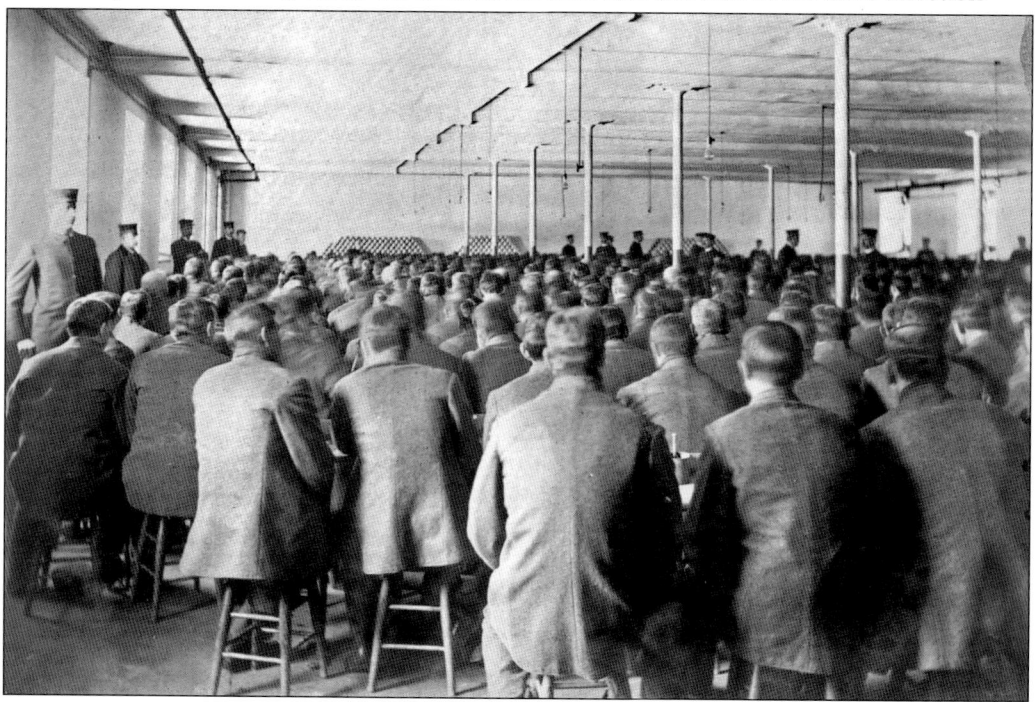

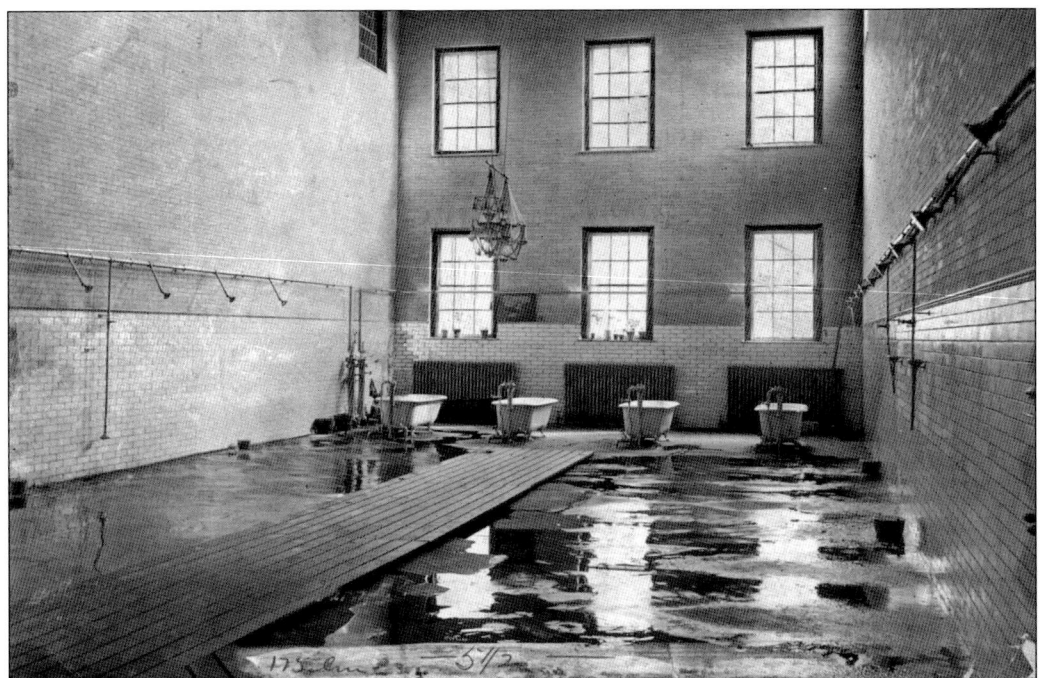

This is a bathroom in one of the cell blocks, around 1905. There are four bathtubs at one end, and multiple showerheads running down both walls. There were no individual controls for the showerheads. The photograph below shows another inmate bathroom. Note the bird cages hanging on the walls and set on the bench next to the bathtub. Keeping pet birds, notably canaries, was a tradition at Auburn Prison. Inmates made the cages from scraps of wood and metal, and many spent years breeding beautiful and musical birds. Inmates were allowed to buy packaged seed from Nichts Feed Store. An inspector from the New York State Commission of Correction, fearing an outbreak of psittacosis (parrot fever), prompted a ban on birds in 1951. Most birds were sent home with inmates' visitors; the remaining birds were sold to a local pet shop.

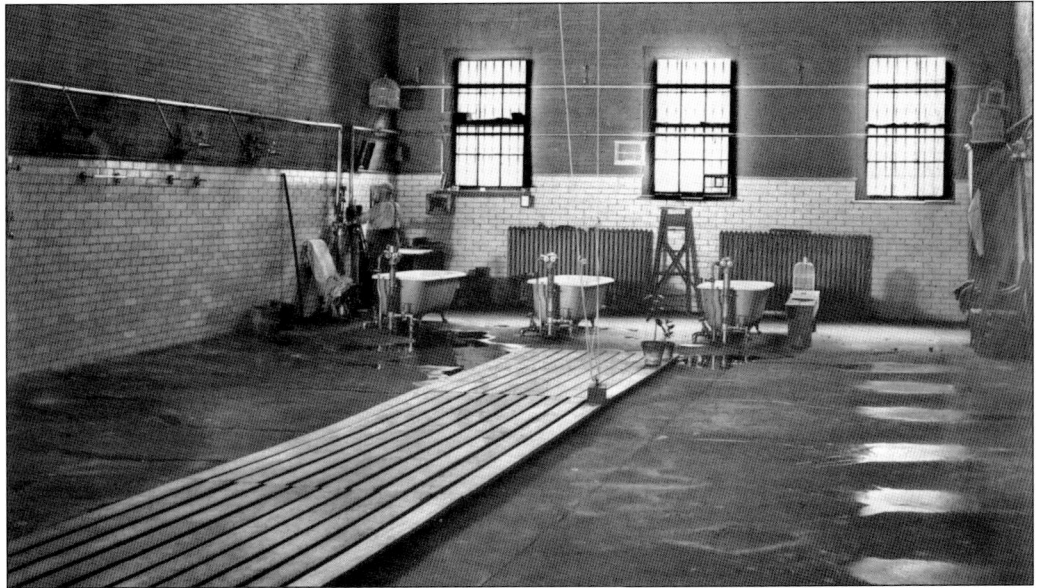

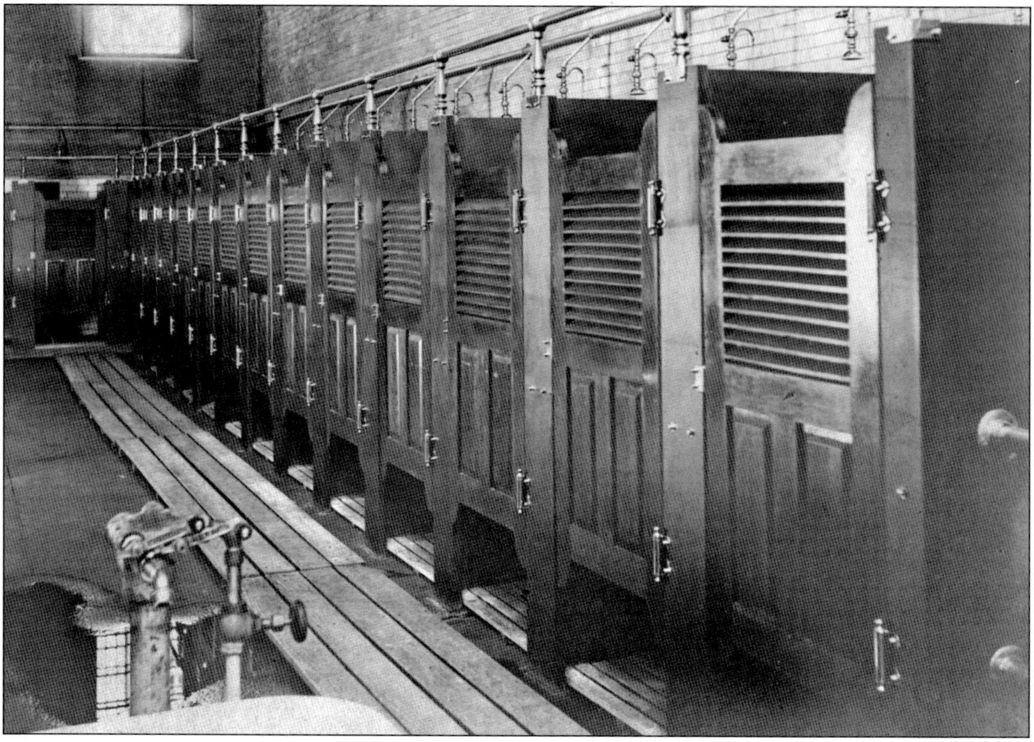

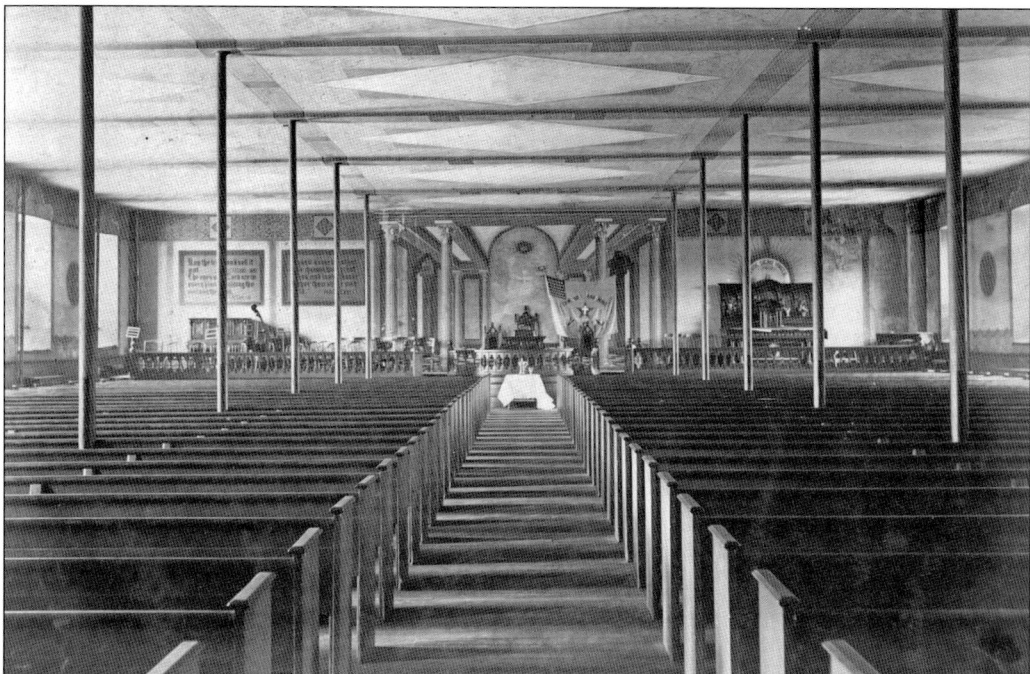

The "new" bathhouse, pictured in 1915, featured individual shower stalls.

Called the chapel, this large assembly room was used for religious services, musical performances, and lectures. Even before the advent of the Mutual Welfare League, the prison played host to shows for inmates who had earned their right to attend through good conduct.

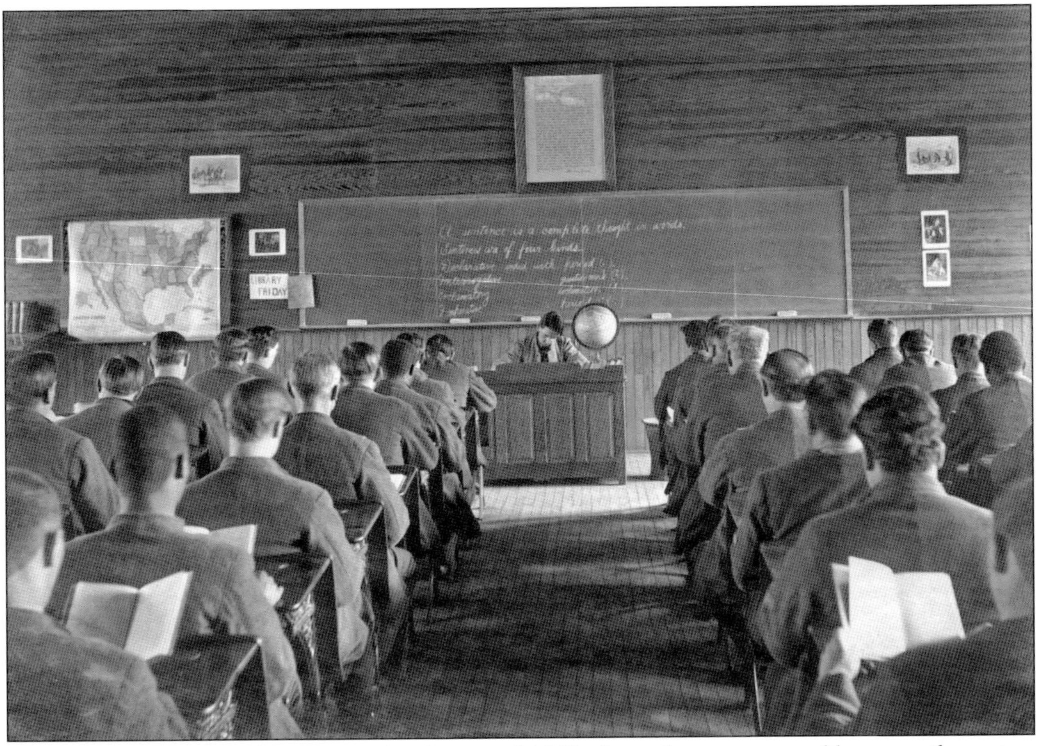

This is a classroom in the prison school, around 1909. Attendance was good because if convicts did not attend chapel, they were locked in their cells from Saturday evening to Monday morning. In 1847, the state authorized the employment of two part-time teachers under the chaplain's direction. Lessons were given on the galleries at night, with the teacher outside with a lantern and a Bible, and the convicts in their cells. The education programs remained in the chaplain's department until the 1920s.

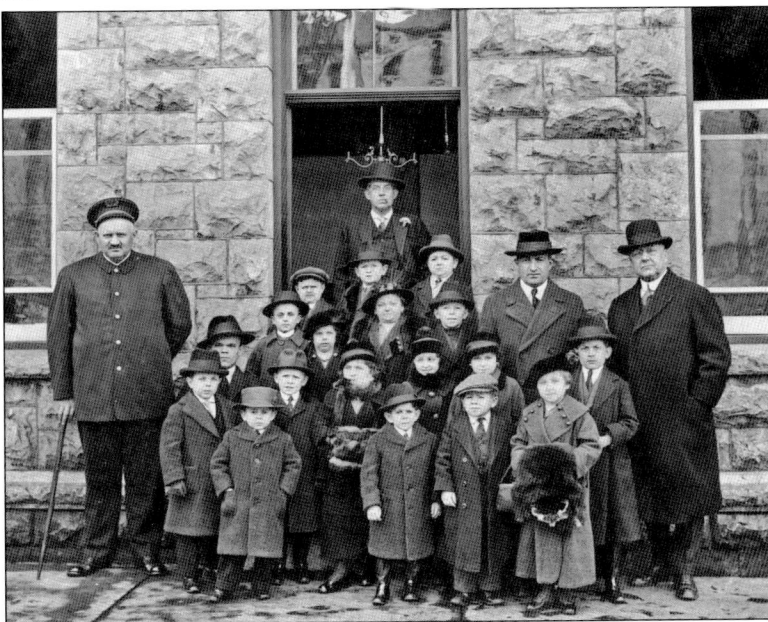

Warden Charles Rattigan (standing in doorway) and principal keeper John Martin (left) are photographed with a troupe of little people entertainers who played at the prison around 1910.

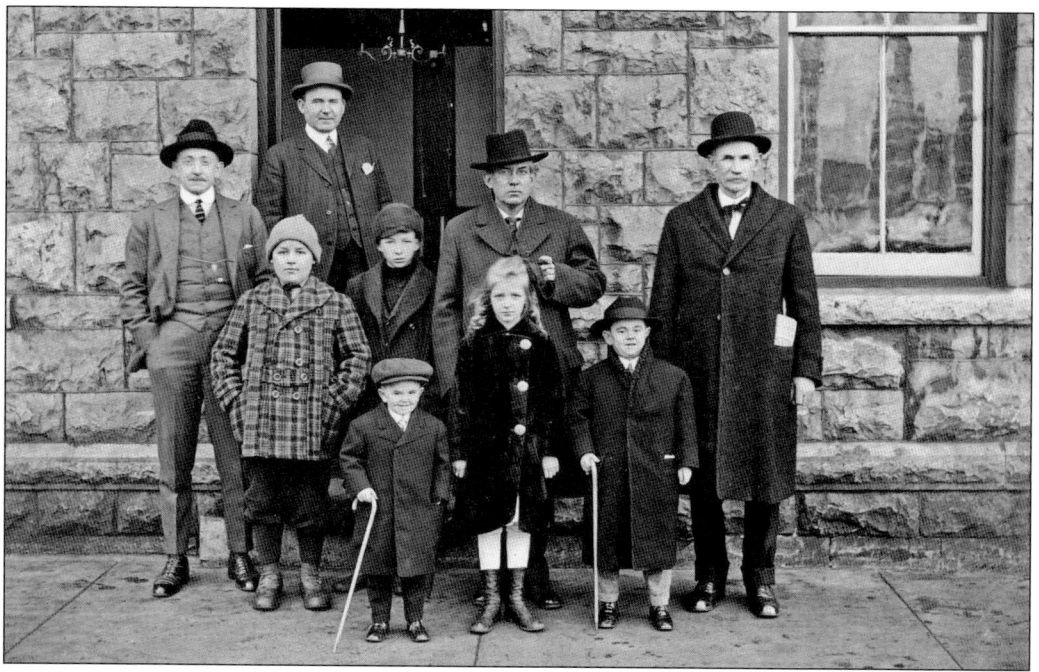

Warden Charles Rattigan (second row, fourth from left), recorded the visit of a vaudeville troupe that performed a show at the prison around 1910.

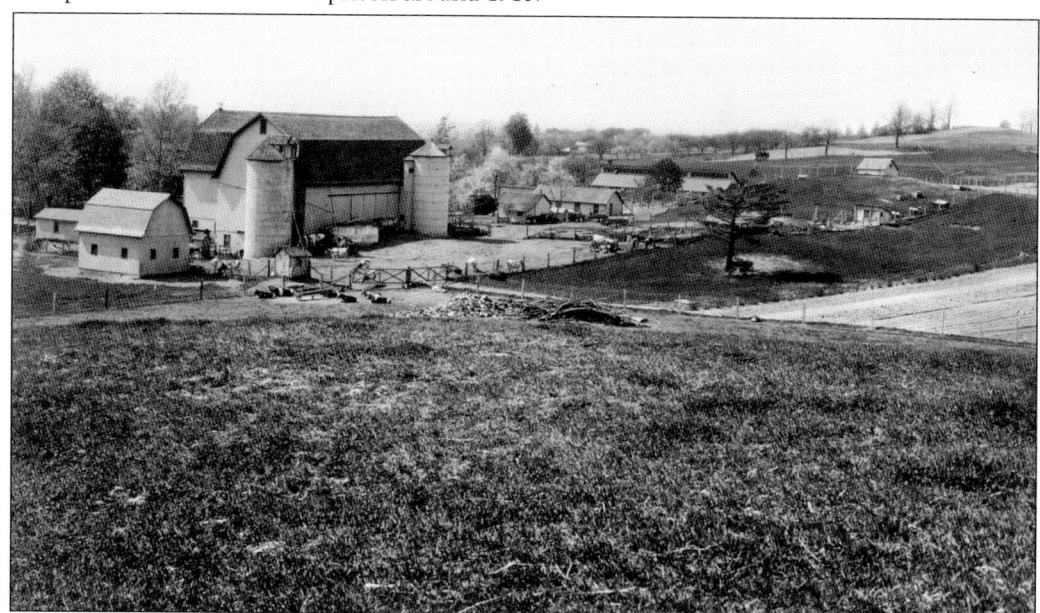

The Auburn Prison farm was photographed in May 1925. Located in Sennett, about 5 miles from the prison, this rural site was used to raise vegetables and dairy products for the prison kitchen. The main farm buildings were on Prison Farm Road, between Genesee and Franklin Streets, which is now called Pine Ridge Road. The buildings were sold to the New York State Division for Youth and later used for the Harriet Tubman Center. The remaining land now serves as the Auburn Correctional Facility Quality of Work Life and Recreation Center and is used for recreational purposes by the corrections officers' union, as well as local nonprofit organizations.

Five

THE ASYLUM AND WOMEN'S PRISON

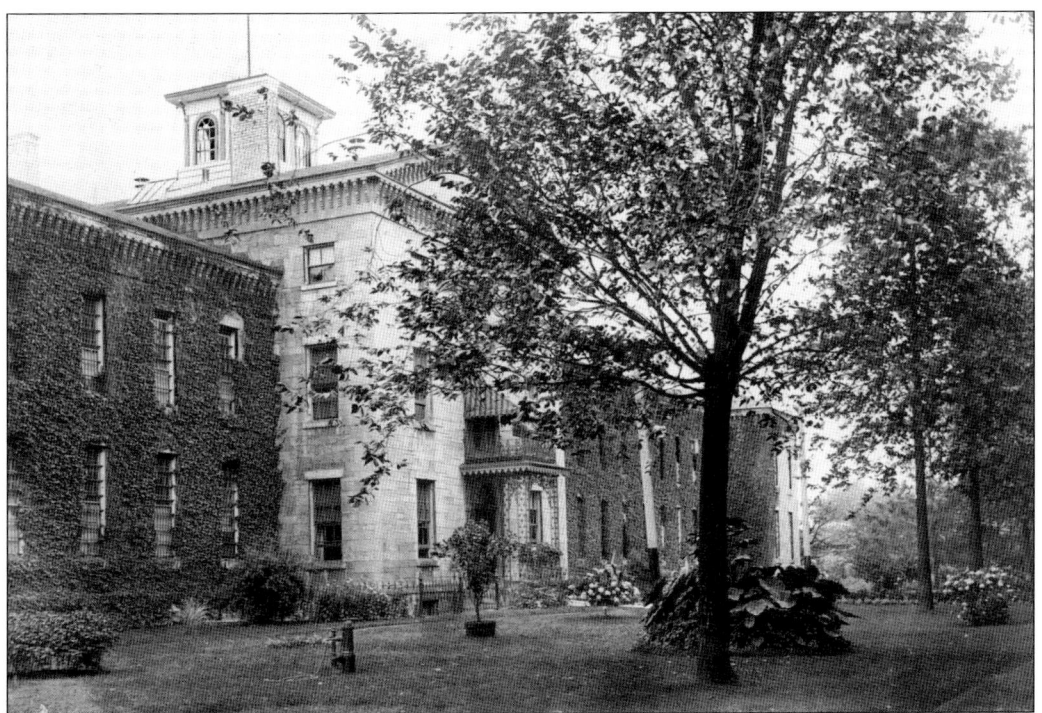

This is the front entrance of the New York State Asylum for the Criminally Insane. In a progressive recognition that the mentally ill should not be treated the same as ordinary criminals, the state legislature approved an expenditure of $20,000 to build an asylum for "lunatic criminals" at Auburn Prison in 1857. The asylum opened in February 1859. It was immediately adjacent to Auburn Prison but was surrounded by its own 12-foot wall.

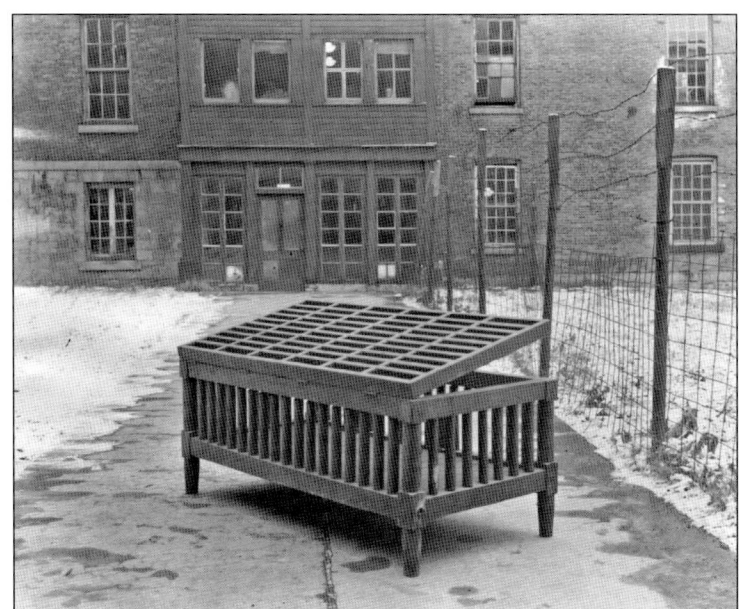

This is how the insane criminals were transported to Auburn. As brutal as this appears, once they arrived the lunatics had much better accommodations than the convicts housed in the regular prison. The asylum grounds eventually included a conservatory, a chapel, carpenter and blacksmith shops, meat and icehouses, greenhouses, a piggery, and barns. Much of the therapy involved working outside in the gardens and barns.

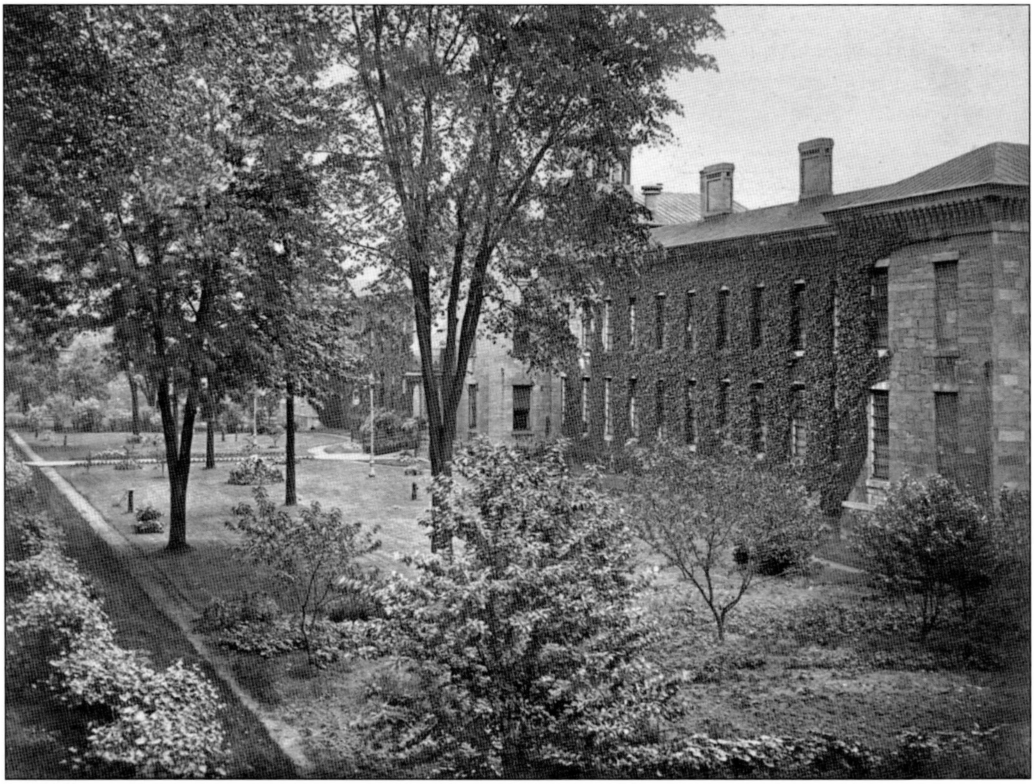

This shows the front side of the asylum for the criminally insane and the care taken to make the grounds attractive. In 1879, the New York State Asylum for Insane Criminals held 121 inmates—109 men and 12 women. Maximum capacity was 160. With rising costs, facilities available elsewhere, and a growing need for a women's prison, the state asylum in Auburn closed in 1893. The buildings were converted to the New York State Prison for Women, which opened the following year.

Women were incarcerated at Auburn Prison in 1825 and were confined in a large room in the attic of the south wing. Their meals were brought to them, and they were tasked with carding wool. When the asylum for the criminally insane closed at Auburn in 1893, the state authorized the building to be used as a prison for women. One of the most famous inmates in the women's prison was Cat Eye Annie, who escaped and was recaptured several times.

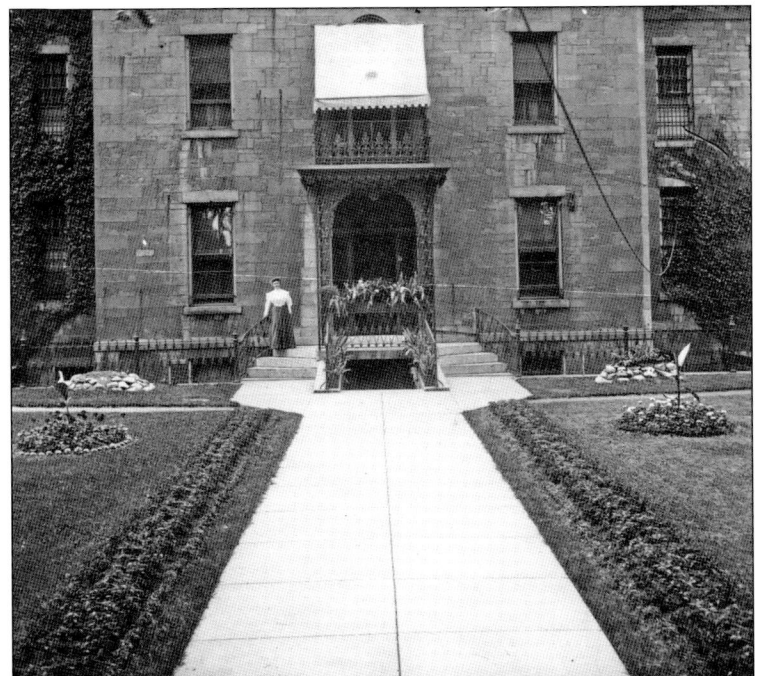

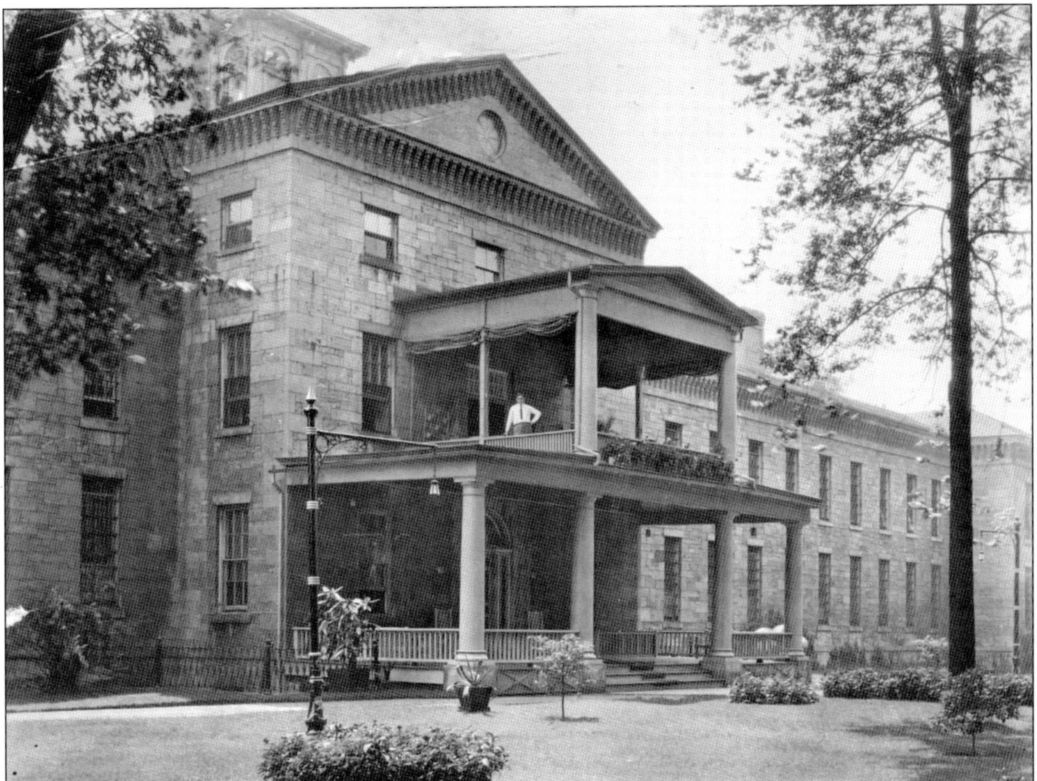

Sometime after the above photograph was taken in 1908, an elaborate two-story porch was added to the front of the women's prison.

This is the Wall Street gate to the grounds of the women's prison in the 1920s. There was also a separate Wall Street gate into the men's prison. (Courtesy of Michael Pettigrass.)

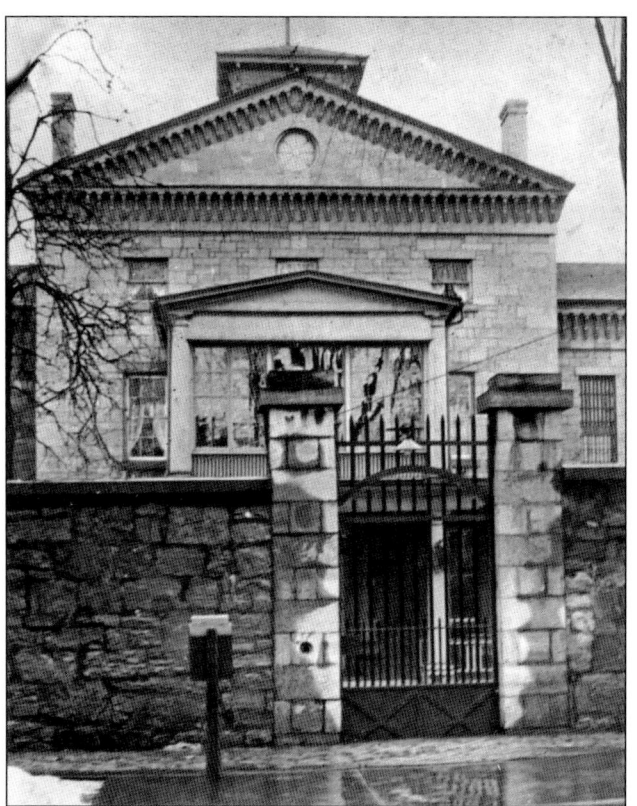

This is the front yard of the women's prison, around 1912. Like the front entrance to Auburn Prison on State Street, passersby looking in the gate saw only a beautifully landscaped yard and an attractive ivy-covered building.

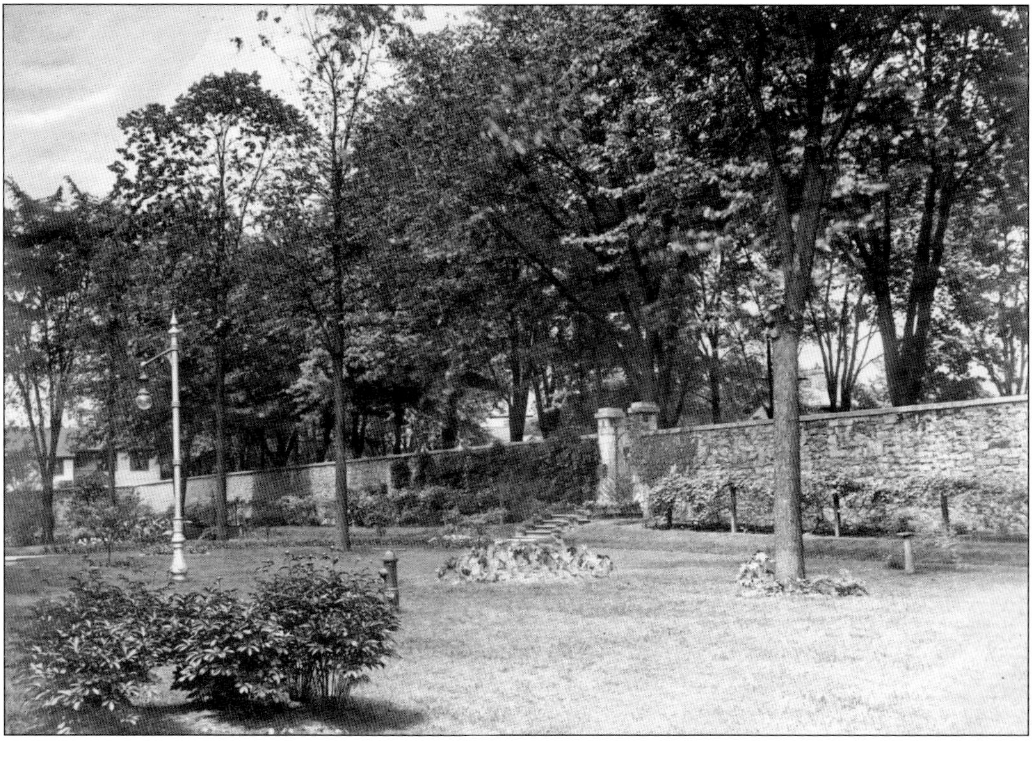

This is one of the rooms in the women's prison at Auburn, with high ceilings and large windows. With 125 rooms, accommodations for as many as 250 women, the women's prison served the entire state until 1934, when part of the Westfield State Farm at Bedford Hills became the women's prison.

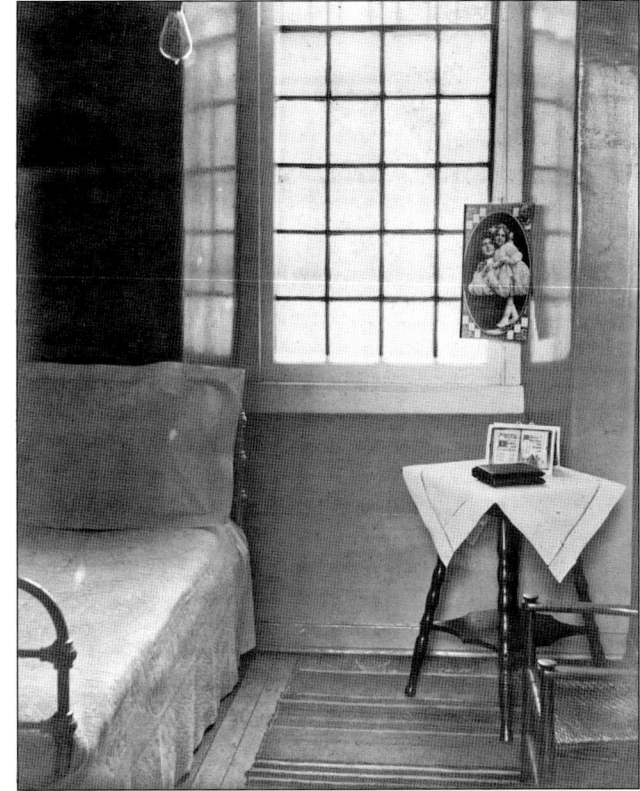

This is one of the main halls of the women's prison, showing the spacious, airy design that characterized the building. The doors on either side open to inmates' rooms. The light fixtures have been converted from gas to electricity.

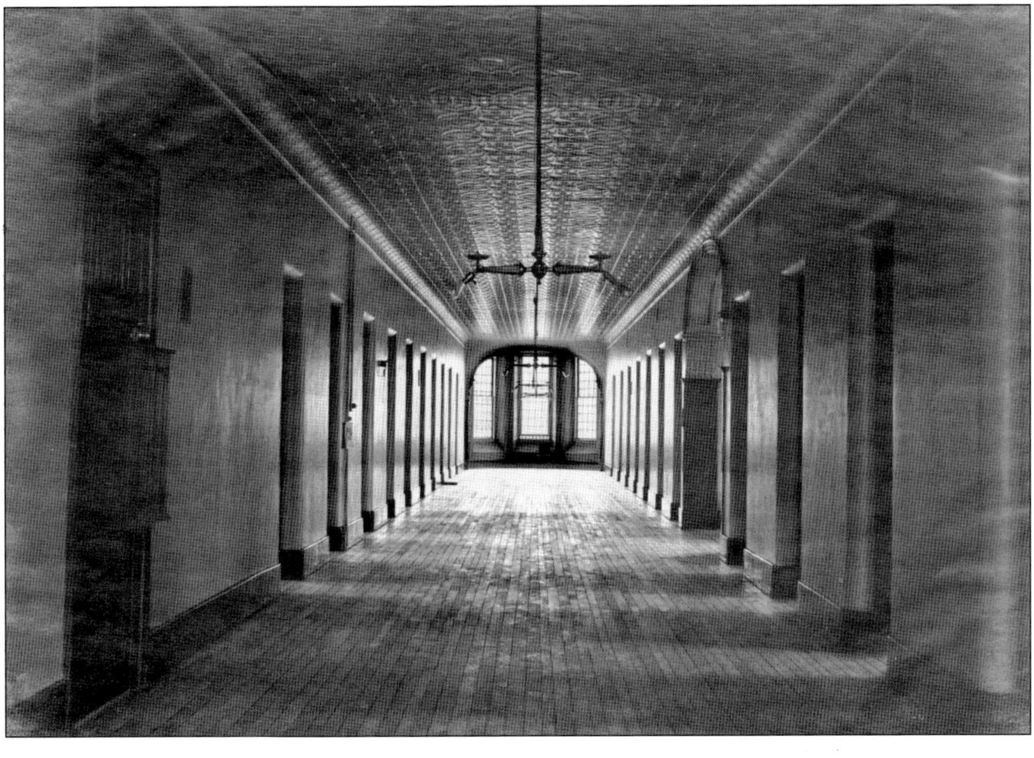

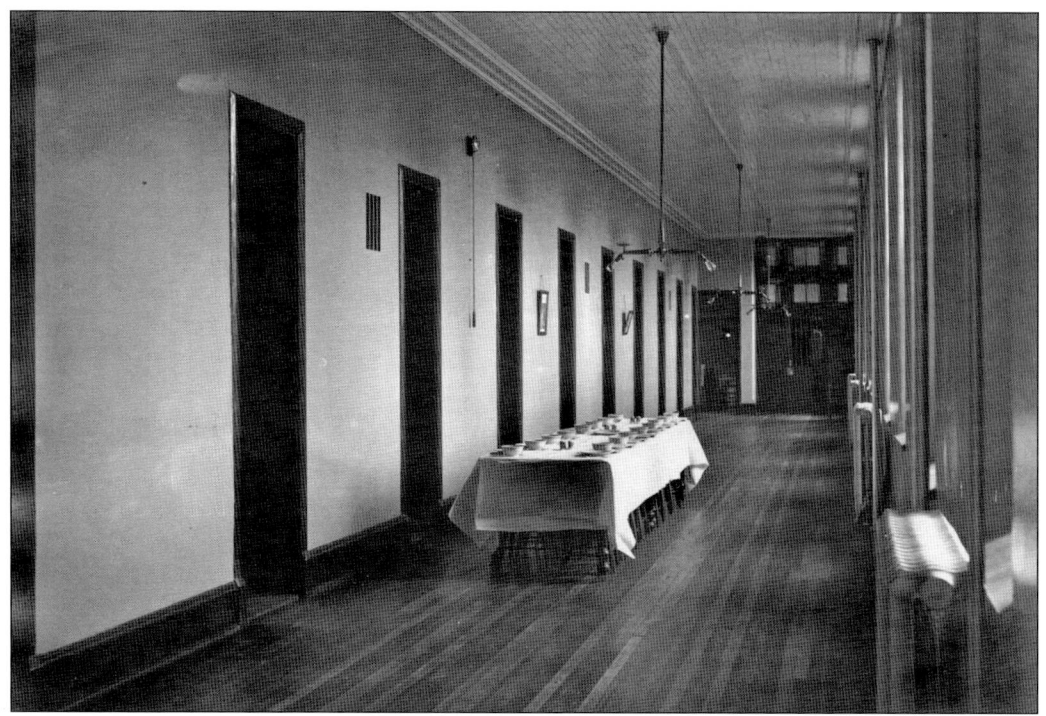
The wide hallways of the women's prison building were sometimes used for dining, classes, and other assemblies.

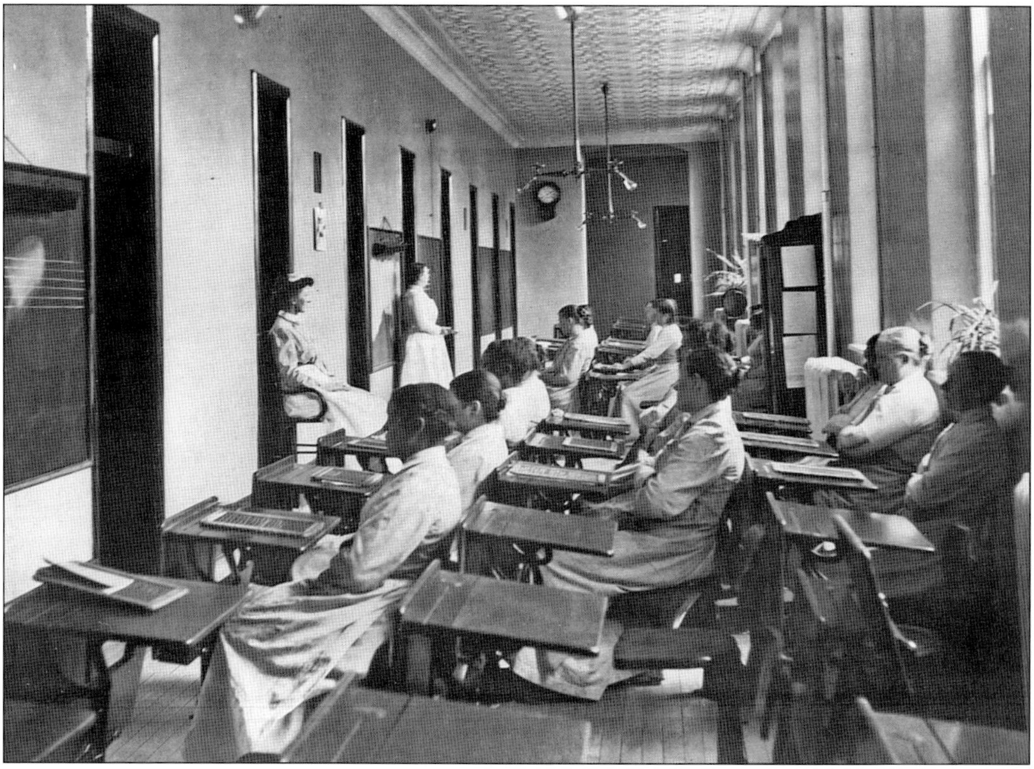

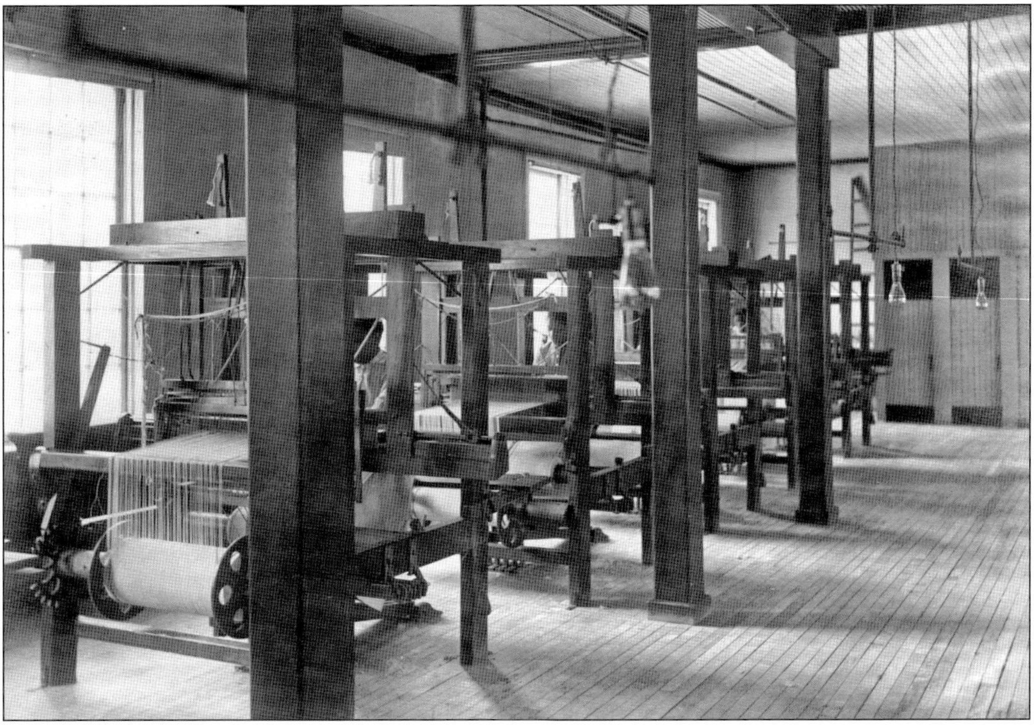

Like their counterparts in the men's prison, the female convicts worked six days a week. They wove blankets and mattress ticking, and sewed most of their clothing and that of the men prisoners.

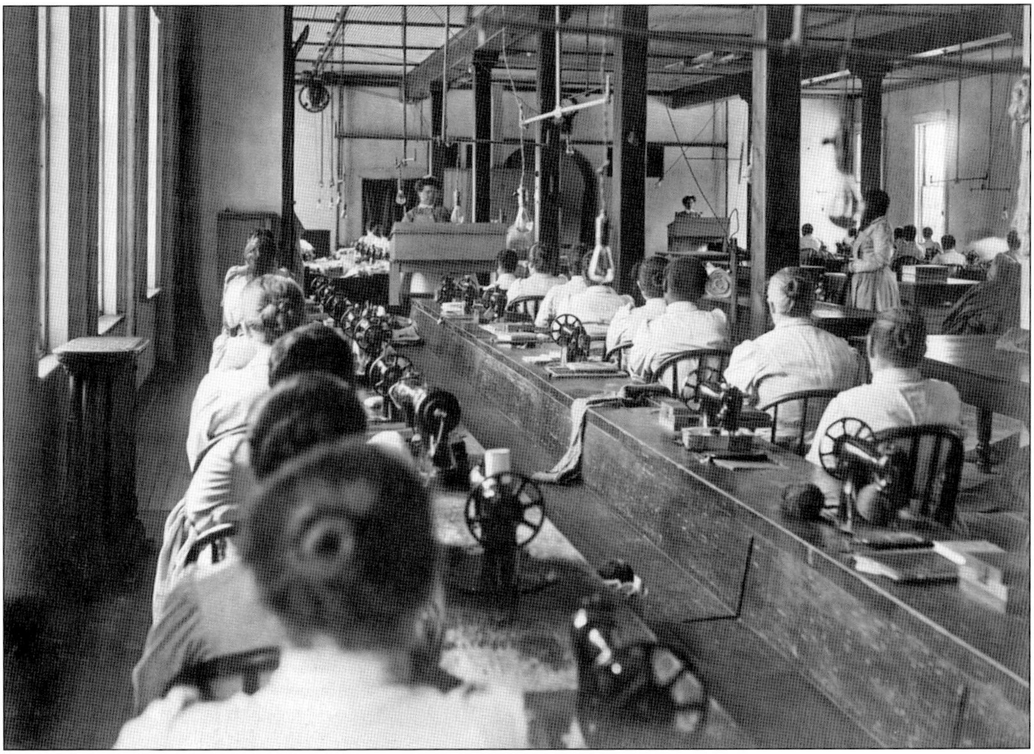

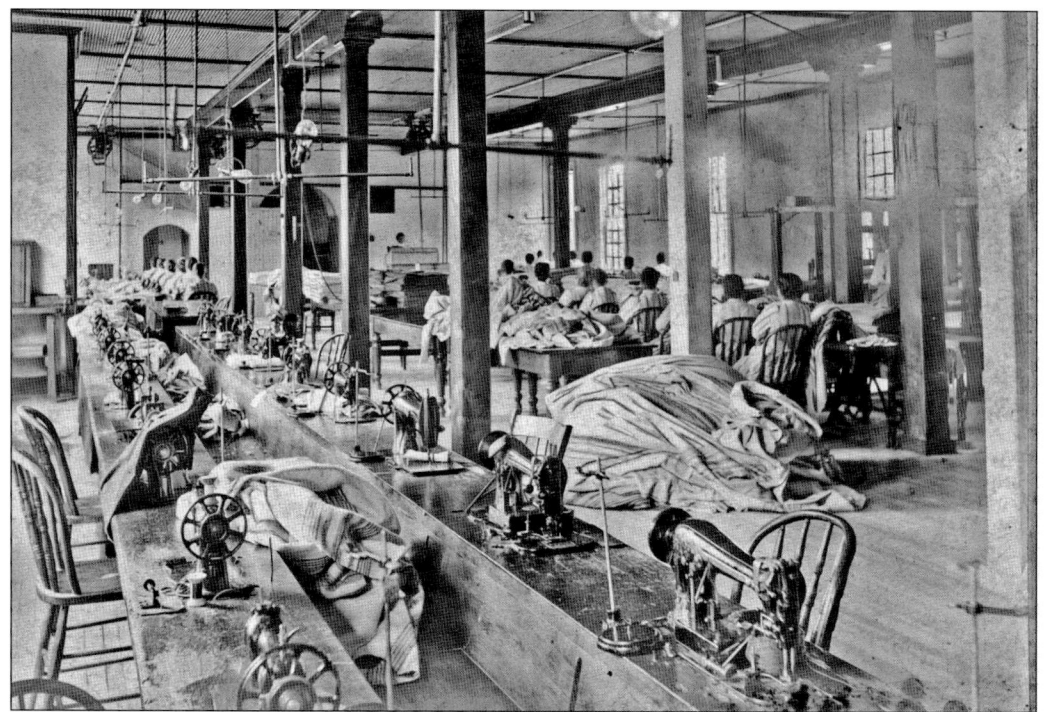
Those women who did not already know how to sew were taught, a skill that might support them after their release. They were also given instruction on personal hygiene and housekeeping.

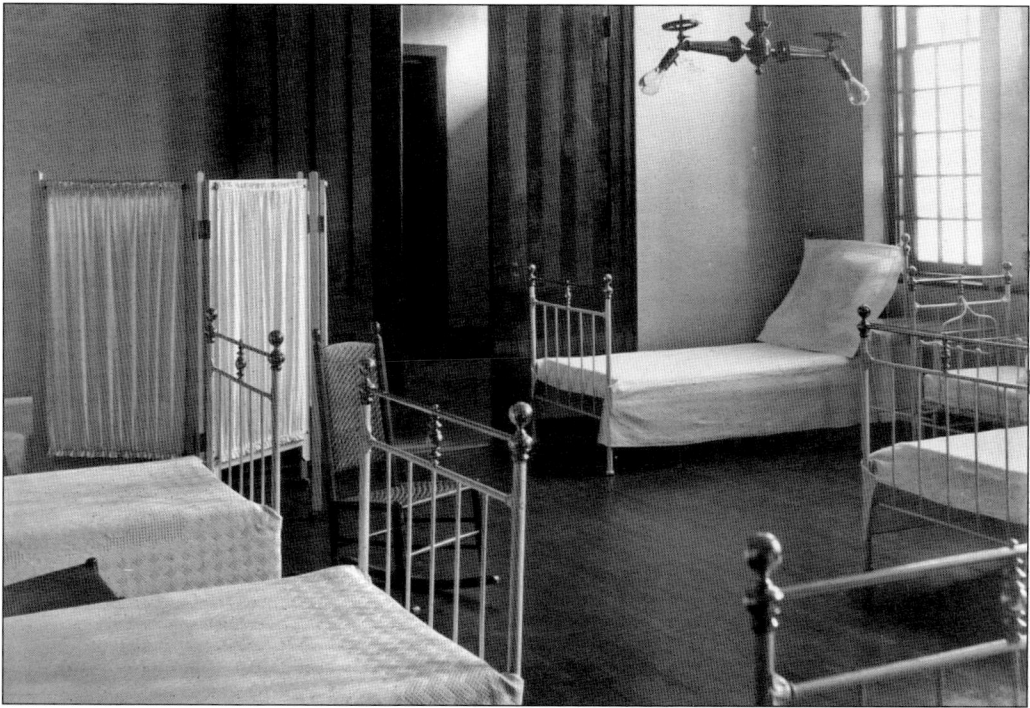
This is the hospital in the women's prison, around 1912. Four female inmates died in the prison in 1912.

Six

The Electric Chair

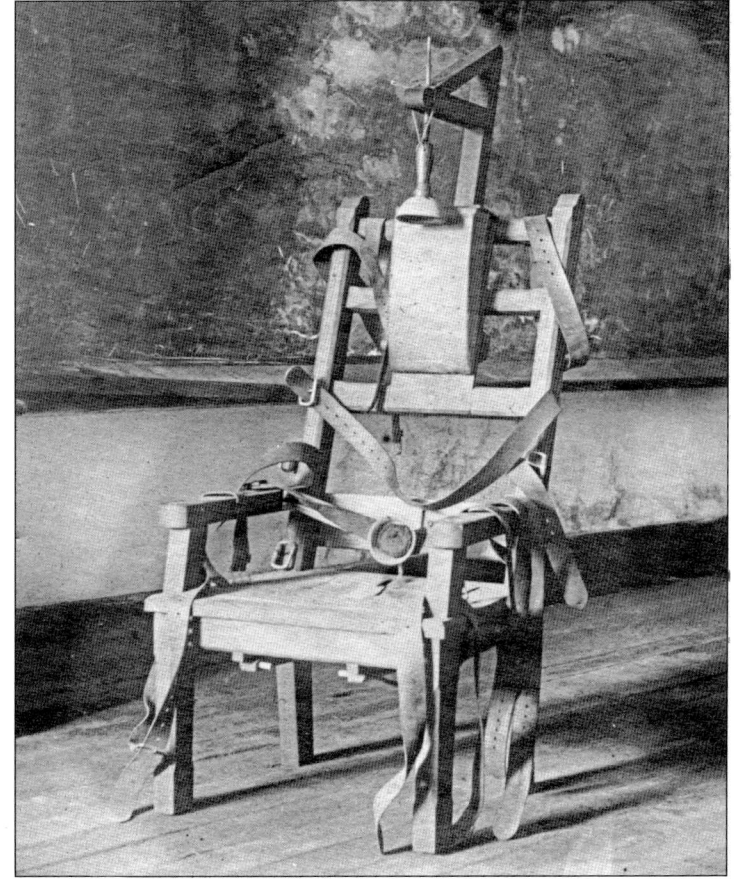

This is the only photograph of the first electric chair, in which William Kemmler died on August 6, 1890. Kemmler was the only man to be executed in New York with one electrode at the base of the spine. Between Kemmler's execution and that of William Tice in 1892, the chair was stored in a prison classroom. A blackboard is visible behind the chair in this photograph.

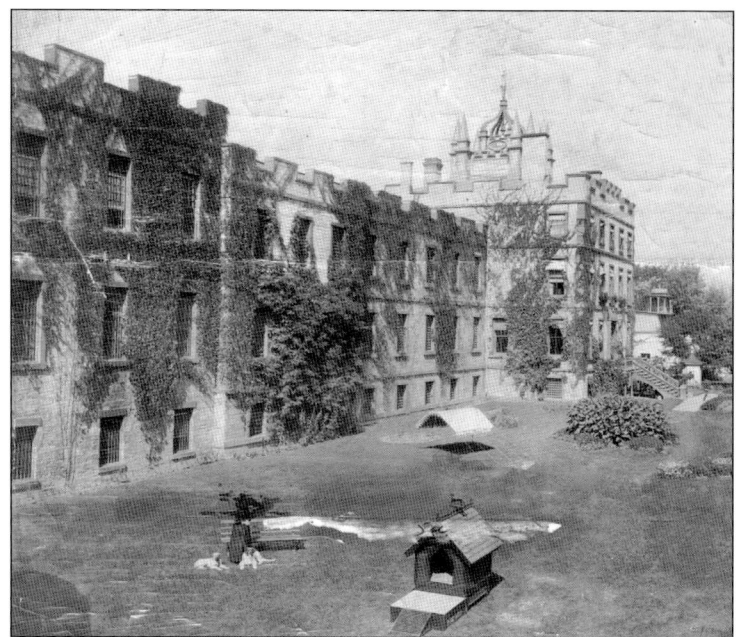

This is the front yard of the prison in 1890. The windows of the room in which Kemmler was executed, in the basement of the administration building, opened onto this yard. The woman and child in the photograph are probably the wife and daughter of warden Charles Durston, who lived at the prison. Mrs. Durston was described in contemporary newspaper reports as keeping large dogs. She visited Kemmler in his cell often while he awaited his execution.

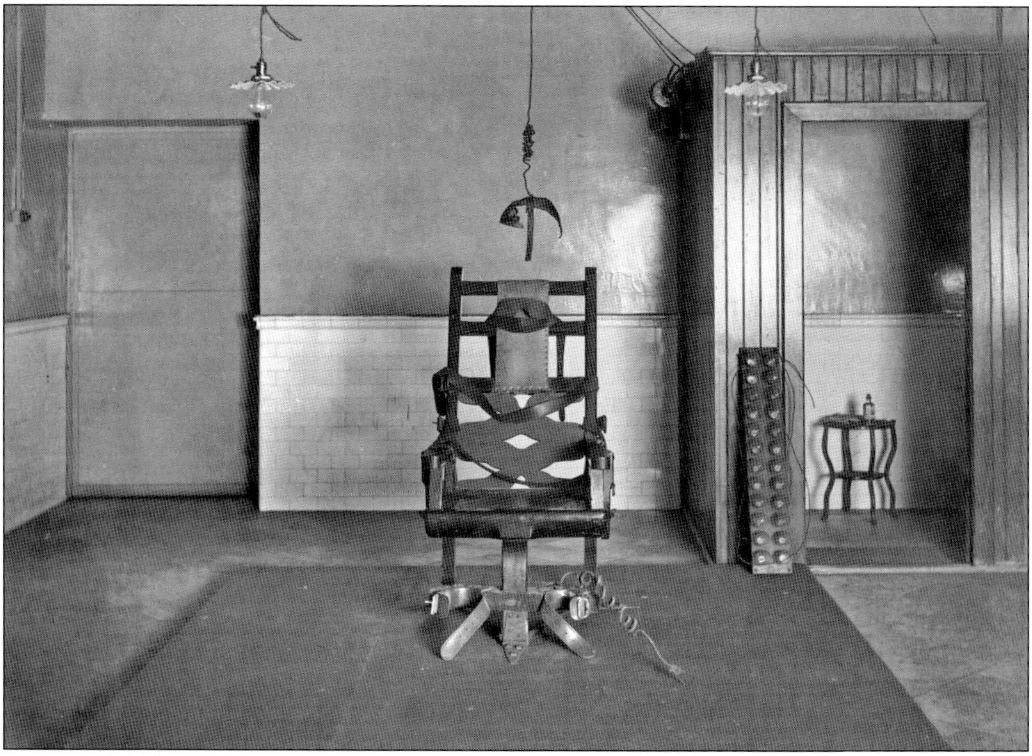

This three-legged chair came into use at Auburn Prison sometime after the execution of Joseph Tice in June 1892. It was the chair used for the execution of William Taylor in July 1893 and all subsequent executions at Auburn. This chair was destroyed in the riot of December 1929, although rumors that it escaped the fire still linger. By law there were as many as 20 witnesses to each execution.

This postcard from a staged photograph was a popular Auburn souvenir. The man was not actually a condemned inmate, and he may have been the same volunteer who posed as an inmate in the 1909 photographic essay.

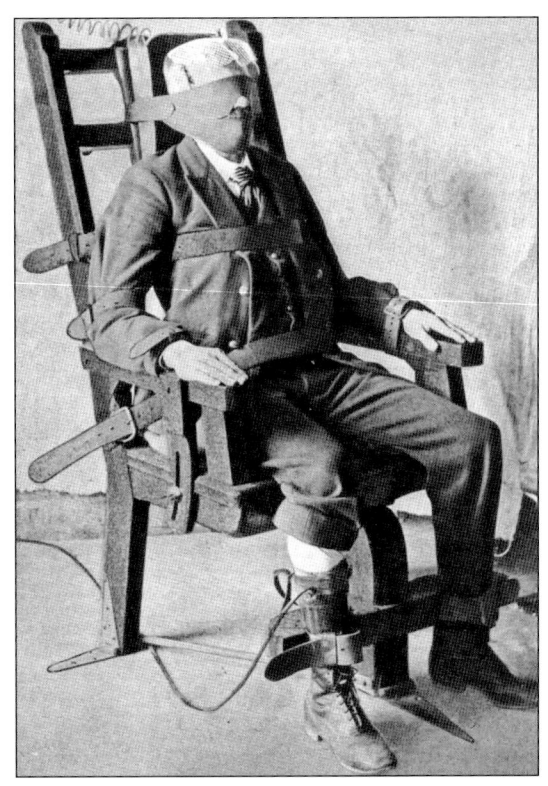

At William G. Taylor's execution in July 1893, the prison dynamo had burned out and failed. Taylor was taken out of the chair, placed on a cot in the death chamber, and was sedated by a doctor. It took over an hour to connect the chair to the city's power lines, and by this time, Taylor had died on the cot. To be sure, the warden had Taylor's body strapped back into the chair and the current turned on.

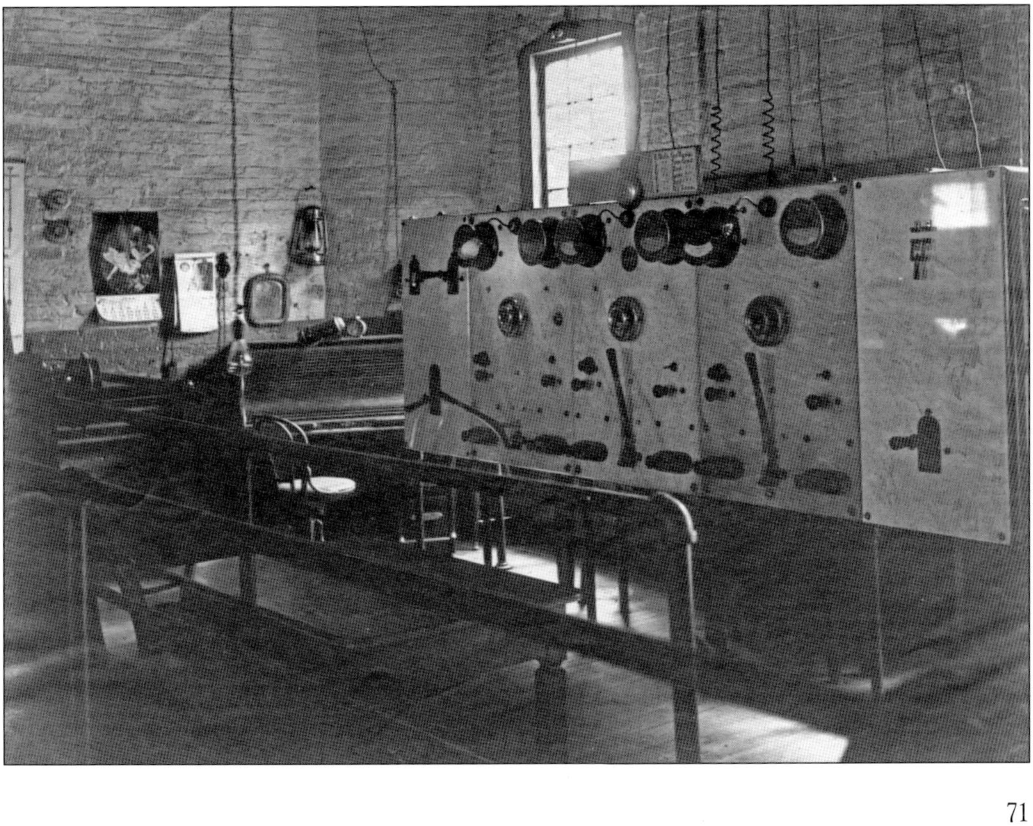

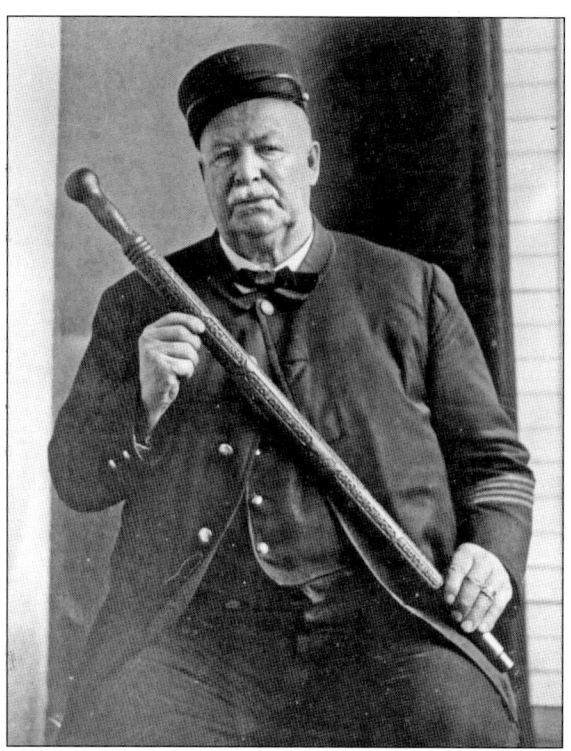

Hospital steward Billy Patterson is pictured with the executioner's cane. Patterson escorted 54 of the 55 condemned prisoners who were executed in Auburn to their deaths. He refused to attend the execution of one man he believed to be innocent. In all, 54 men and one woman, Mary Farmer, died in the Auburn Prison electric chair.

Three of these canes were made by inmates. One was given to Billy Patterson, one to principal keeper John Martin, and one to deputy warden Allen Tupper. This is the cane that belonged to John Martin. Today it is a part of the collection of the Cayuga Museum of History and Art. (Courtesy of Michael Pettigrass.)

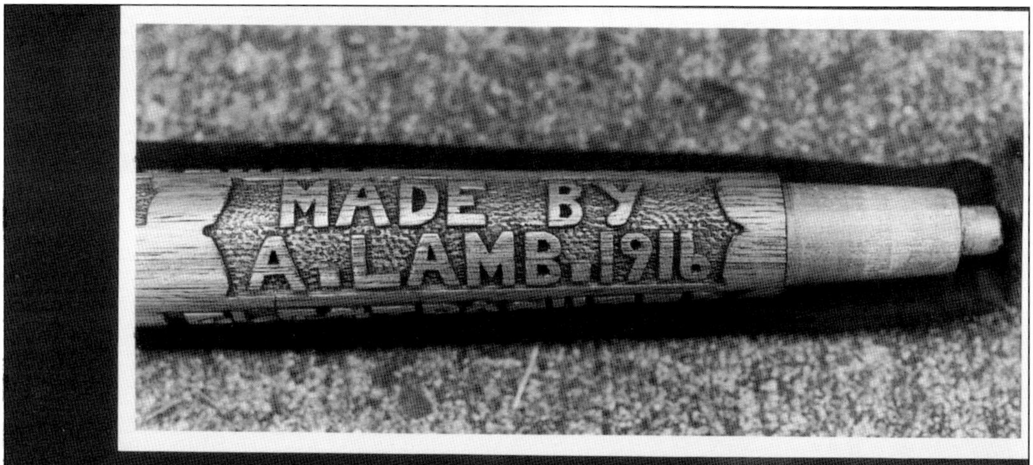

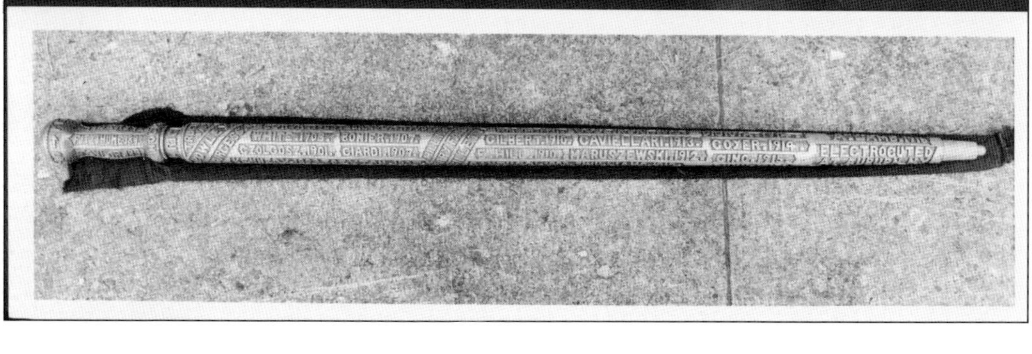

Seven

Thomas Mott Osborne and Prison Reform

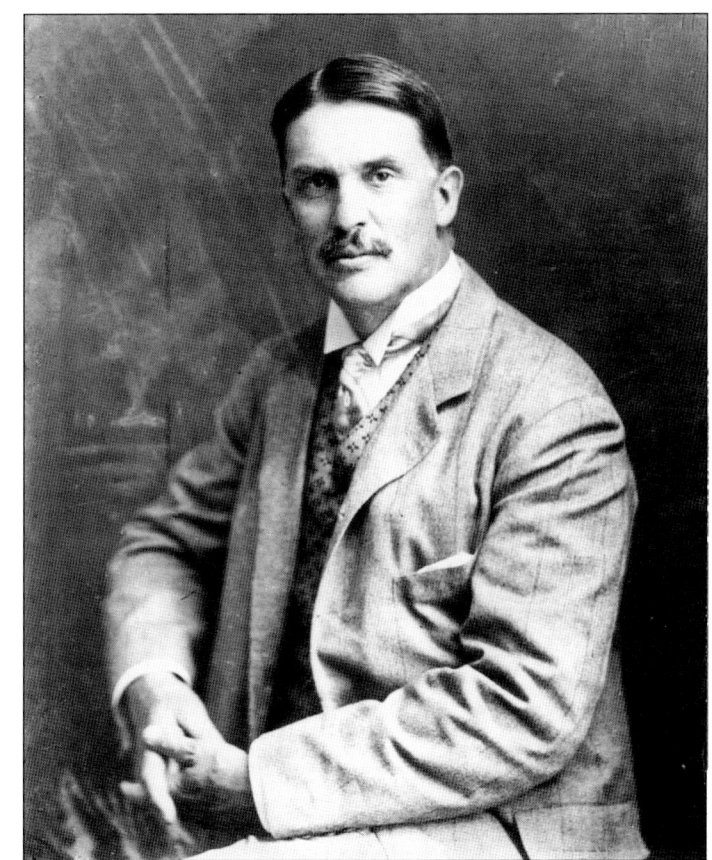

Thomas Mott Osborne, a former mayor of Auburn, was appointed by New York governor William Sulzer as chairman of a commission on prison reform in 1913. Wanting to see for himself how the convicts lived, Osborne arranged with warden Charles Rattigan to go into Auburn Prison undercover. He was incarcerated at Auburn Prison on September 29, 1913, under the name Tom Brown. He stayed for one week, living as a regular inmate.

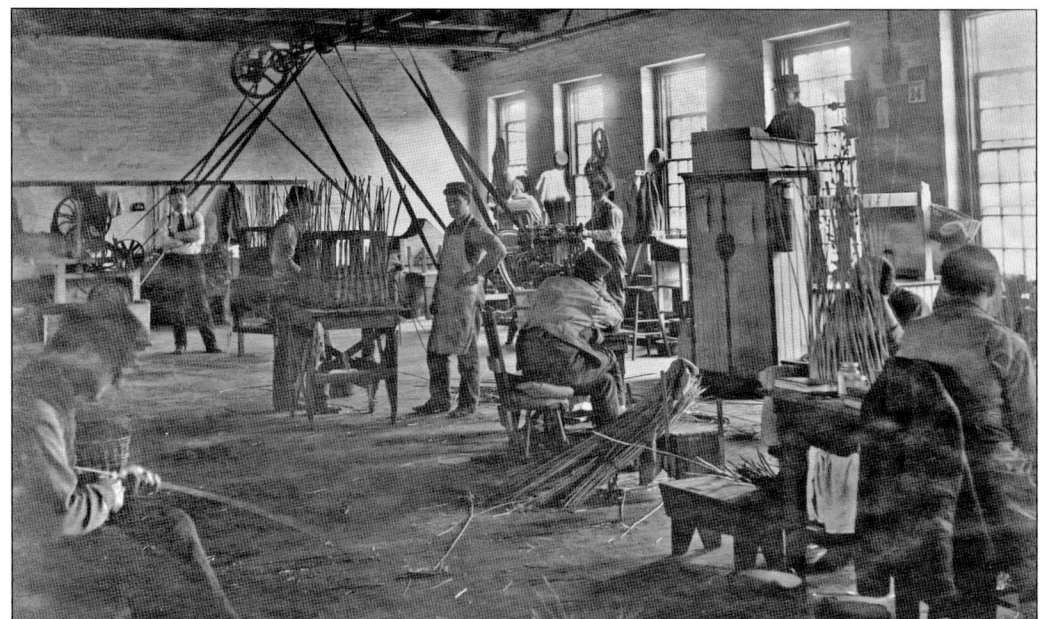

During his week of incarceration in 1913, Thomas Mott Osborne worked in the prison basket shop. He believed the prison should be treated as a community, and the prisoners should have some say in governing that community. Osborne stressed the value of educating, rather than punishing, the prisoners. He was the driving force behind the creation of the Mutual Welfare League, established at Auburn Prison in December 1913.

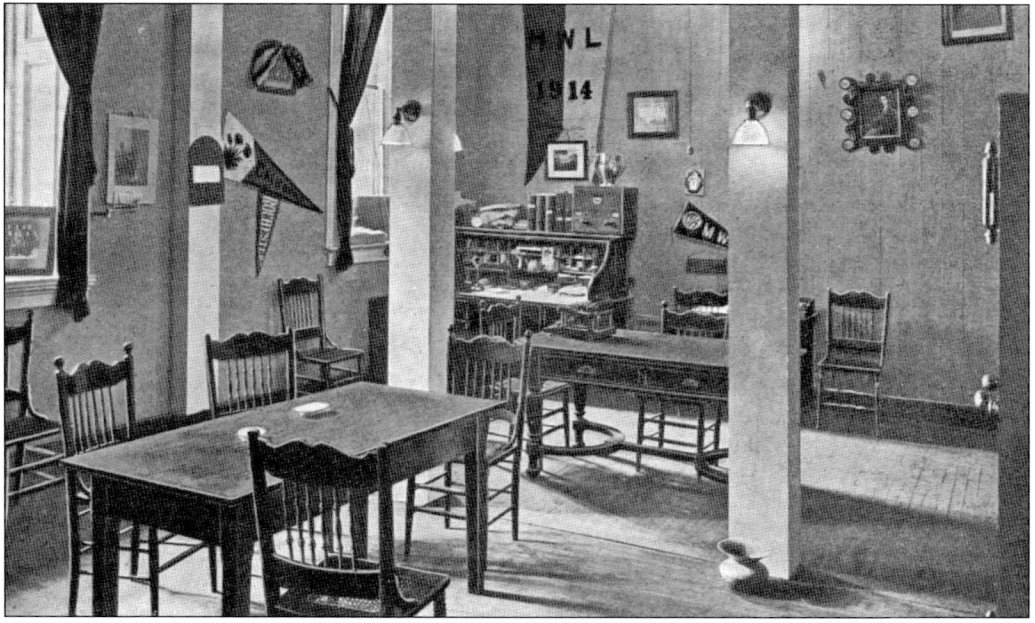

This is a postcard image of the Mutual Welfare League office at Auburn Prison, around 1915. Inmates elected delegates to the league, and the league took over some of the management of the prison population, including punishment of inmates. Some of the humane improvements that came out of the Mutual Welfare League were expanded yard recreation time, weekly movies, entertainments, an inmate band, and vocational education programs.

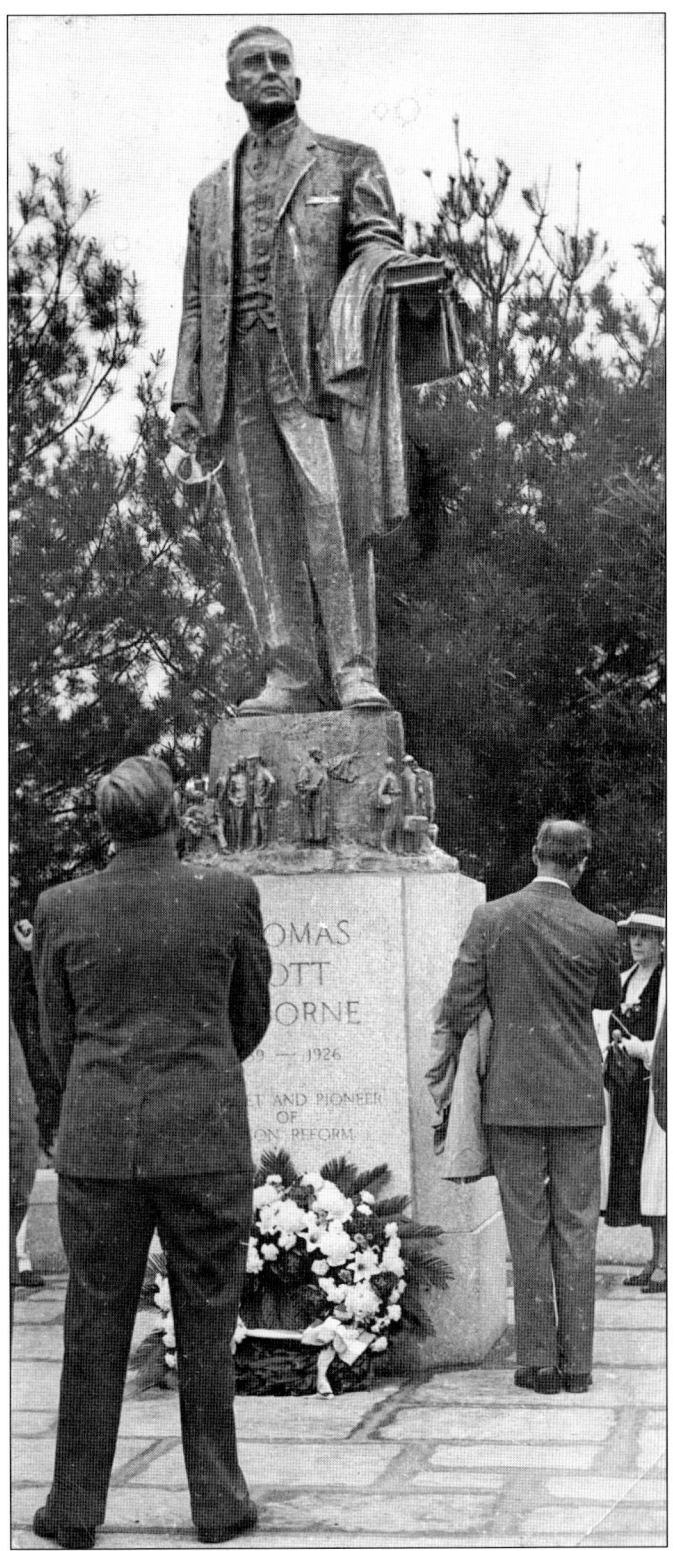

A statue of Thomas Mott Osborne was dedicated in Auburn in 1931. The base of the statue is ringed with 21 small figures depicting prison life. The statue was originally on the grounds of the Auburn Academic High School, presently East Middle School, but it was moved to stand outside the police station due to persistent vandalism. A duplicate of this statue, minus the base, is in the Corrections Museum, which is run by the New York State Department of Correctional Services Training Academy in Albany.

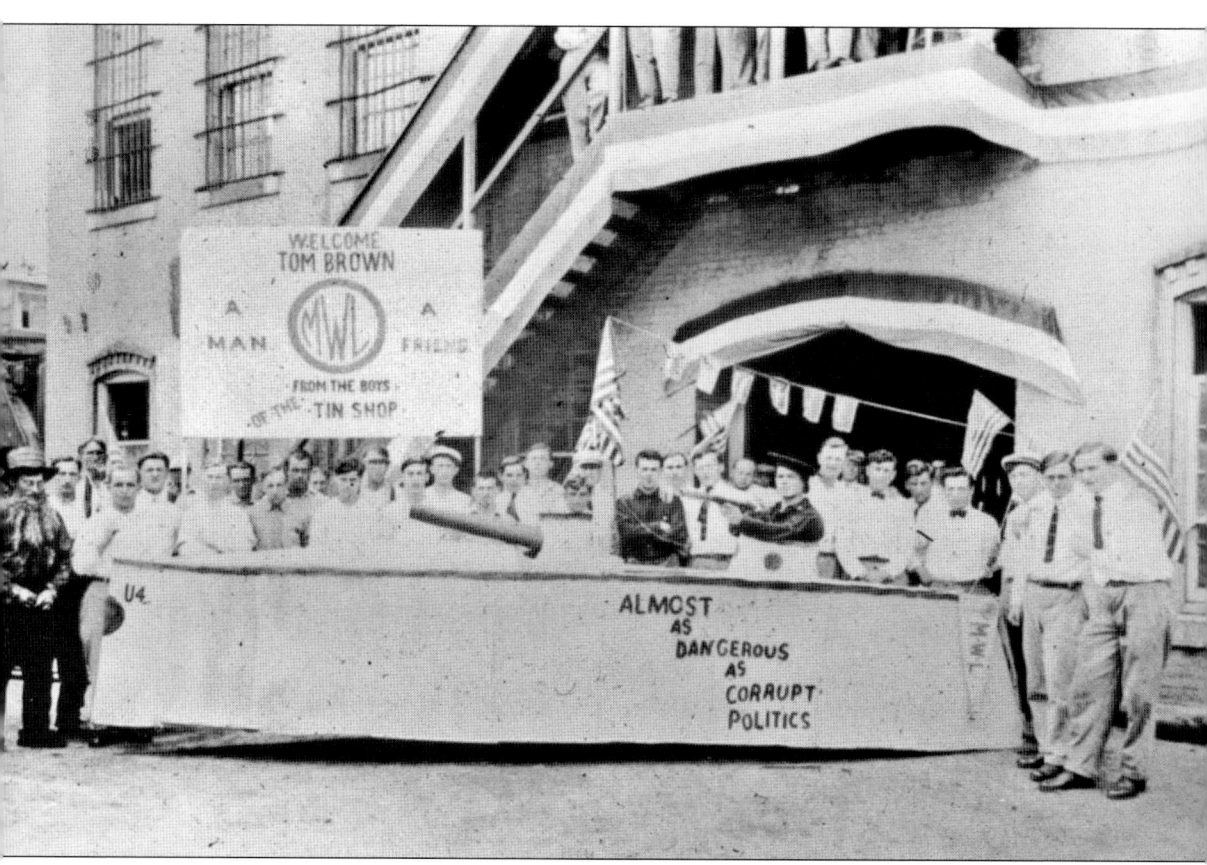

Osborne was feted as a hero whenever he returned to Auburn Prison. This model of a navy gun ship may have greeted Osborne on a visit to Auburn during his tenure as commandant of the U.S. naval prison at Portsmouth, New Hampshire from 1917 to 1920. The popular feeling among inmates was that corrupt politicians had ended Osborne's service as warden of Sing Sing. (Courtesy of Michael Pettigrass.)

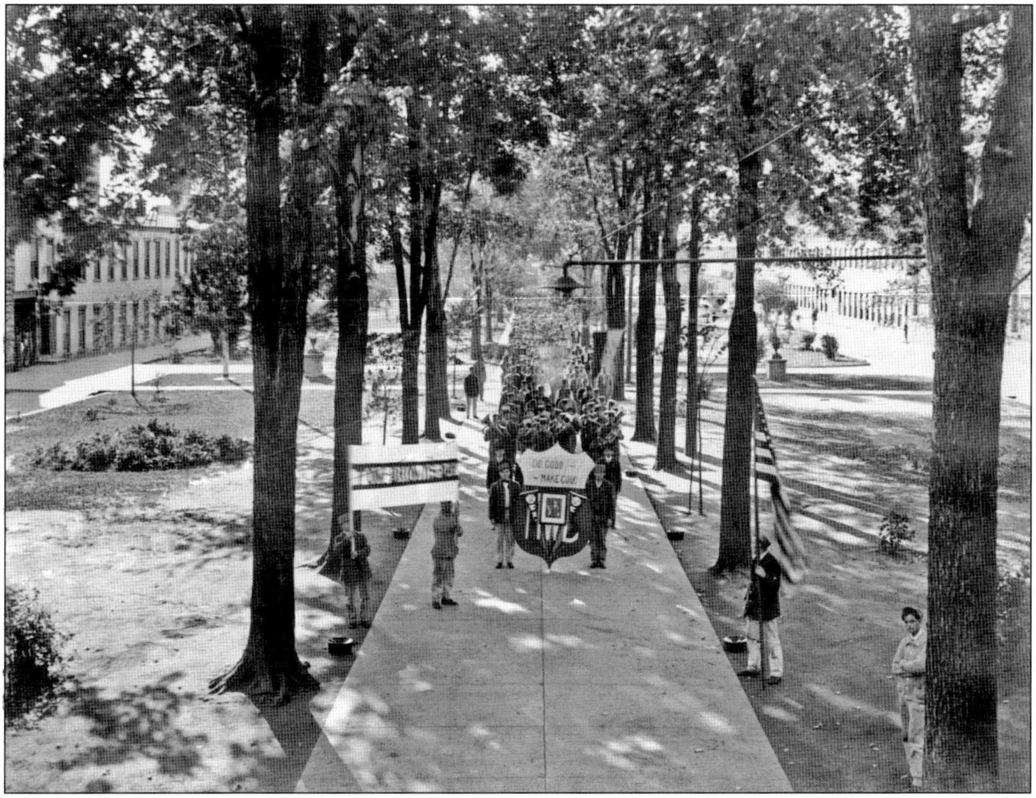

One of the most well documented events at Auburn Prison was the celebration of Tom Brown Day in July 1914, the first anniversary of the founding of the Mutual Welfare League. The prison declared a holiday, with a parade in the yard, games, sporting events, and speeches. Here the parade is headed by the Mutual Welfare League banner, stating their slogan, "Do good—Make good."

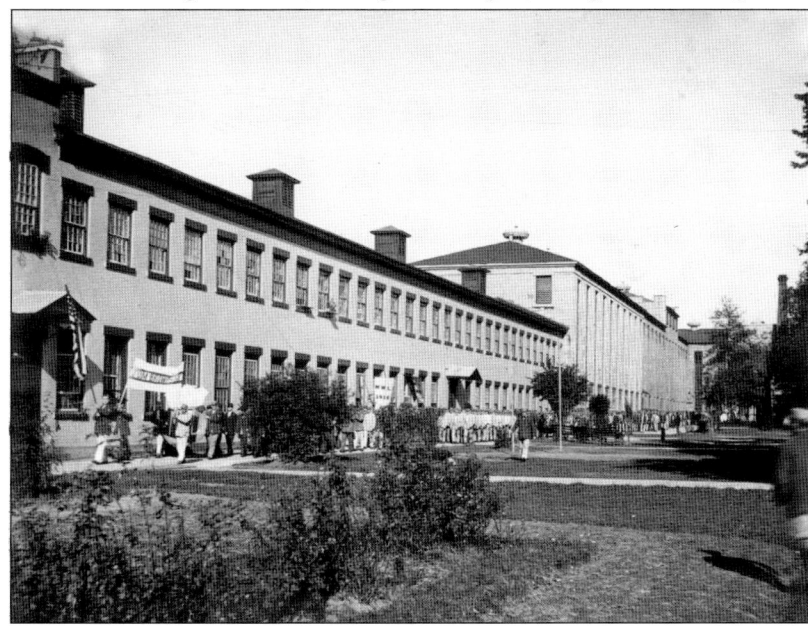

The inmates' parade circled the yard several times at the start of the celebration.

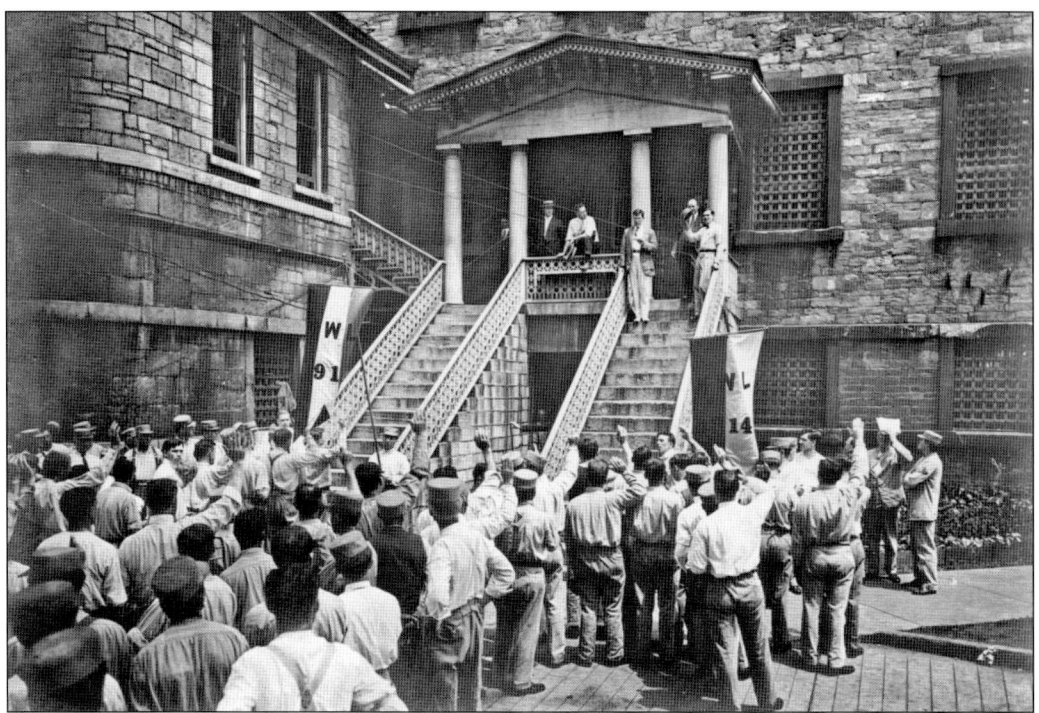

No celebration is complete without someone making a speech. Here the inmates appear to be voting by a raise of hands.

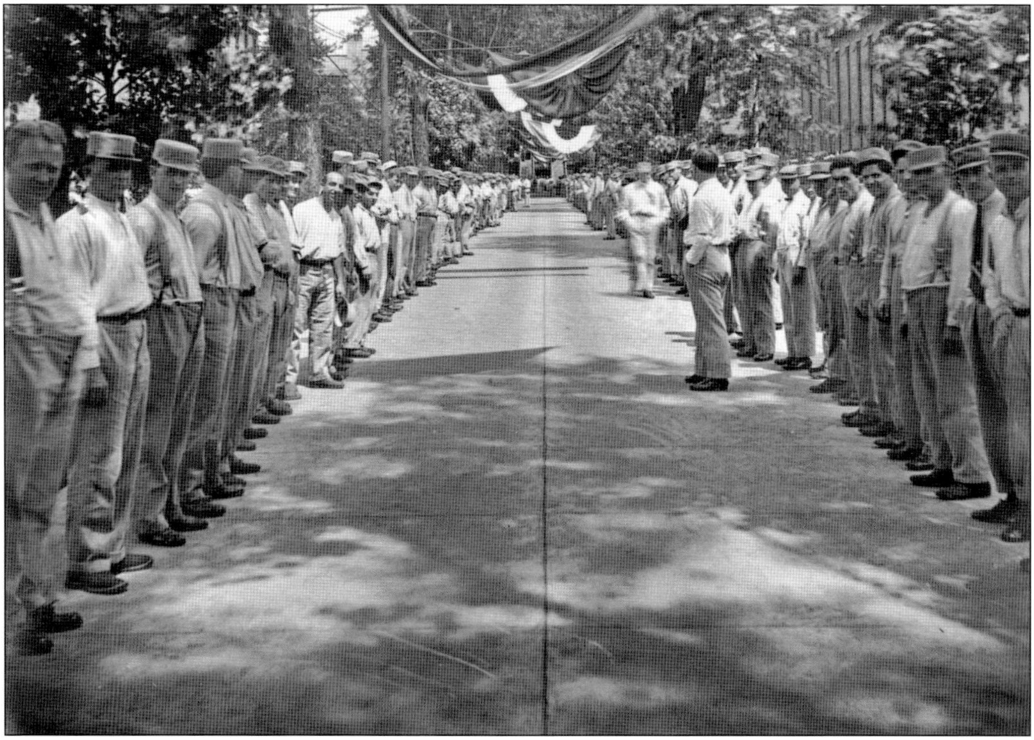

Inmates line up along the main path in the yard to cheer on their favorites in a footrace.

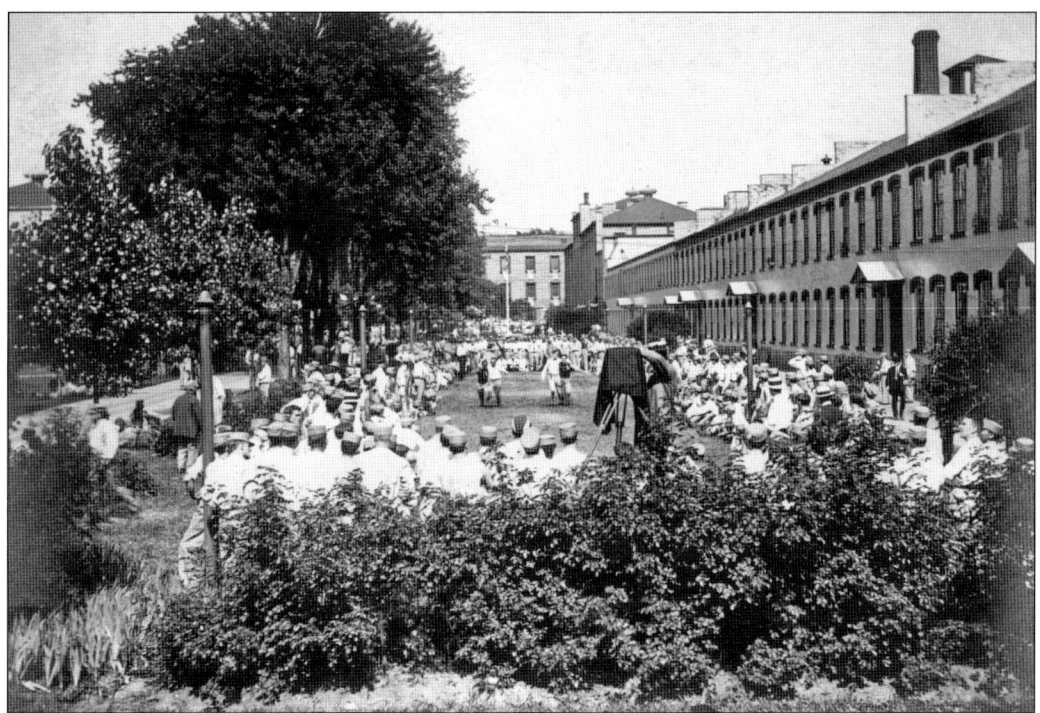

Here is the three-legged race. It is clear why there are so many photographs of this day's events. The cameraman who took this photograph recorded another in the act.

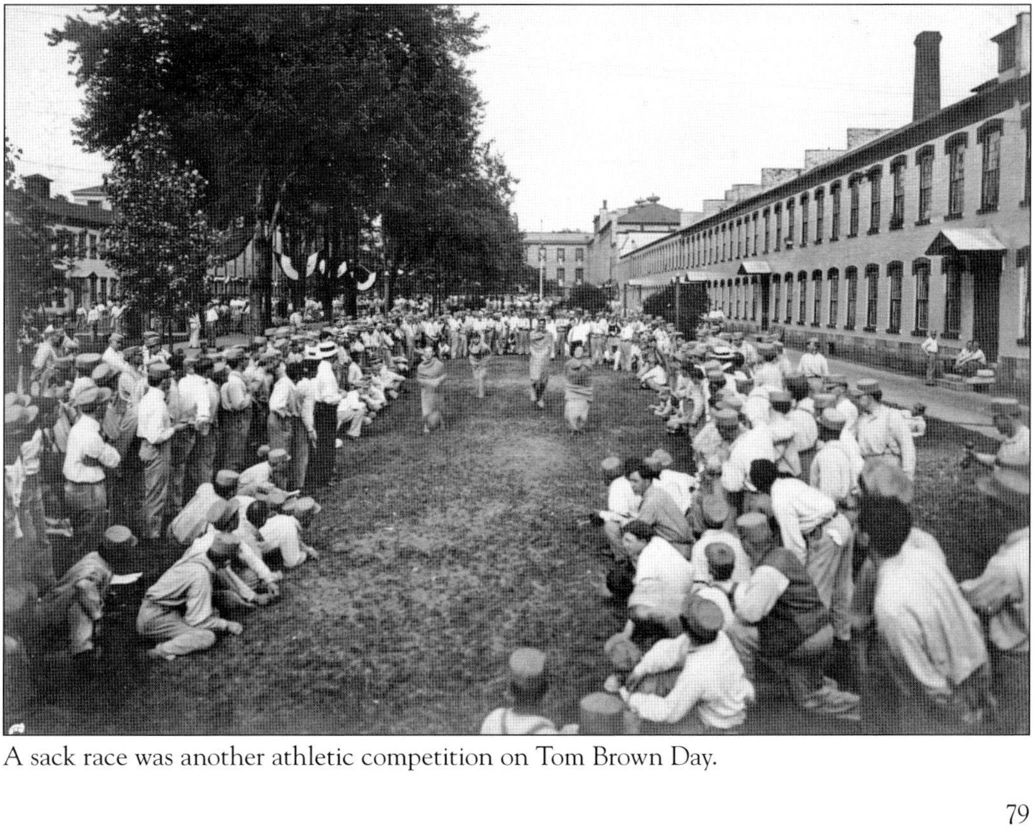

A sack race was another athletic competition on Tom Brown Day.

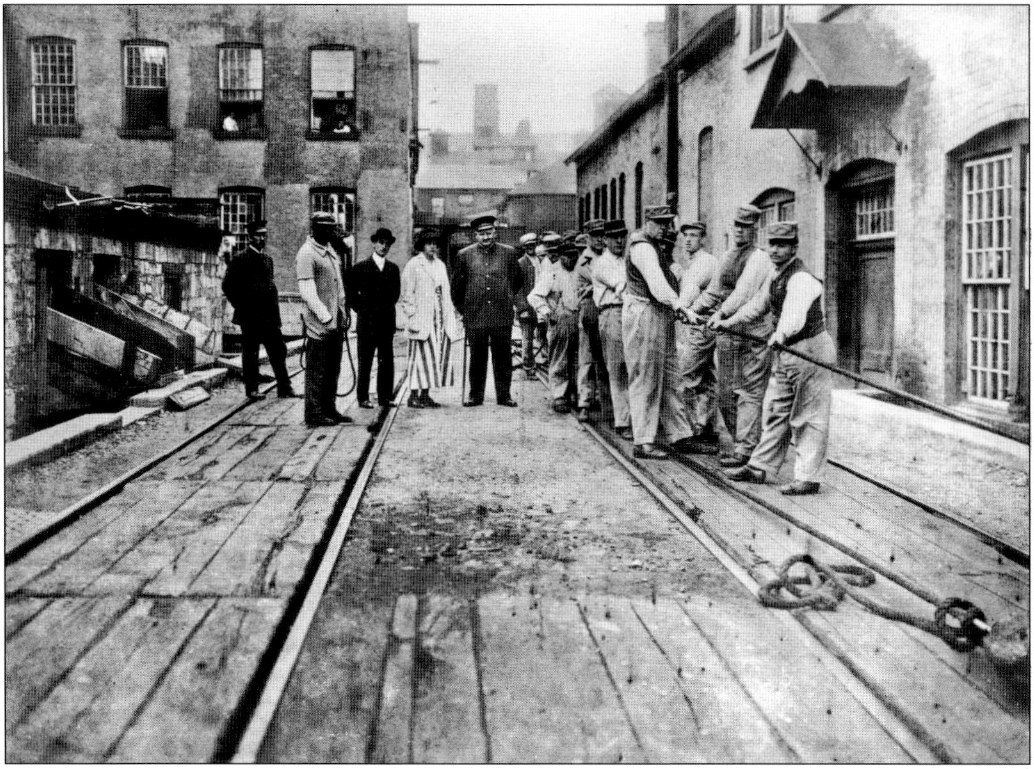

Thomas Mott Osborne reportedly returned to Auburn Prison as Tom Brown several times in the years following his week of incarceration, to work alongside the regular inmates. In this photograph from the collection of principal keeper John Martin, who appears in the center, Osborne is with the crew hauling the heavy ropes. He is indicated by an arrow.

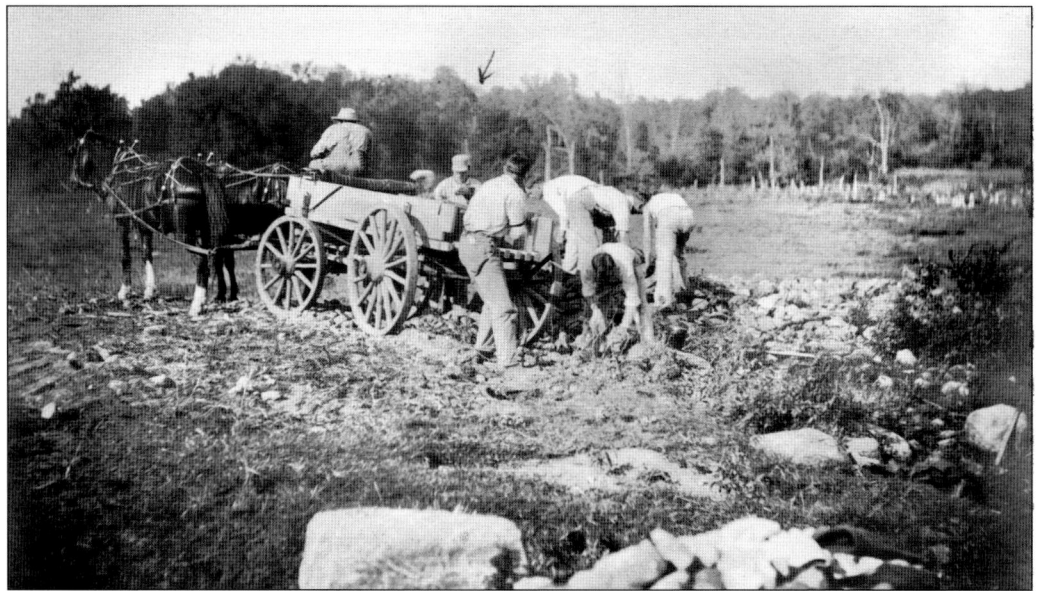

In this photograph from the collection of warden Charles Rattigan, Osborne is working with a prison road crew. He is again indicated by an arrow.

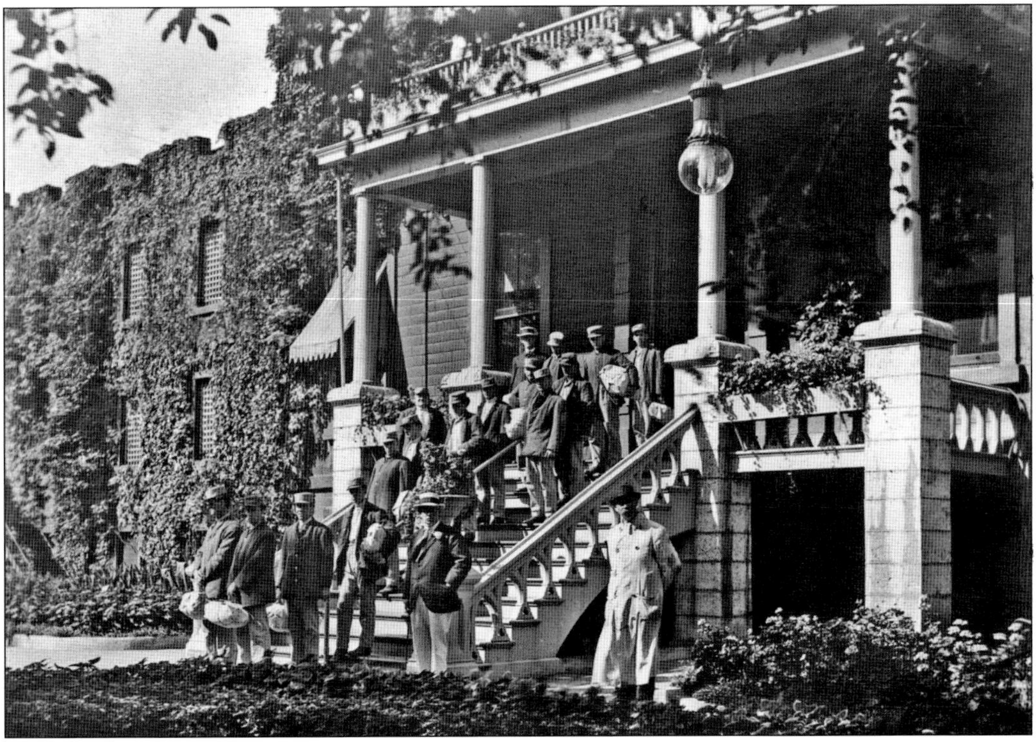

The Mutual Welfare League helped to establish work camps. Trusted inmates were taken out of the prison, sometimes for the entire summer, to work on the roads around central New York. The inmates stayed in vacant farm houses, were often fed by local farm wives, and worked on bettering the deplorable condition of area roads. It was a winning situation for all concerned: the roads improved greatly at little cost to the townships, and the men enjoyed a season in the open air outside of the noisome condition of the prison. Here a group of men leave the prison for a road camp, carrying their belongings with them, in 1914.

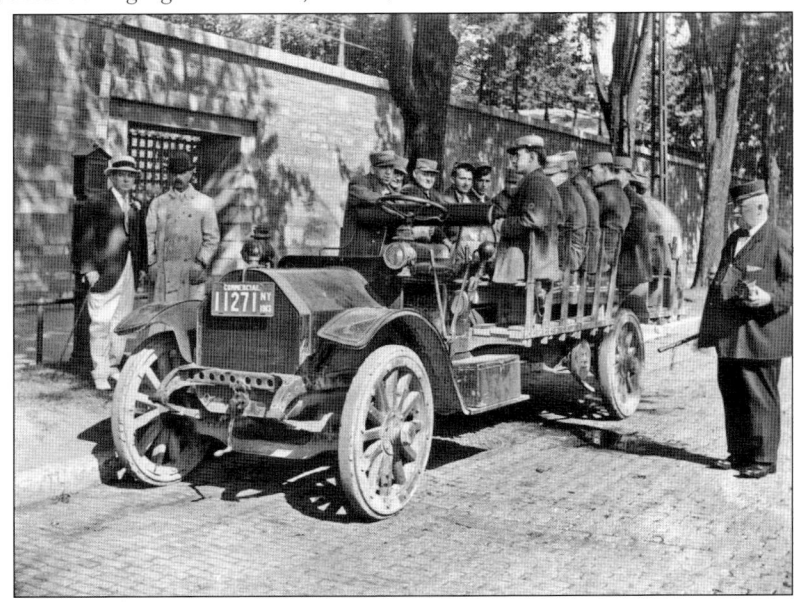

This group of men is being driven to the road camp in 1914. Warden Charles Rattigan (far left), with cane, is there for the photograph, taken outside the prison's Wall Street gate, as is hospital steward Billy Patterson (far right), in the street.

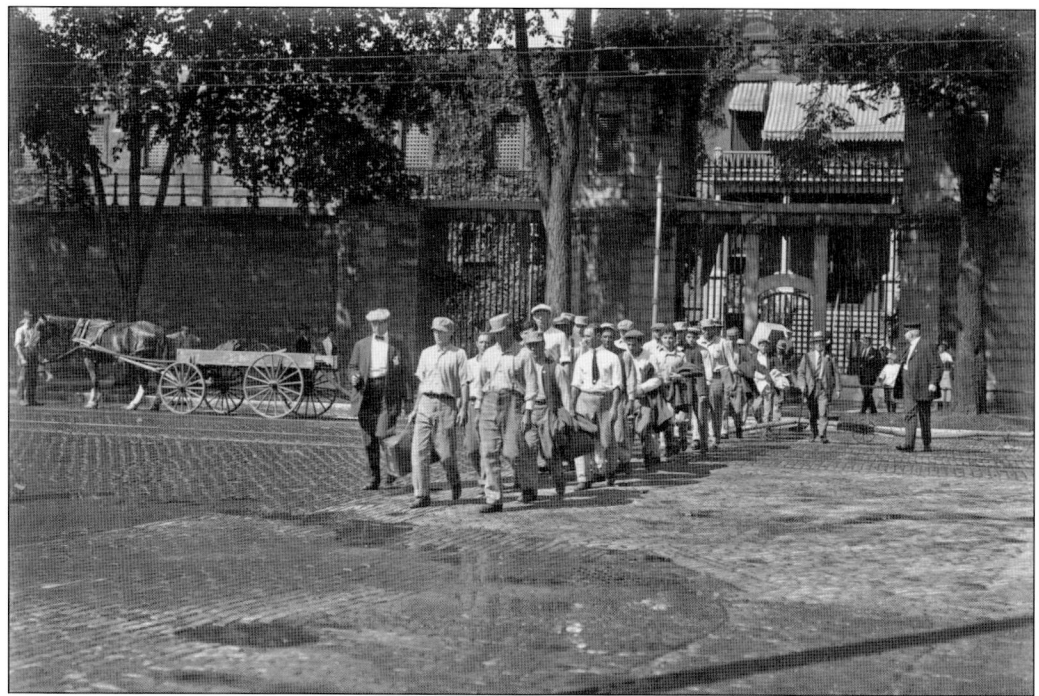

This group of men, carrying their suitcases, are leaving the prison's main gate and crossing the street to the railroad station on their way to a road camp.

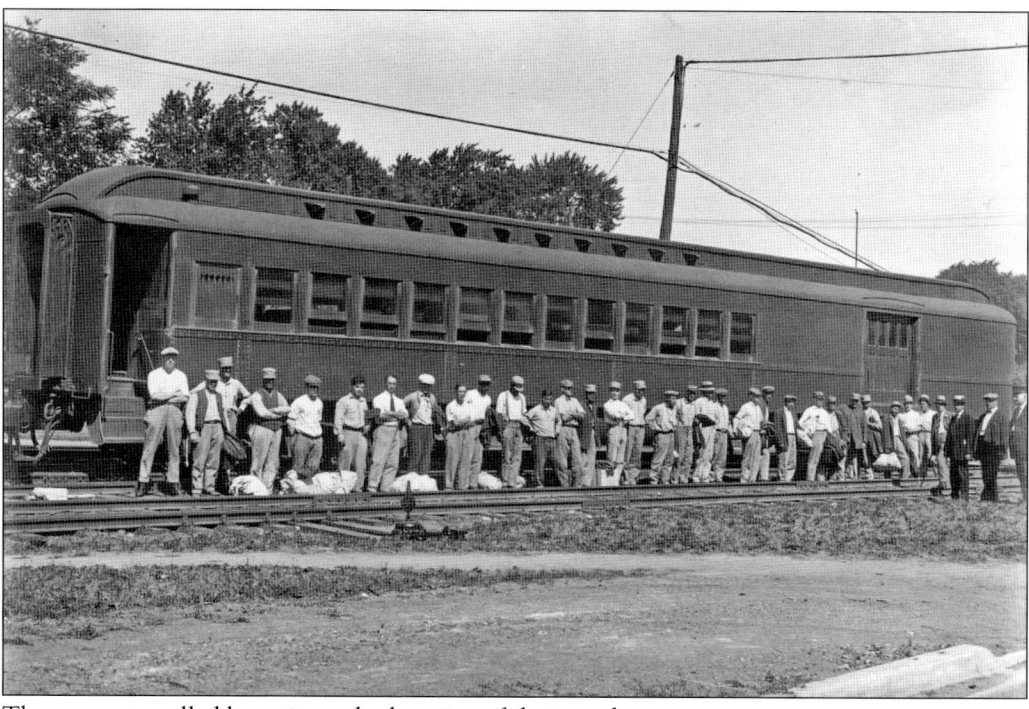

These men travelled by train to the location of their road camp.

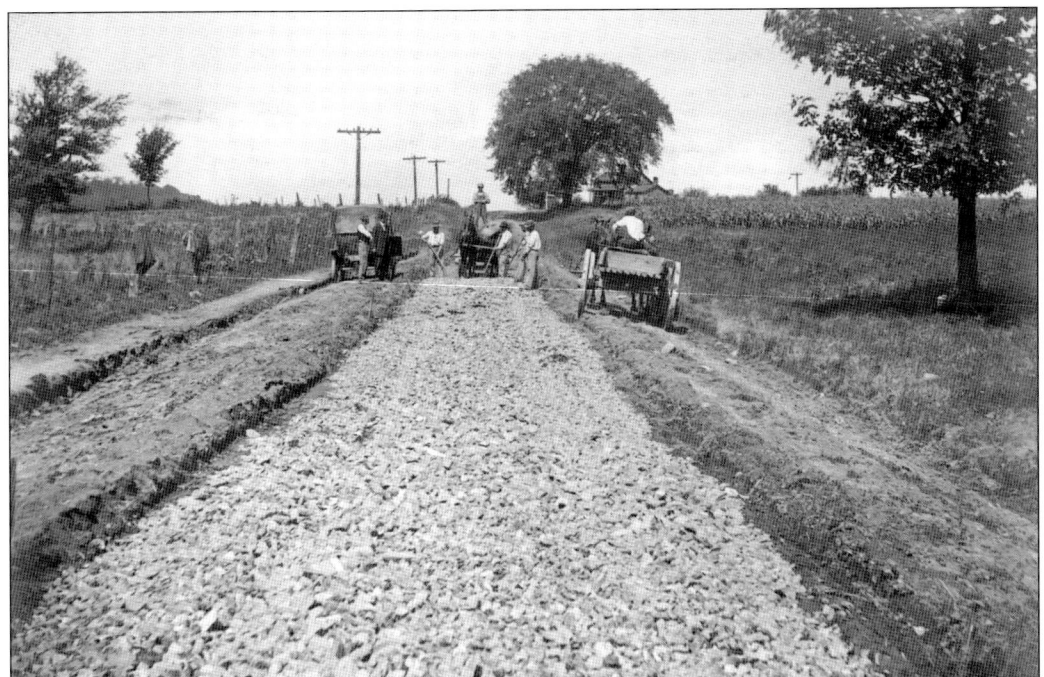

Most of the roads were just dirt before the work crews started. They graded and widened the roads, and added ditches on either side, all under the direction of officials from the various towns that requested the service from the prison.

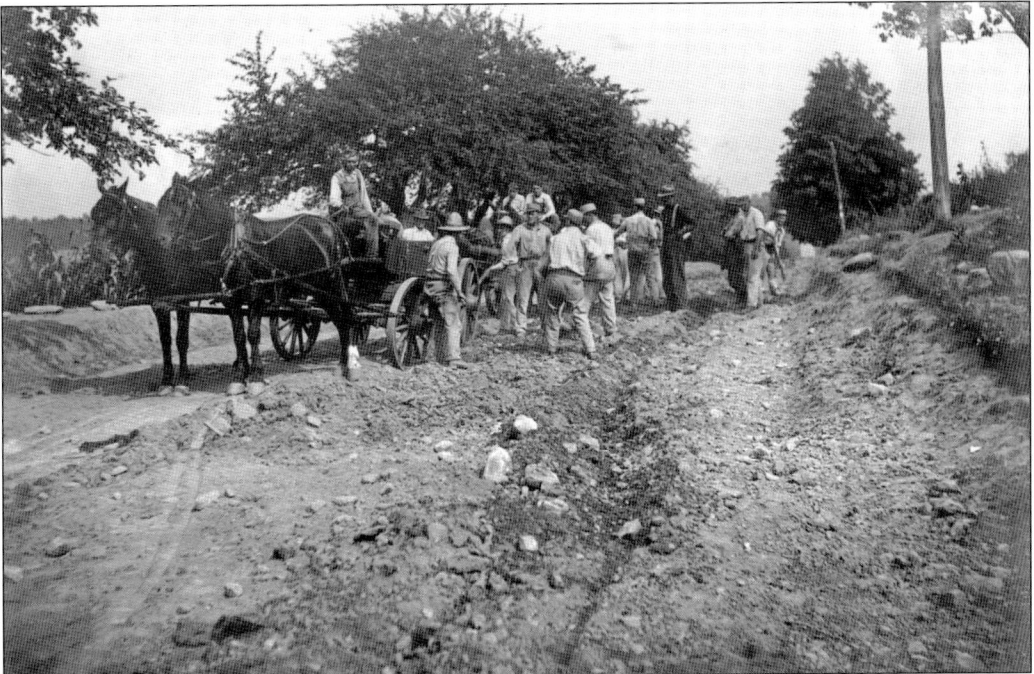

While automobiles were becoming more common, much of this kind of work was still done by manual labor and horses. The prisoners worked for free, but the owners of the horses had to be paid. The inspector who drove out to the site was D. J. Grant.

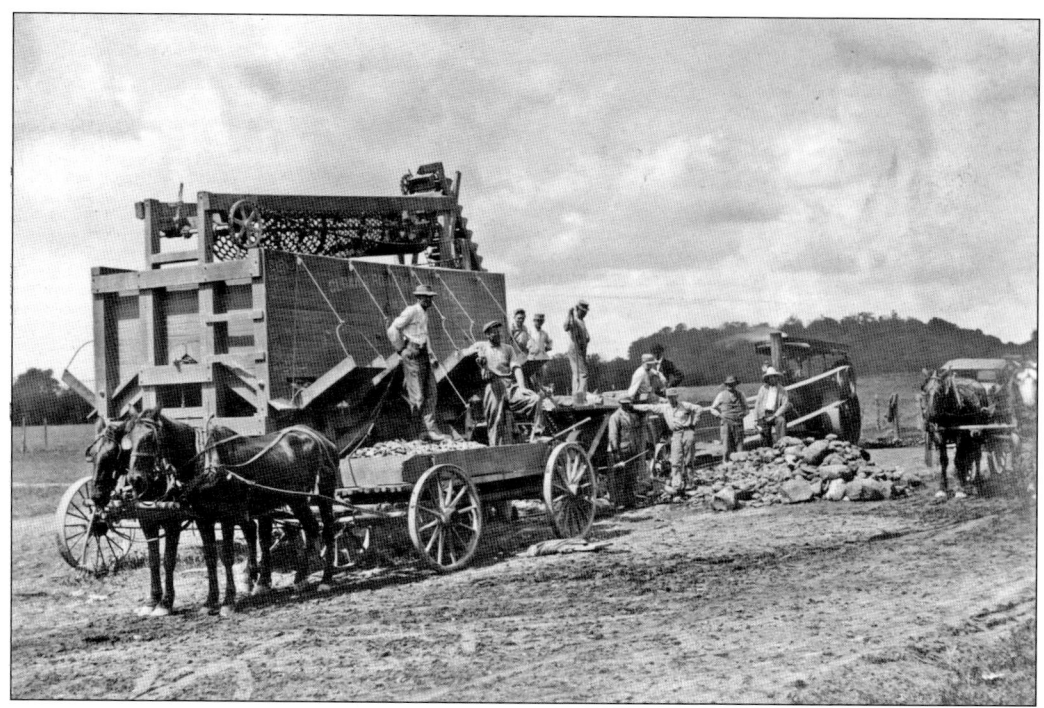

In the town of Meridian, many of the roads were built with multiple layers of crushed stone in decreasing sizes. Although the labor could be backbreaking, the men welcomed the opportunity to be outside of the prison, working in the fresh air and eating fresh food.

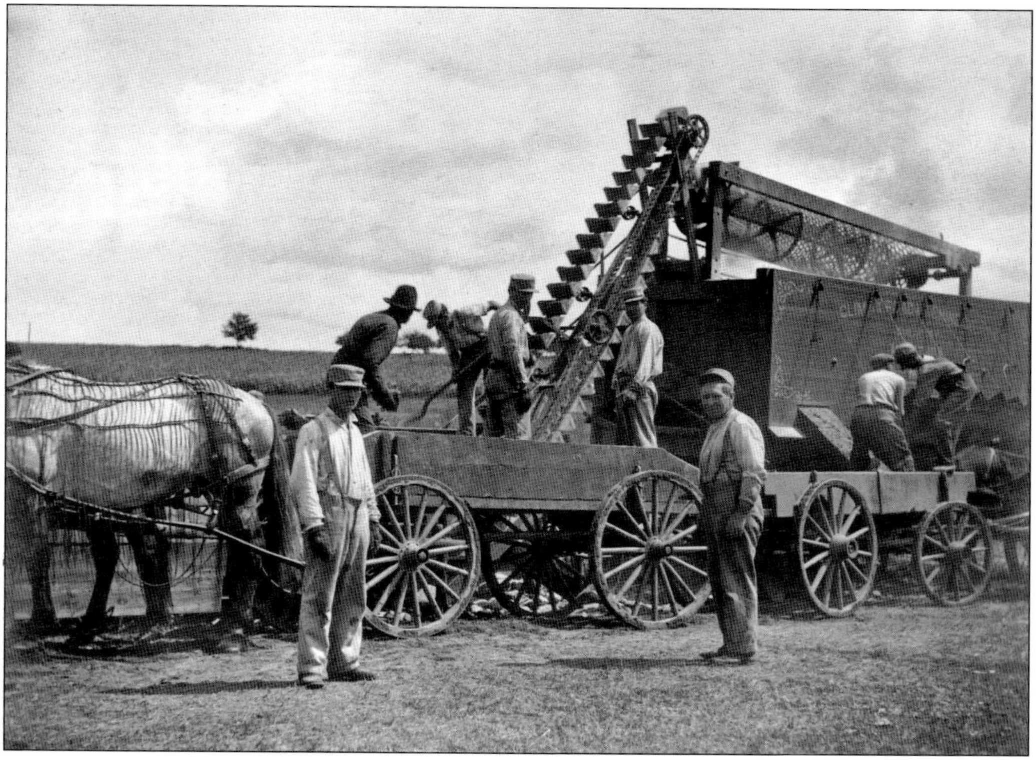

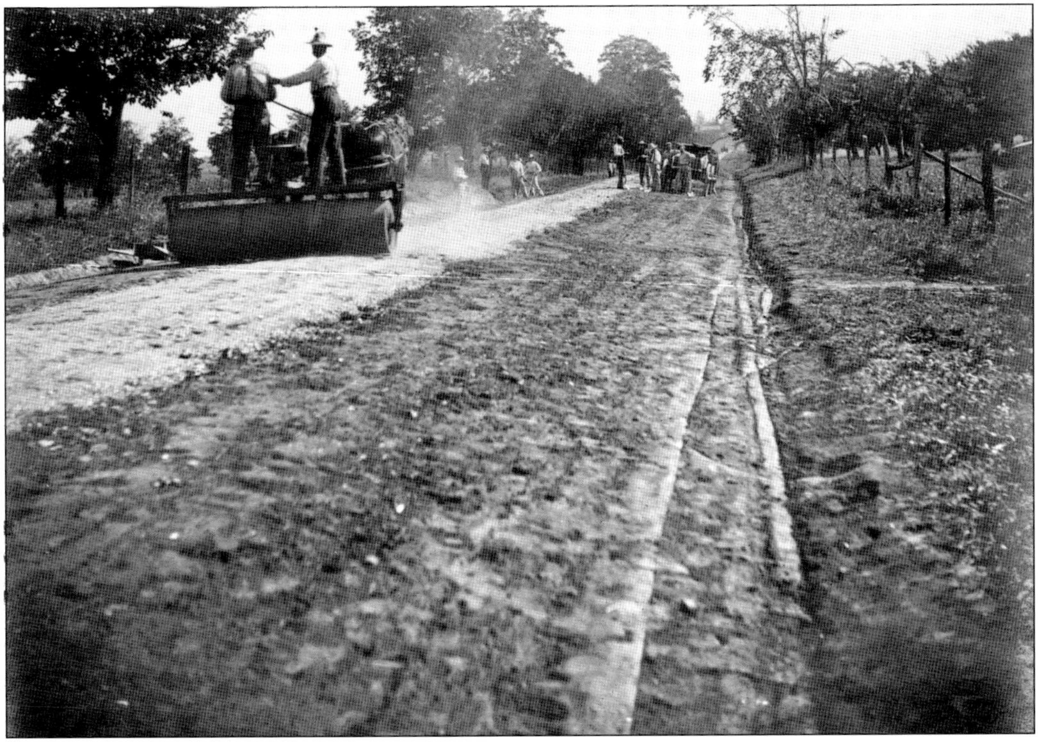

In Fleming, New York, this road was both crowned and widened.

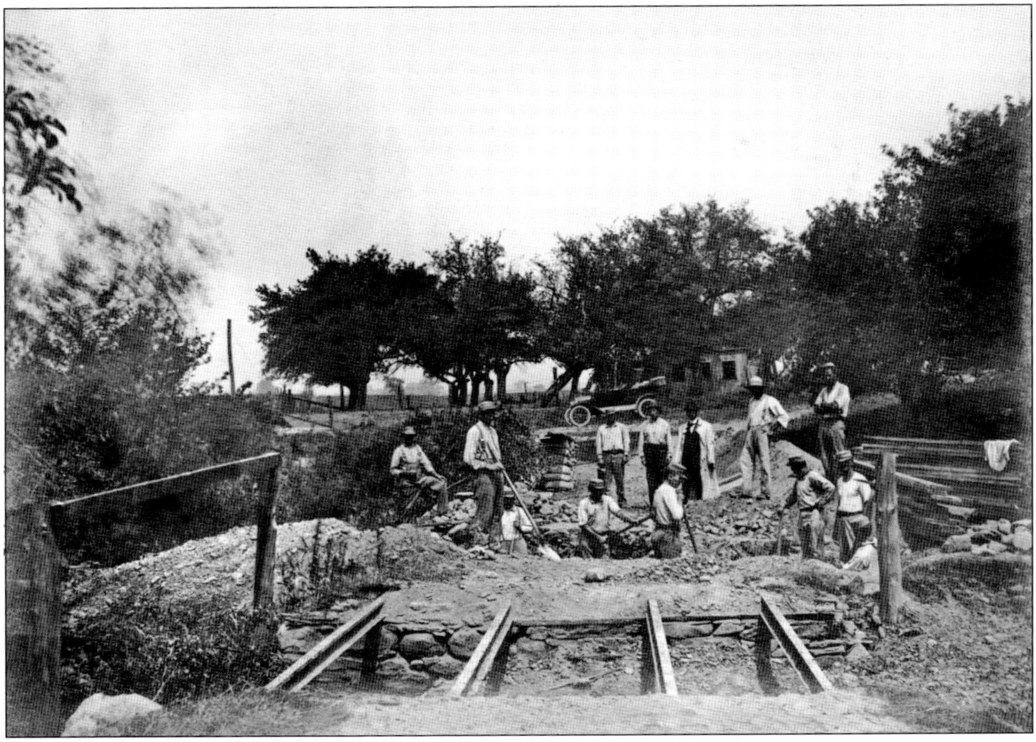

In addition to roads, the work crews built bridges and culverts.

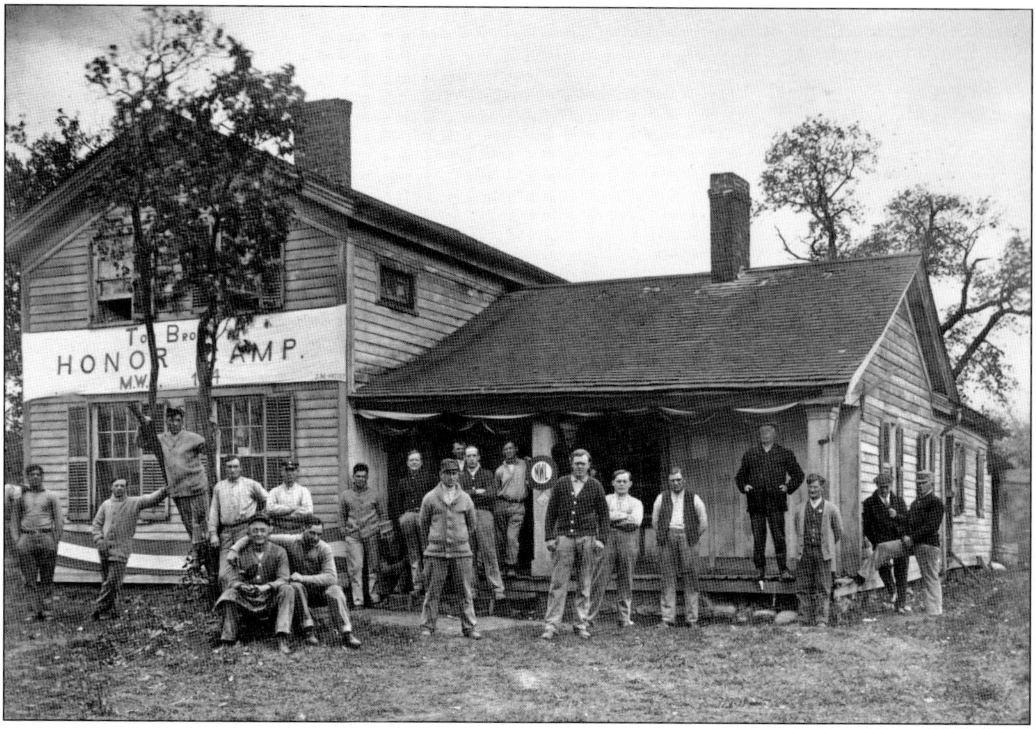

The road camps were called honor camps because only those prisoners who had no conduct violations were eligible to go. The prisoners stayed in vacant farm houses supplied by the town, and much of their food was purchased from nearby farms. This camp was named for Tom Brown, Thomas Mott Osborne's pseudonym, and was located in the village of Meridian in the town of Cato.

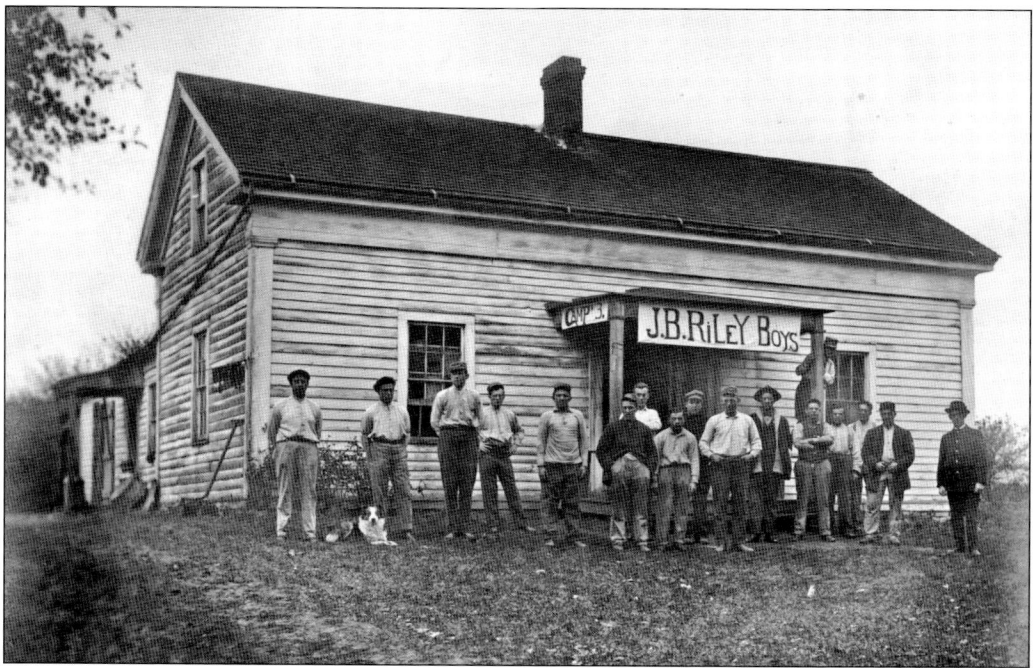

This camp, named for J. B. Riley, was in the town of Ira.

This camp, number one, was named for warden Charles Rattigan.

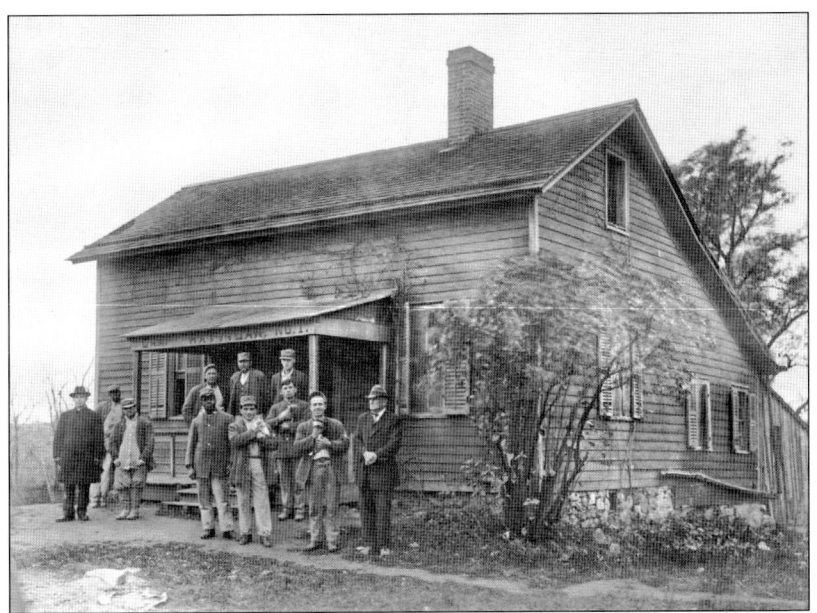

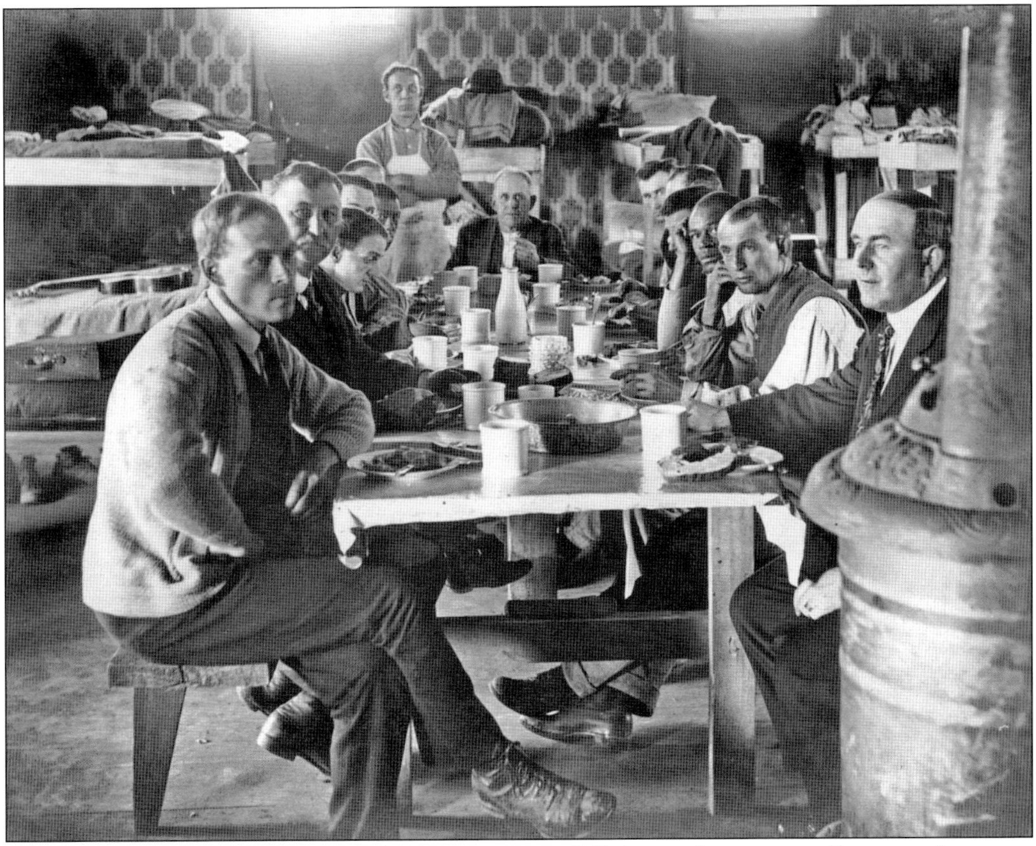

This is an interior shot of one of the honor camps. While conditions were Spartan, they were more comfortable than those inside the prison. The three men at the end of the table, wearing ties, were likely officials from the township.

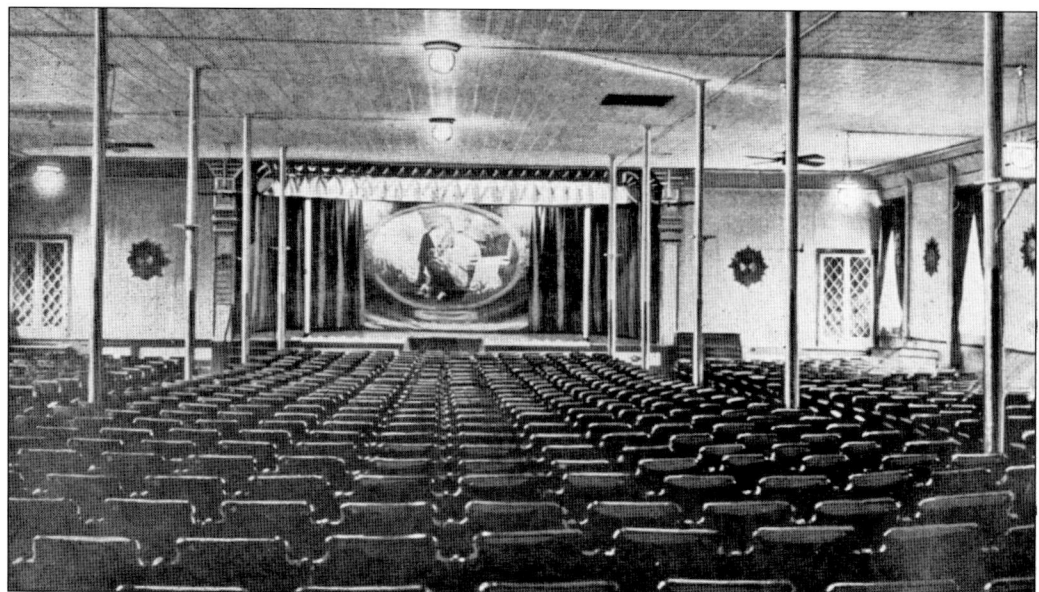

Another change instituted by the Mutual Welfare League was a significant increase in the entertainment opportunities in the prison. There were movies, lectures, theatrical productions, and more. Some were produced by the inmates themselves, and others were regular vaudeville shows brought into the prison. The largest prison assembly room was renovated to resemble a public theater.

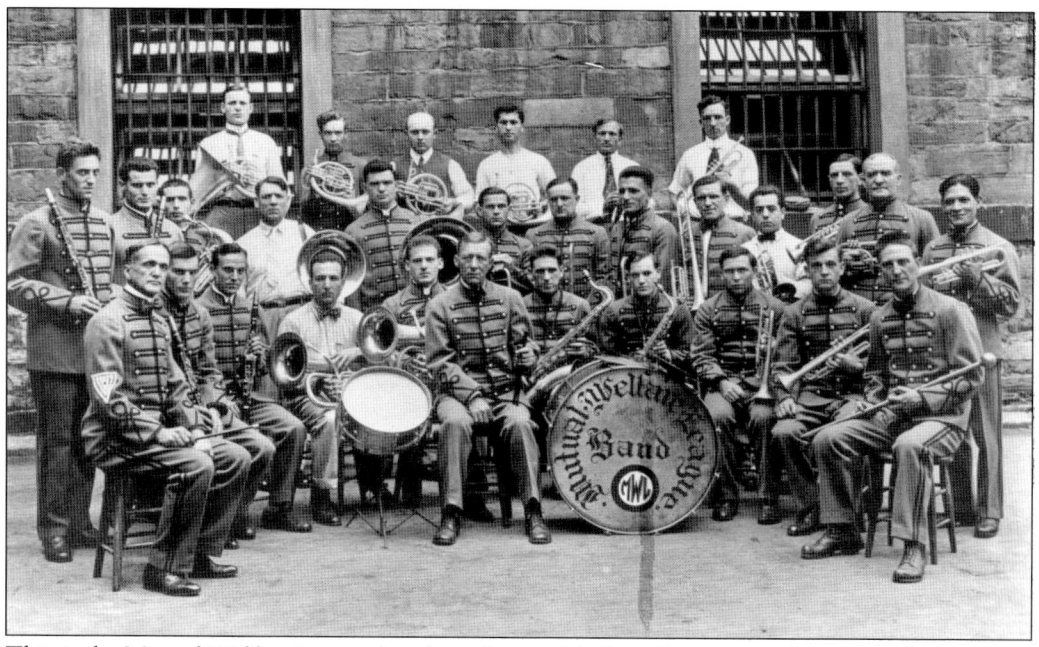

This is the Mutual Welfare League band, made up of Auburn Prison inmates, around 1915. Note the quality of the uniforms.

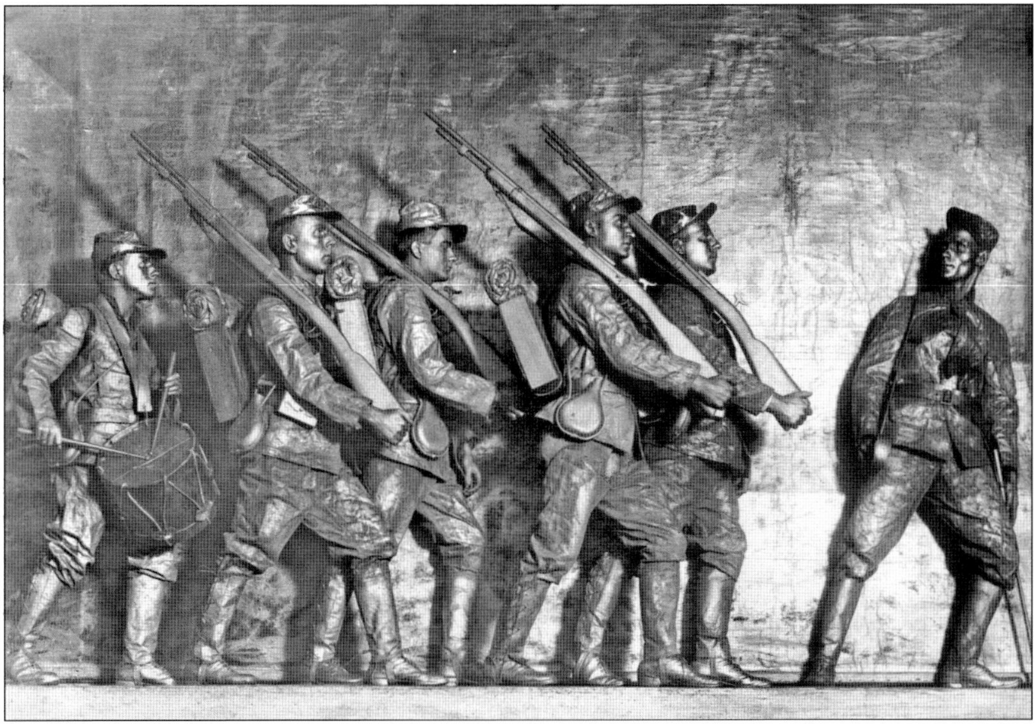

The inmates created most of their own entertainment. One of the most unusual was the "living statues," in which a group would recreate a scene from history or classical literature.

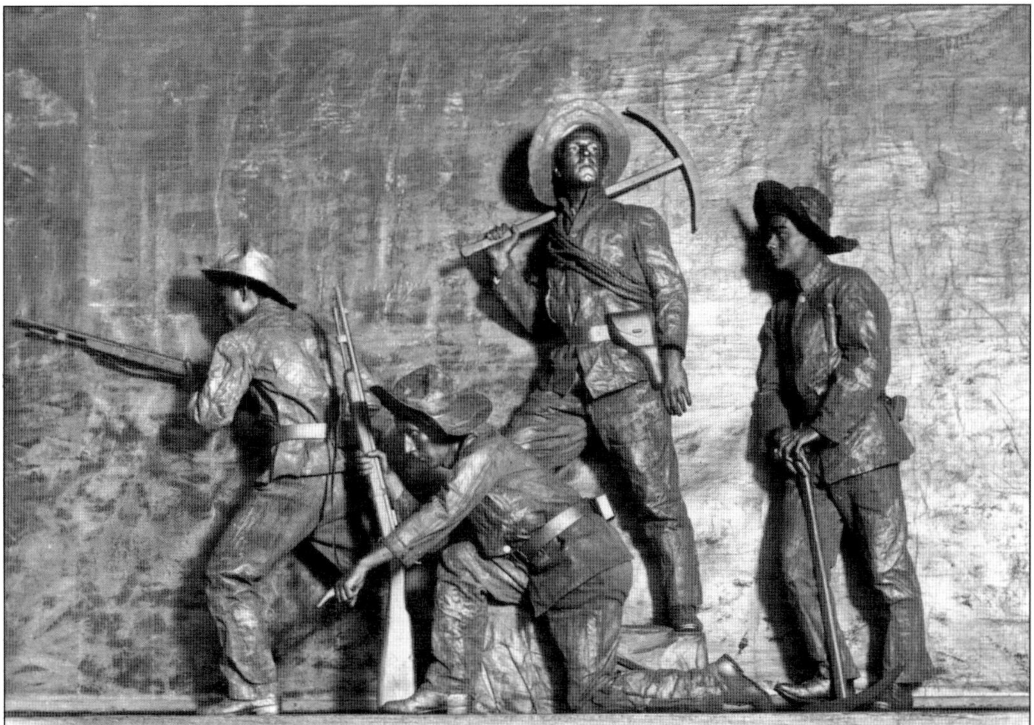

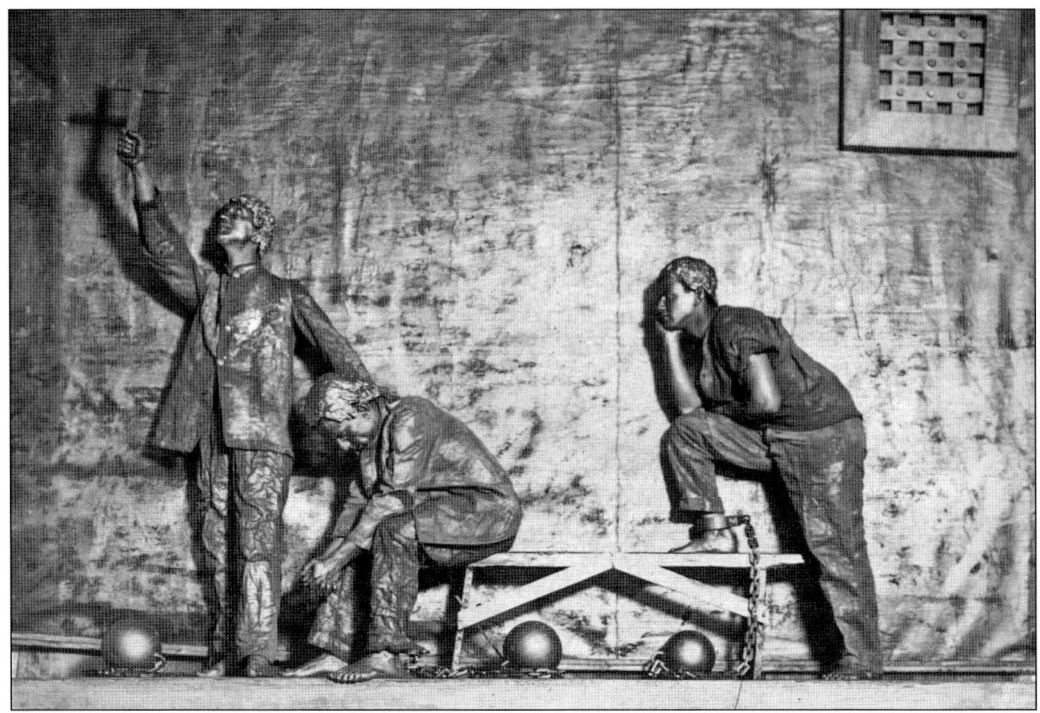

Here a clergyman consoles a despairing prisoner while another looks on in a "living statues" program from around 1915. The ball and chain were certainly not in use at Auburn Prison at this time.

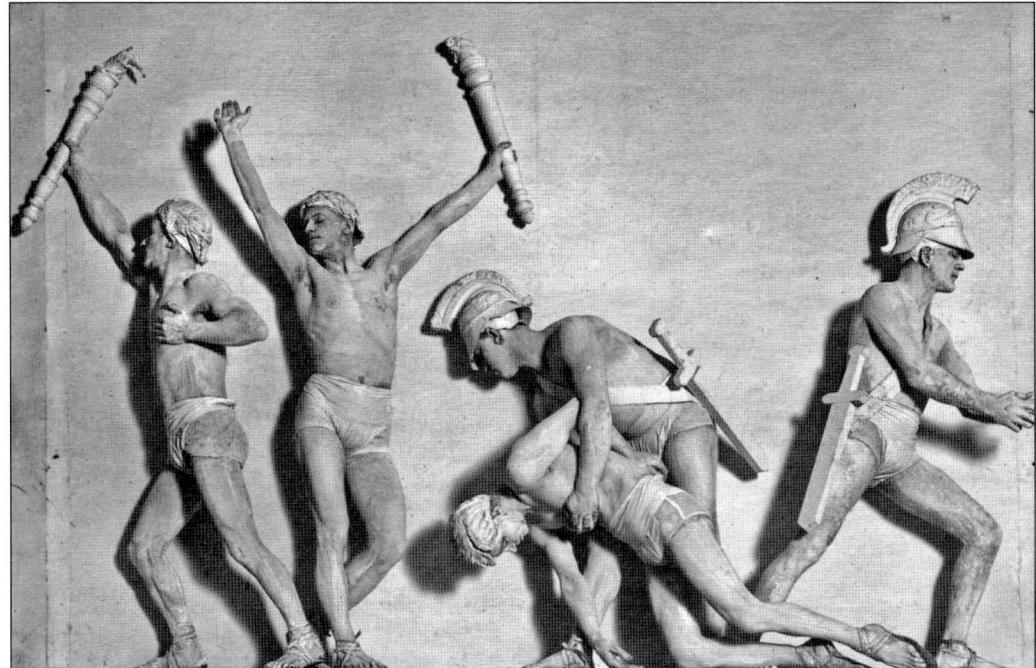

Is this a scene from the Olympics or from the Grecian wars? In either case, it is the inmates' interpretation of the event.

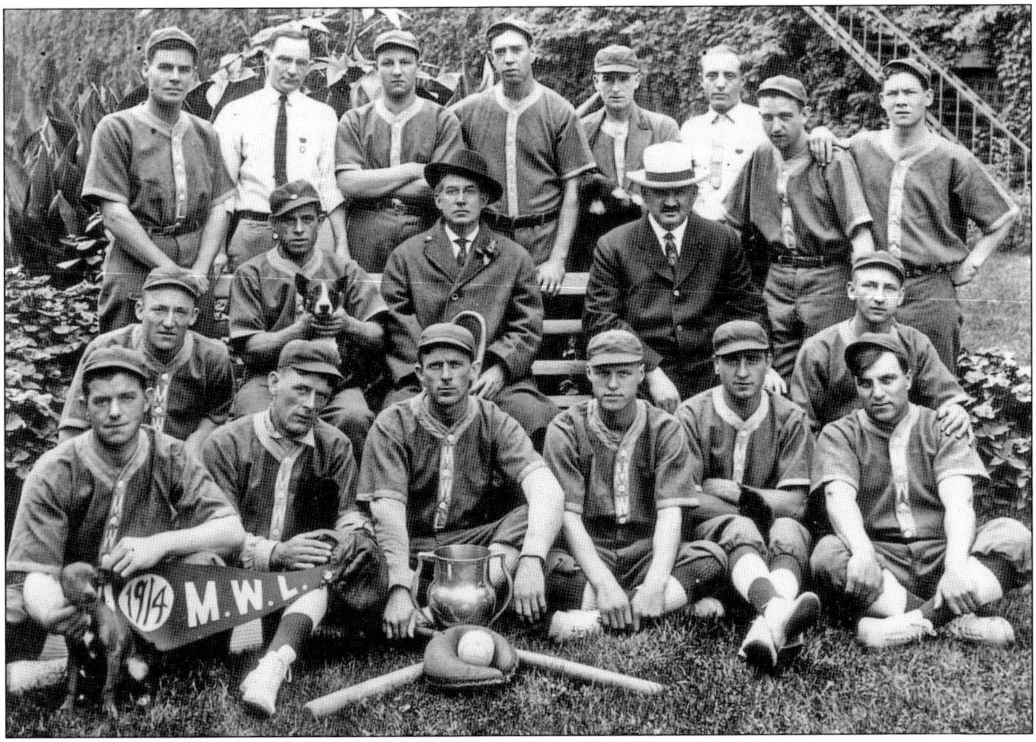

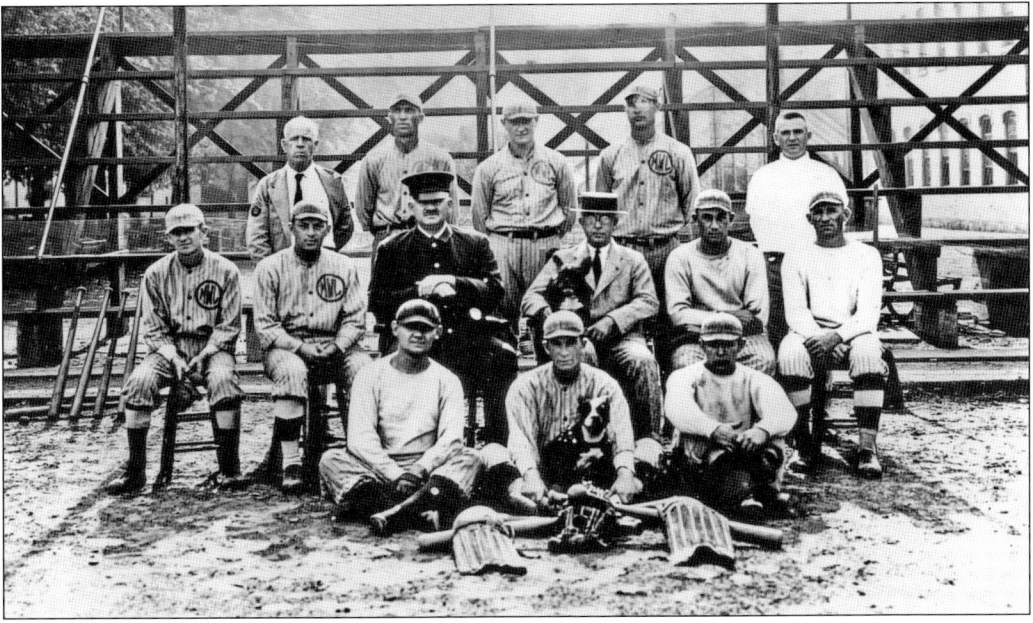

The Mutual Welfare League pushed for more access to sports. Here is the Mutual Welfare League baseball team from 1914. Warden Charles Rattigan (left) and principal keeper John Martin are seated at center. (Courtesy of Michael Pettigrass.)

Here is the Mutual Welfare League (MWL) baseball team in the 1920s. Warden Edgar Jennings, in Panama hat, sits next to principal keeper John Martin on the bench. The MWL team played teams from the city of Auburn on the baseball diamond on the prison grounds.

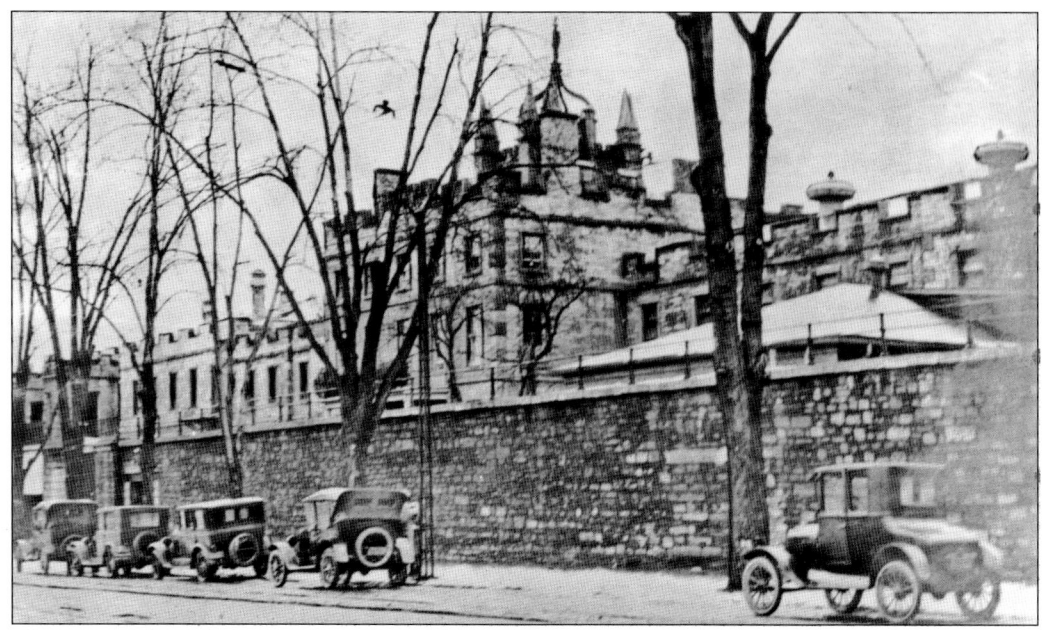

The prison, directly across the street from the New York Central Railroad station, was the first sight to greet many visitors to Auburn.

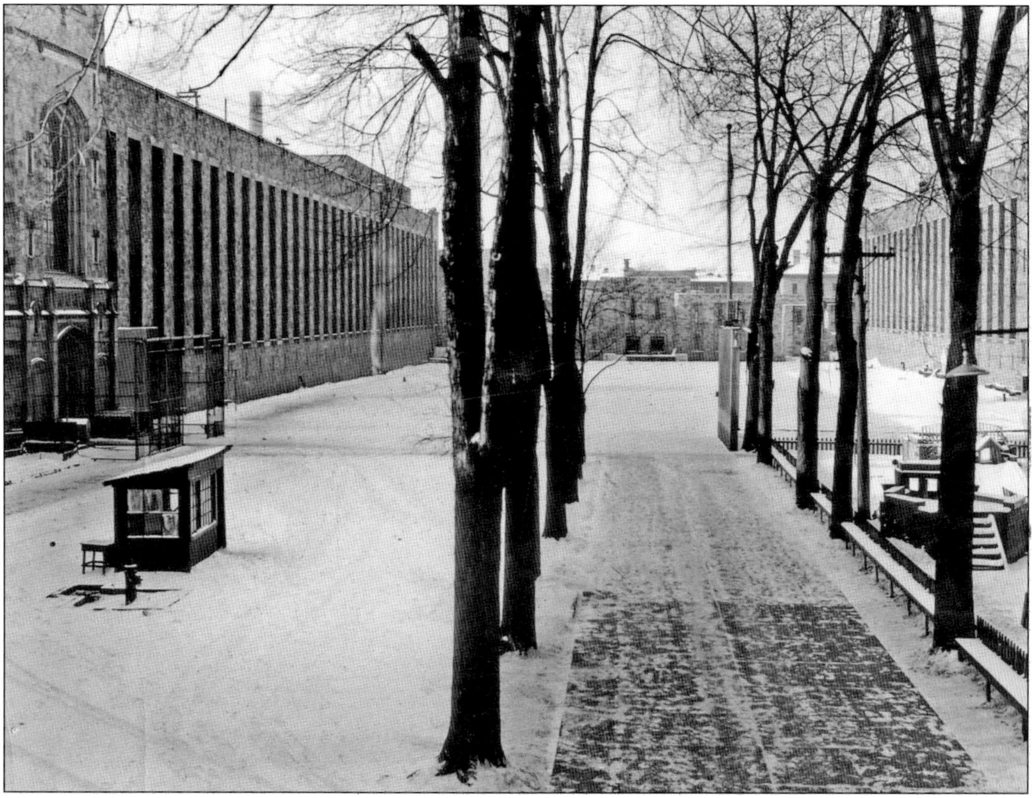

This is a snowy day in the prison yard in 1920. To the right is the miniature golf course that was a product of the Mutual Welfare League's call for more recreational activities for inmates.

Eight
DEADLY RIOTS IN 1929

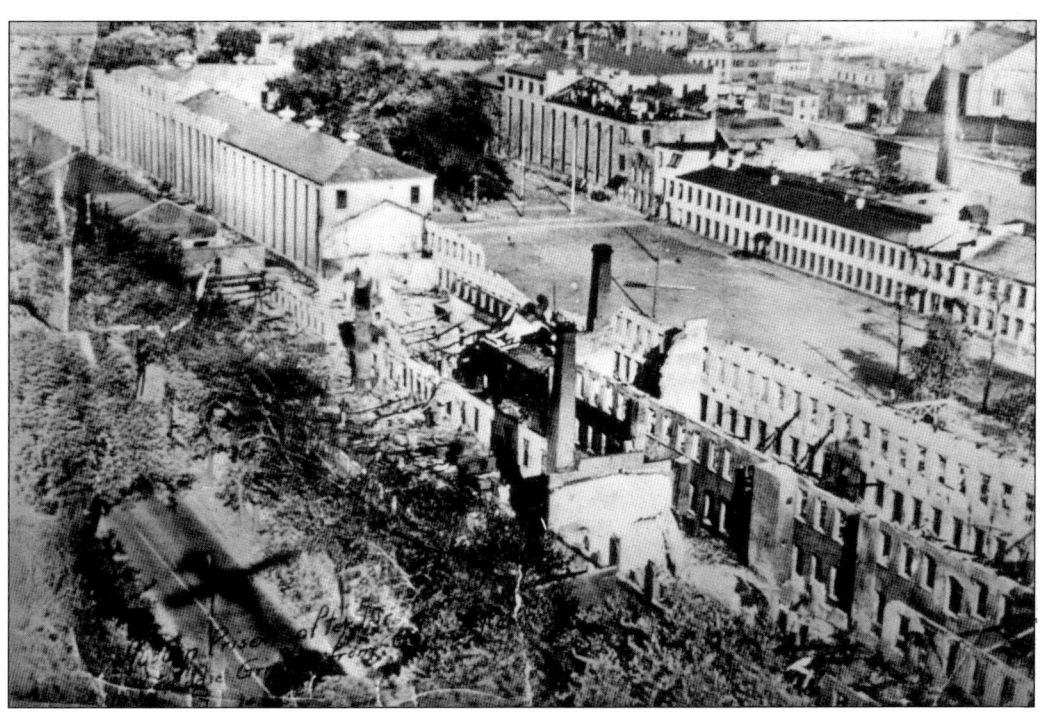

The worst troubles at Auburn Prison occurred on July 28 and December 11, 1929—the hottest and coldest days of the year. On July 28, inmates sprayed acid in an officer's face and gained access to the arsenal. Four prisoners escaped over the wall. The riot spread to the inmate population, and the prison shops were set on fire. Six buildings were destroyed. (Courtesy of Michael Pettigrass.)

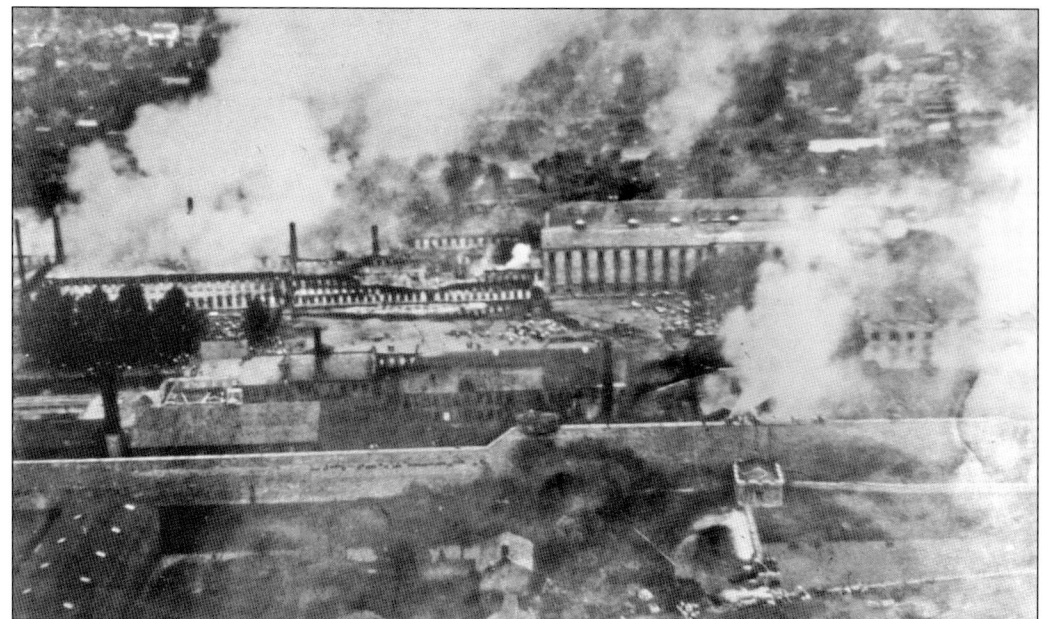

There was little to burn in the stone cell block buildings, but the wooden-roofed workshops burned easily. The fires were eventually brought under control with the help of the Auburn Fire Department, but not before much of the prison lay in ruins. Two inmates were killed and one wounded. Two officers were shot, one was burned by acid, one was beaten, and one was overcome by gas. After several hours, the rioters were subdued and locked in their cells. (Courtesy of Michael Pettigrass.)

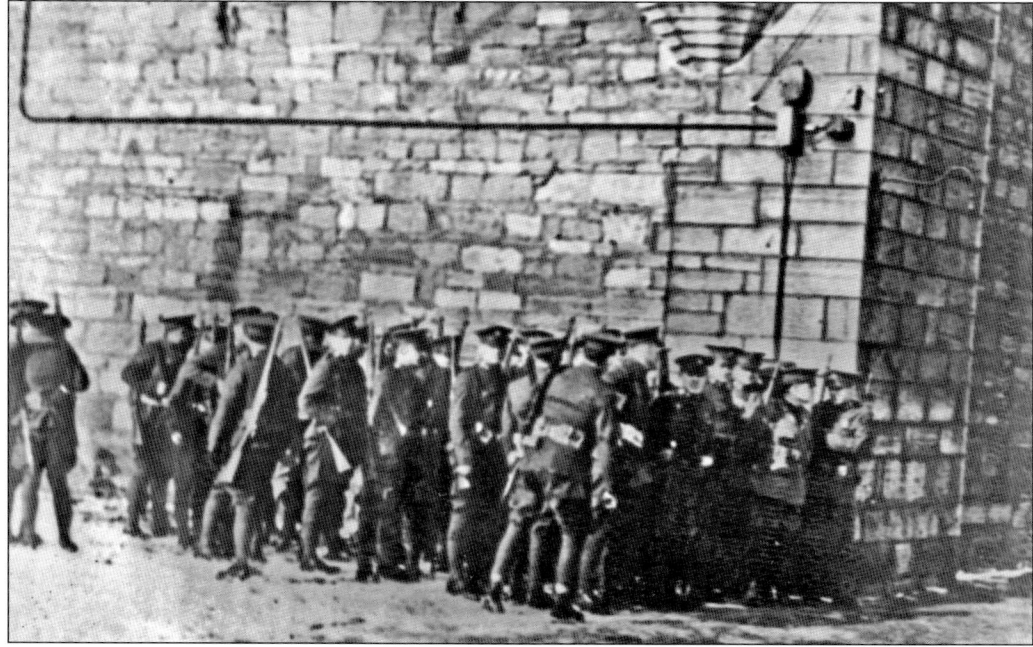

Company I of the New York National Guard was called out to help quell the riot in the prison in July 1929. Because the inmates had breached the prison's arsenal, it was feared that a major gun battle would be launched.

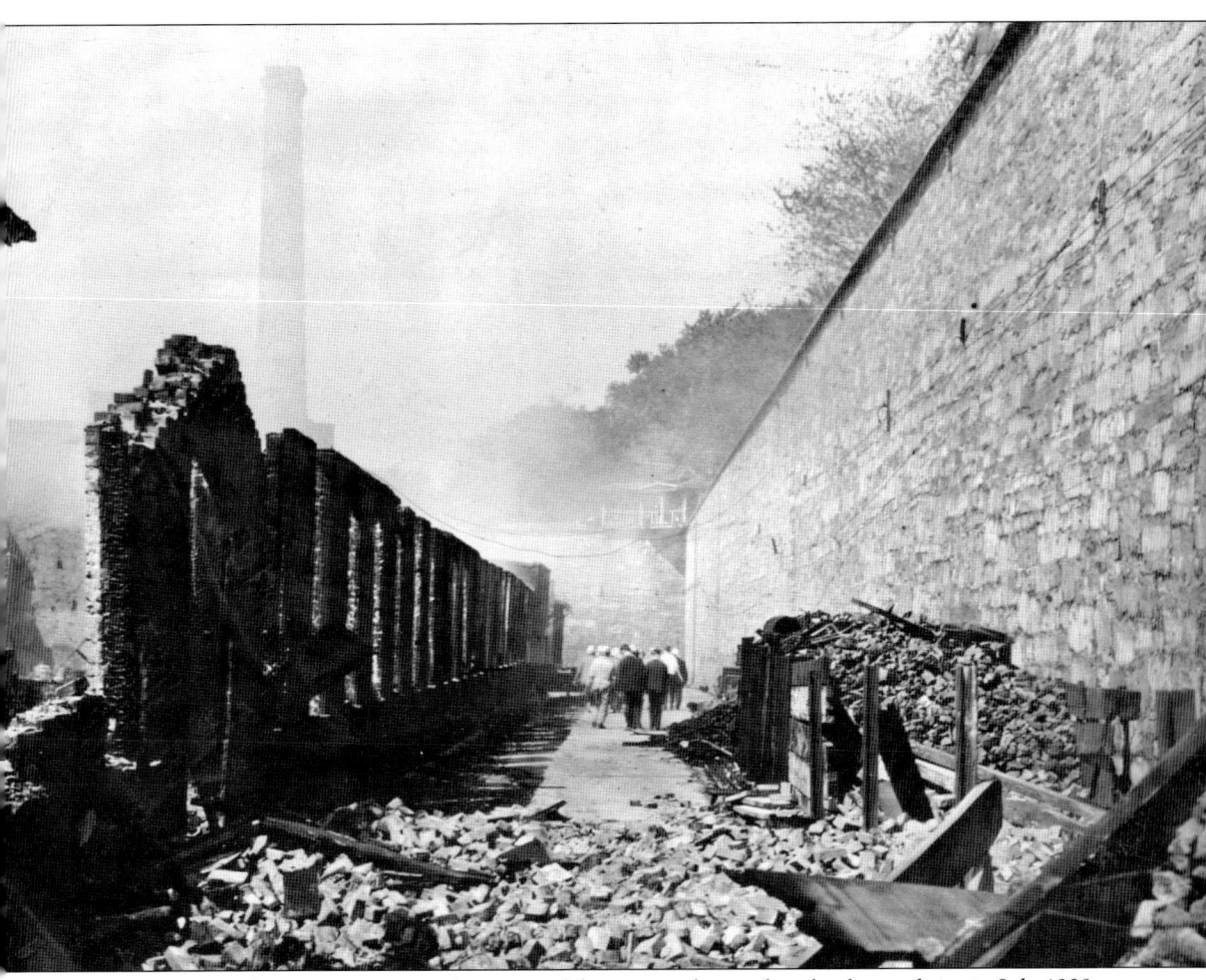
Here is a group of reporters touring the ruins of the prison shops after the fire and riot in July 1929. This photograph was taken inside of the north wall.

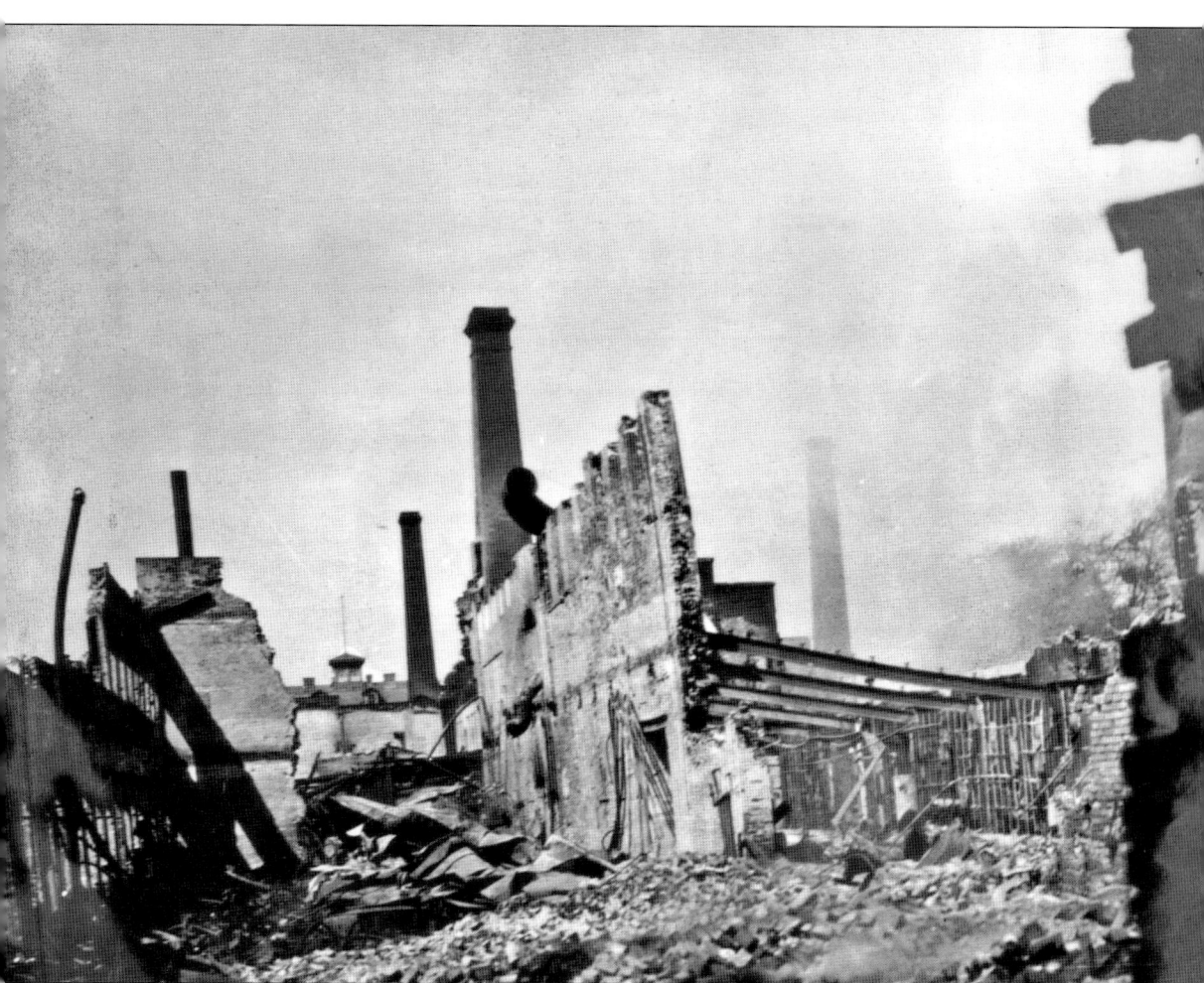

Many of the industrial shops were completely destroyed, leaving the inmates with nothing to keep them busy. Auburn Prison was overcrowded in July 1929. There were 1,768 inmates, although cell capacity was only 1,285. Reasons behind the riots included routinely longer sentences and the decrease in early release for good conduct. With longer sentences and little hope of parole, inmates had little to lose by rioting. (Courtesy of Michael Pettigrass.)

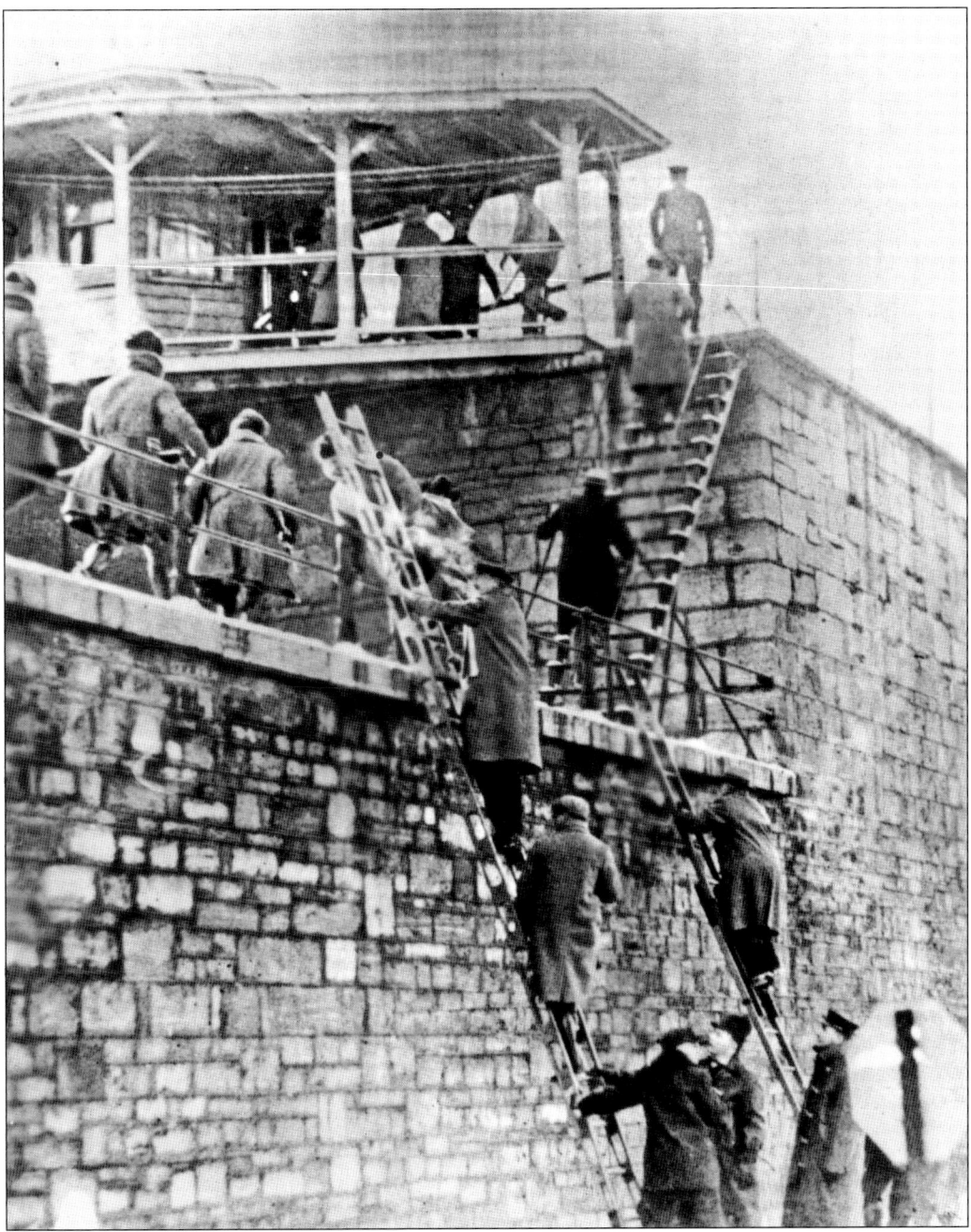

A second riot occurred in December 1929 when prisoners used guns hidden in the prison since the July riot. Hundreds of Auburn residents who heard the gunfire ran to State Street to help defend their community. This was the first time the New York State troopers were called out as a military unit. The troopers, in fur hats and boots, manned the walls of the prison.

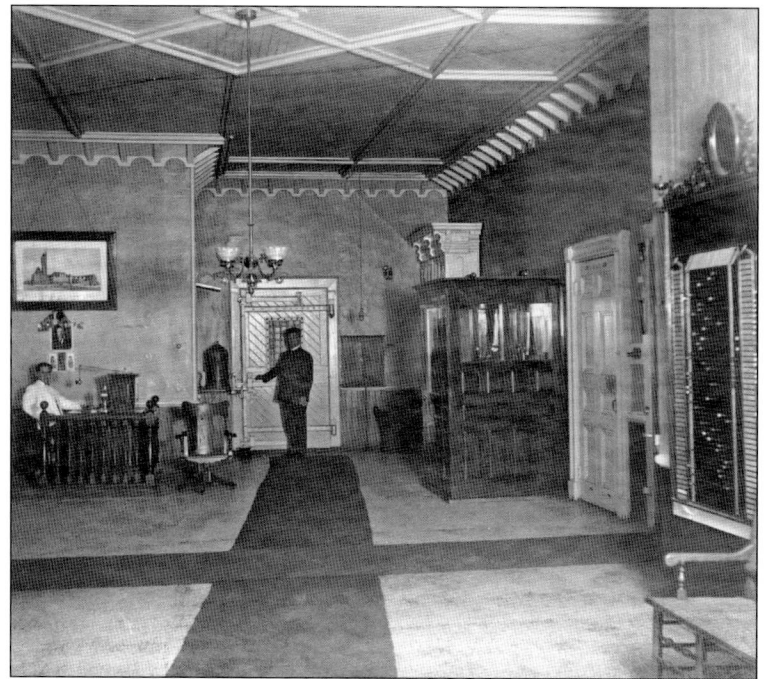

This guard room was one of the main locations during the December 1929 riot. Gustav Stickley carved the decorative top of the "count board" in the right corner of the photograph when he worked at the prison in the 1890s.

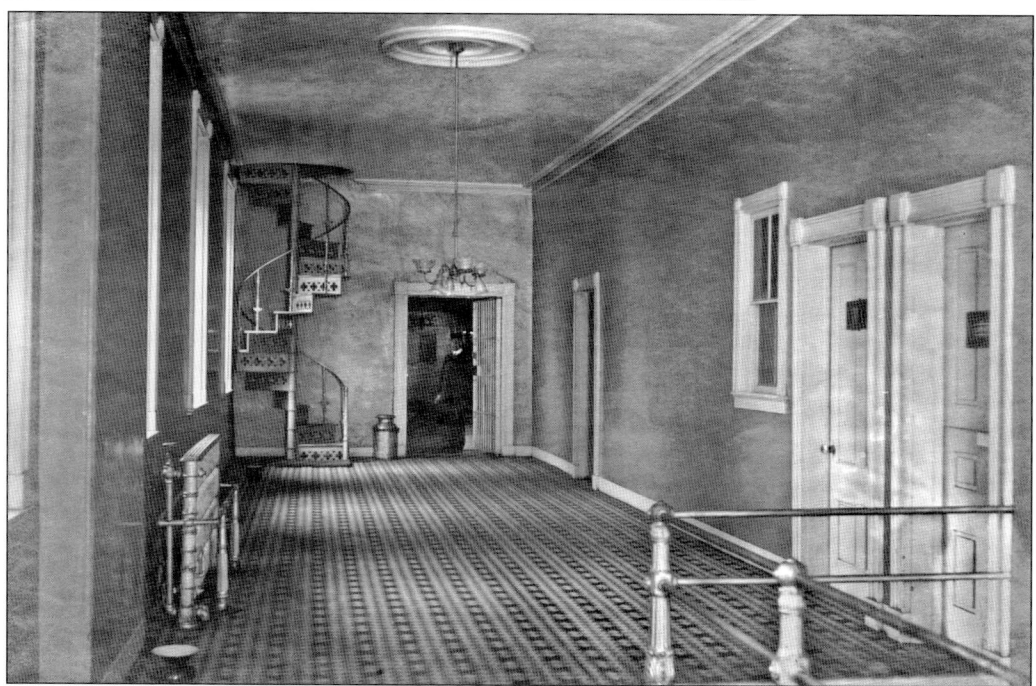

This is the front hall where warden Edgar Jennings and the captured officers were held hostage. The rioters demanded their own release in return for the hostages' lives. When officials refused, both rioters and hostages were subdued with the use of poisonous gas. In total, in addition to murdered principal keeper George Durnford, eight prisoners were killed, and nine people, including two prisoners, were wounded. Three convicts were later executed at Sing Sing for their roles in the riots.

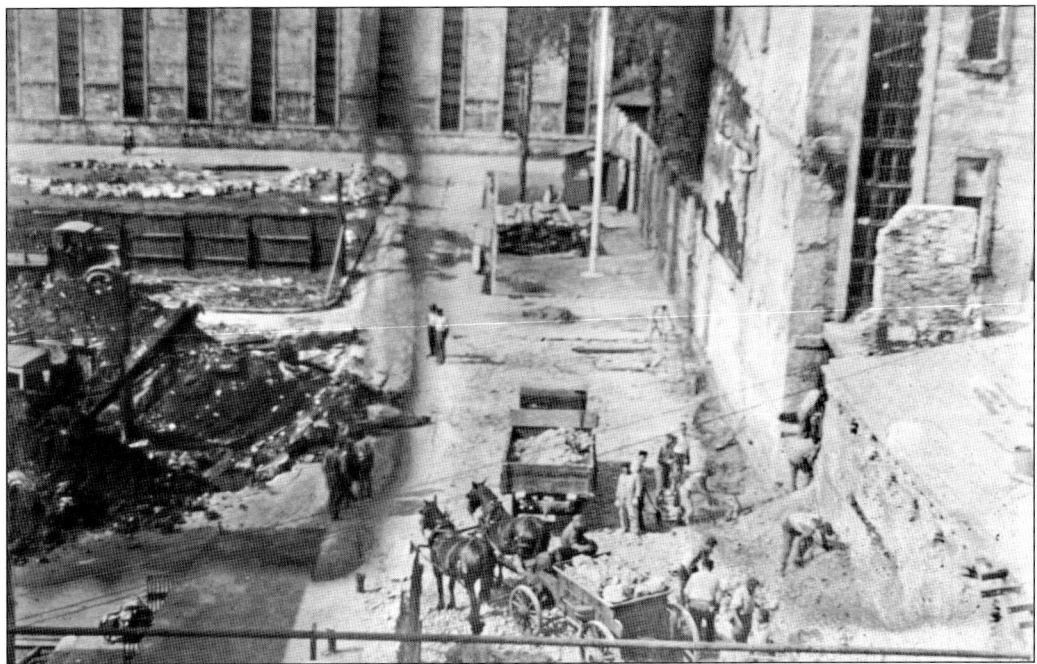

After the fear caused by the December riot, many Auburn residents wanted New York State to move the prison out of the city, perhaps to the site of the prison farm 5 miles away in rural Sennett. Despite the political pressure, the state concluded that moving the prison was simply too expensive. The decision was made to reconstruct and enlarge the prison on the existing site. (Courtesy of Michael Pettigrass.)

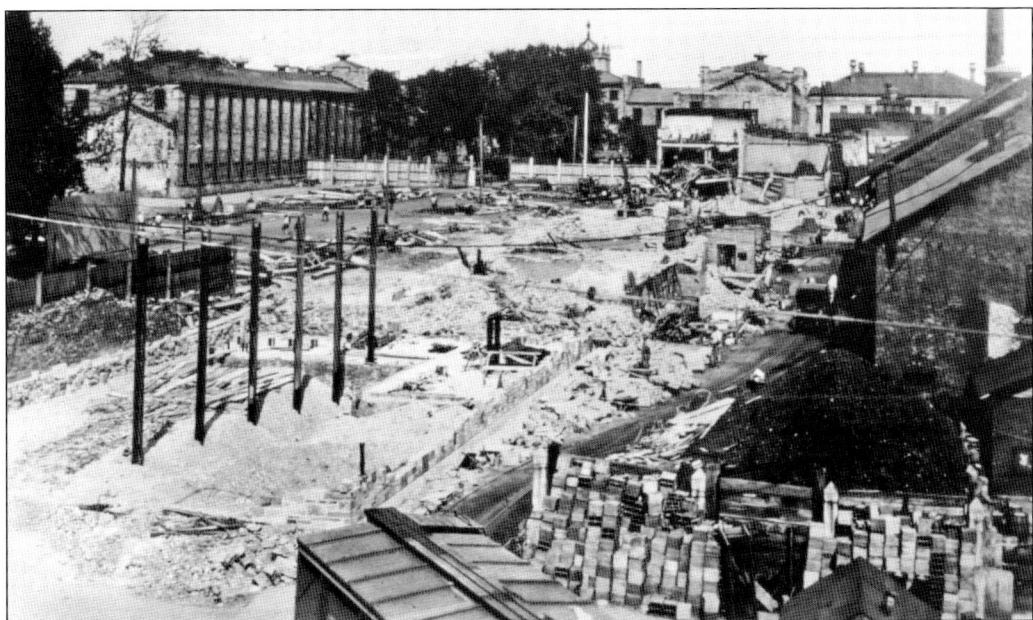

The prison complex became a giant construction site. Fortunately for Auburn, hard hit by the stock market crash and the beginning of the Great Depression, the reconstruction of the prison employed hundreds for more than 10 years. (Courtesy of Michael Pettigrass.)

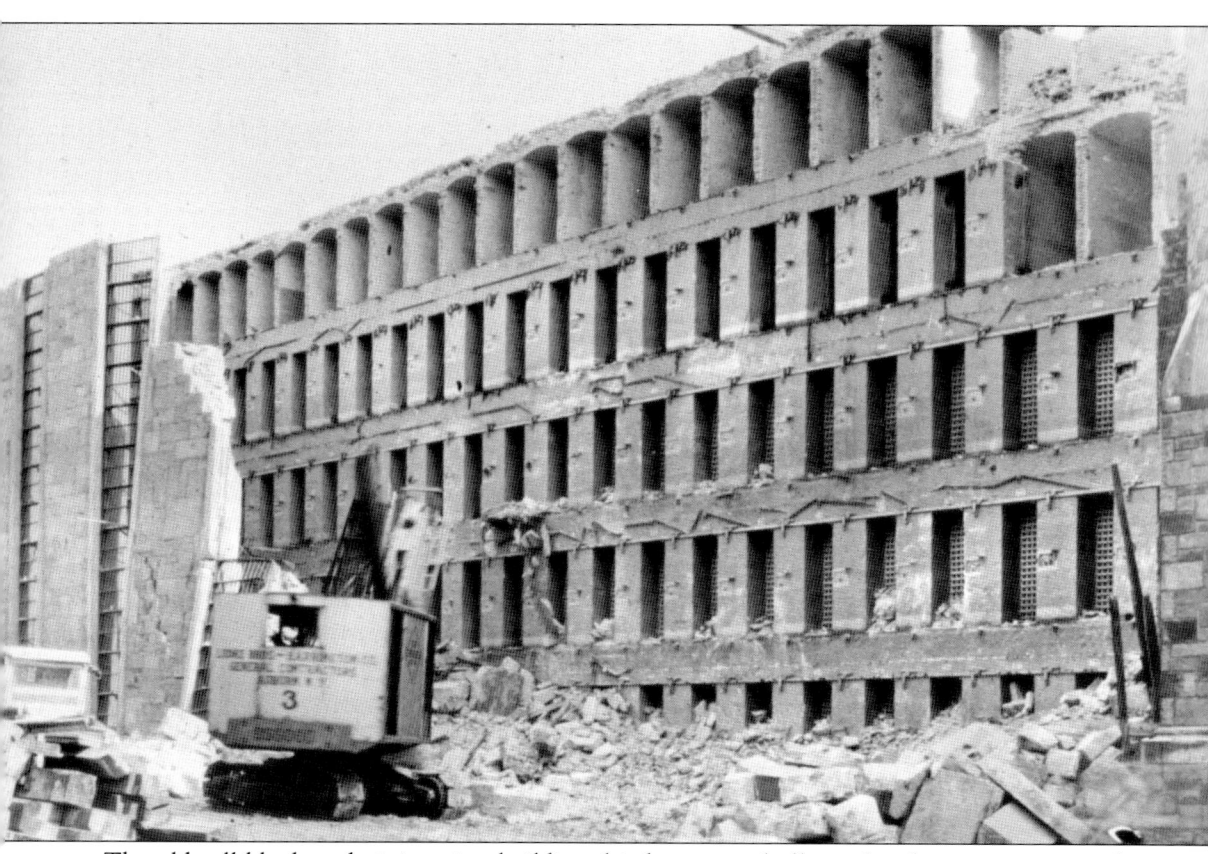

The old cell blocks, administration building, kitchen, mess halls, and auditorium were razed. (Courtesy of Michael Pettigrass.)

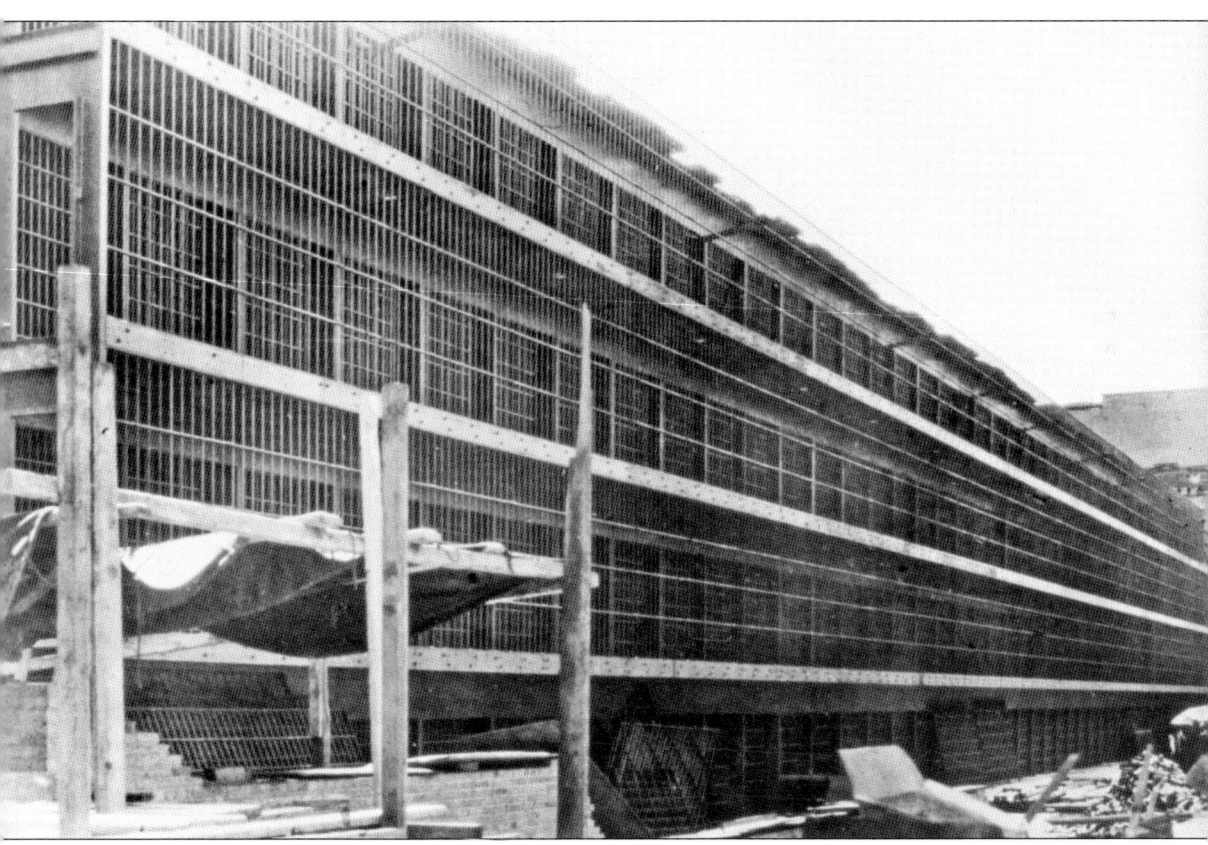
The new cell blocks were built in the same location as the originals. The new cell blocks featured steel-walled cells that were 6 feet wide; 8 feet, 7 inches deep; and 7 feet, 11 inches high. These cell blocks remain in use in Auburn Correctional Facility today. (Courtesy of Michael Pettigrass.)

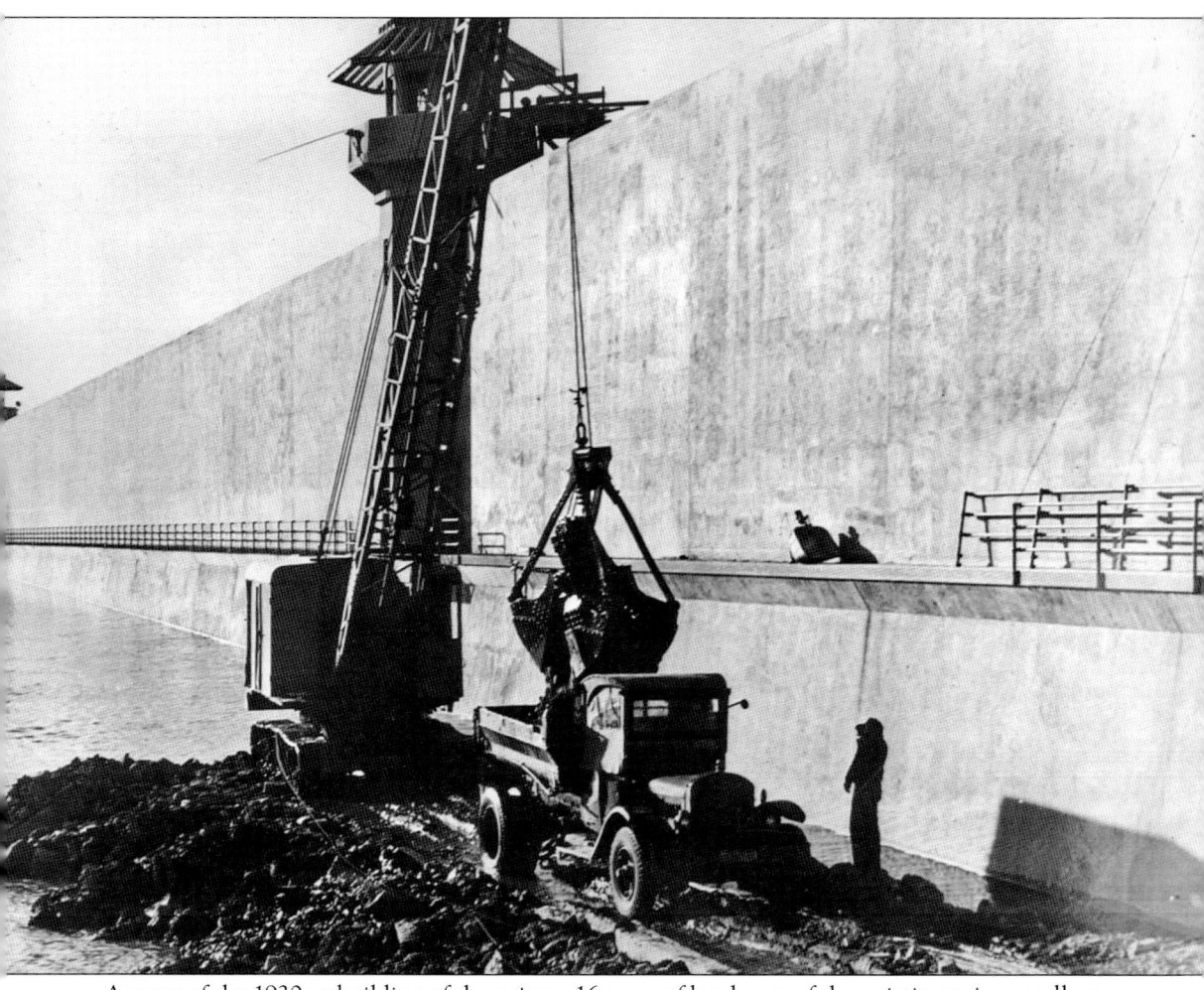

As part of the 1930s rebuilding of the prison, 16 acres of land west of the existing prison wall were purchased. A modern industrial complex was erected on the site. Construction of a tall, cement wall to surround the newly enlarged prison grounds was begun in 1934. The new wall is as high as 40 feet in places and encircles the entire prison complex.

Nine
THE MODERN PRISON

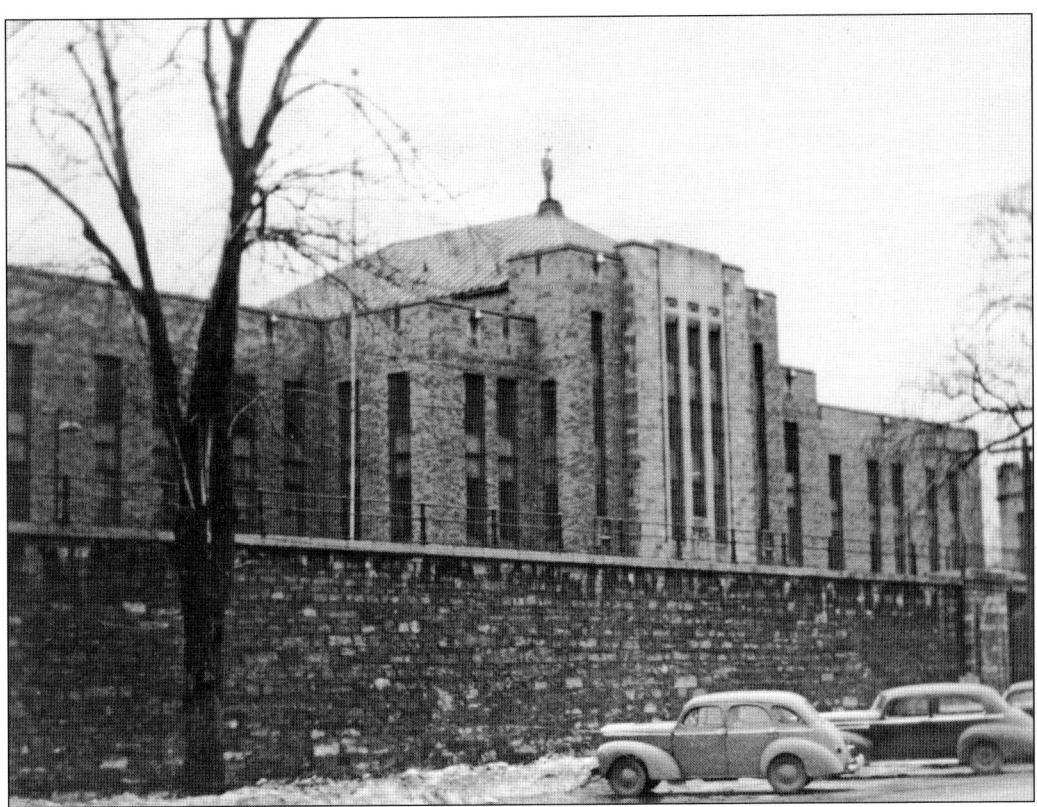

This photograph was taken from State Street, around 1940. The new administration building had been finished, and Copper John was returned to his post, but the original wall and the central turrets remained.

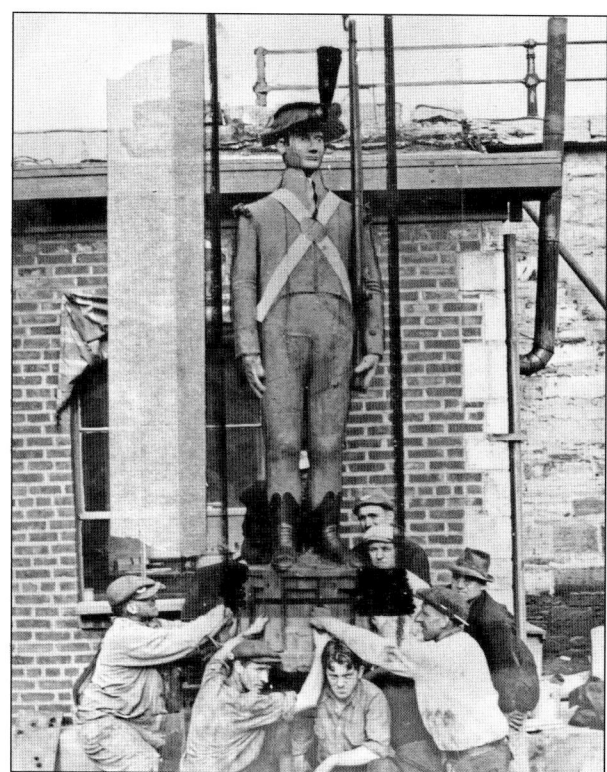

When the old administration building was razed, Copper John was taken down while the new building was under construction. He was a featured guest at the New York Department of Corrections display at the New York State Fair in 1938. (Courtesy of Michael Pettigrass.)

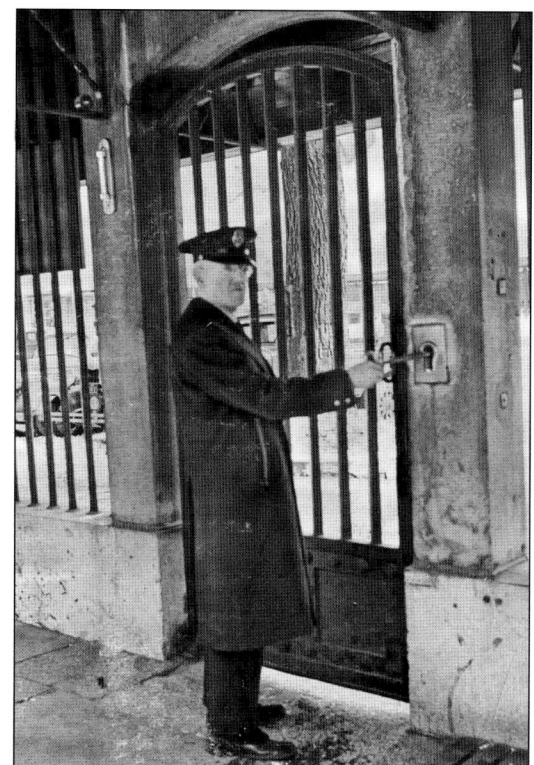

This is Officer John Mahoney with the giant key to the State Street gate, around 1930.

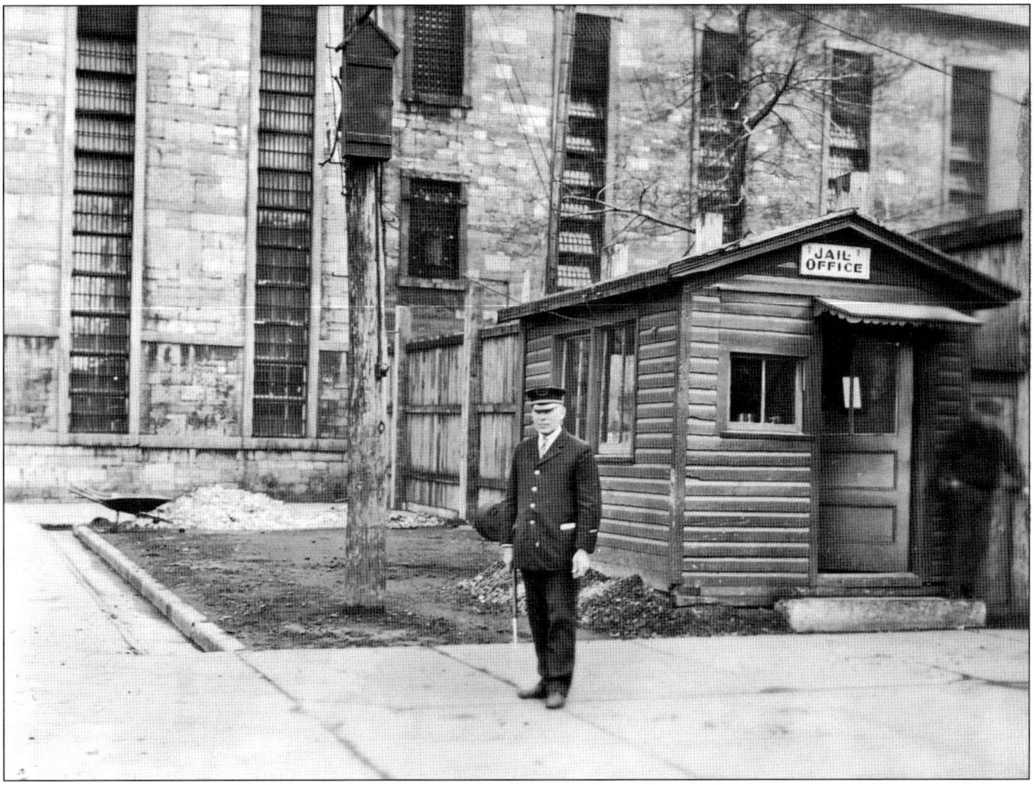

This is principal keeper Edward B. Beckwith in January 1930. P. K. Beckwith became the third principal keeper in a row to be murdered by inmates when he was stabbed to death in the mess hall in March 1931. He was stabbed seven times. P. K. George Durnford was shot and killed during the riot of December 1929. His predecessor, principal keeper James Durnin, had been stabbed to death outside the mess hall on November 17, 1927.

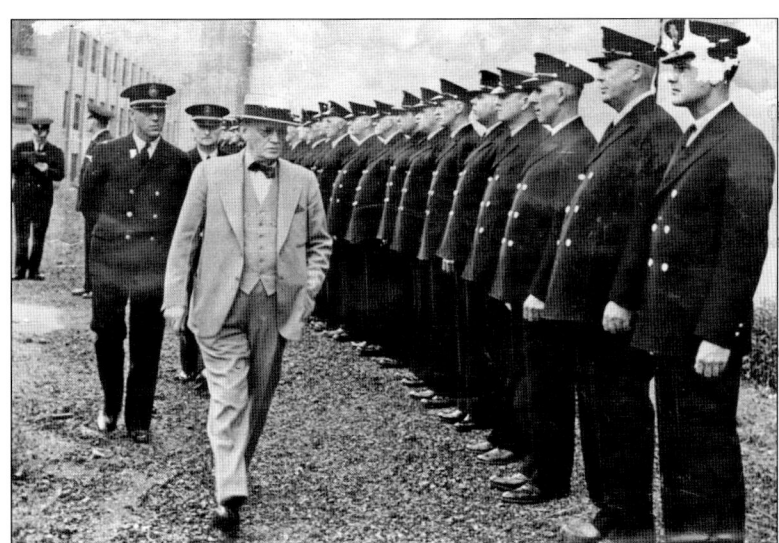

Warden Joseph H. Brophy, front, principal keeper Vernon Morhaus, second from left, and Capt. John Foster inspect a company of guards at Auburn Prison in this undated photograph. Warden Brophy and his successor, Warden Foster, supervised the rebuilding of the prison throughout the 1930s.

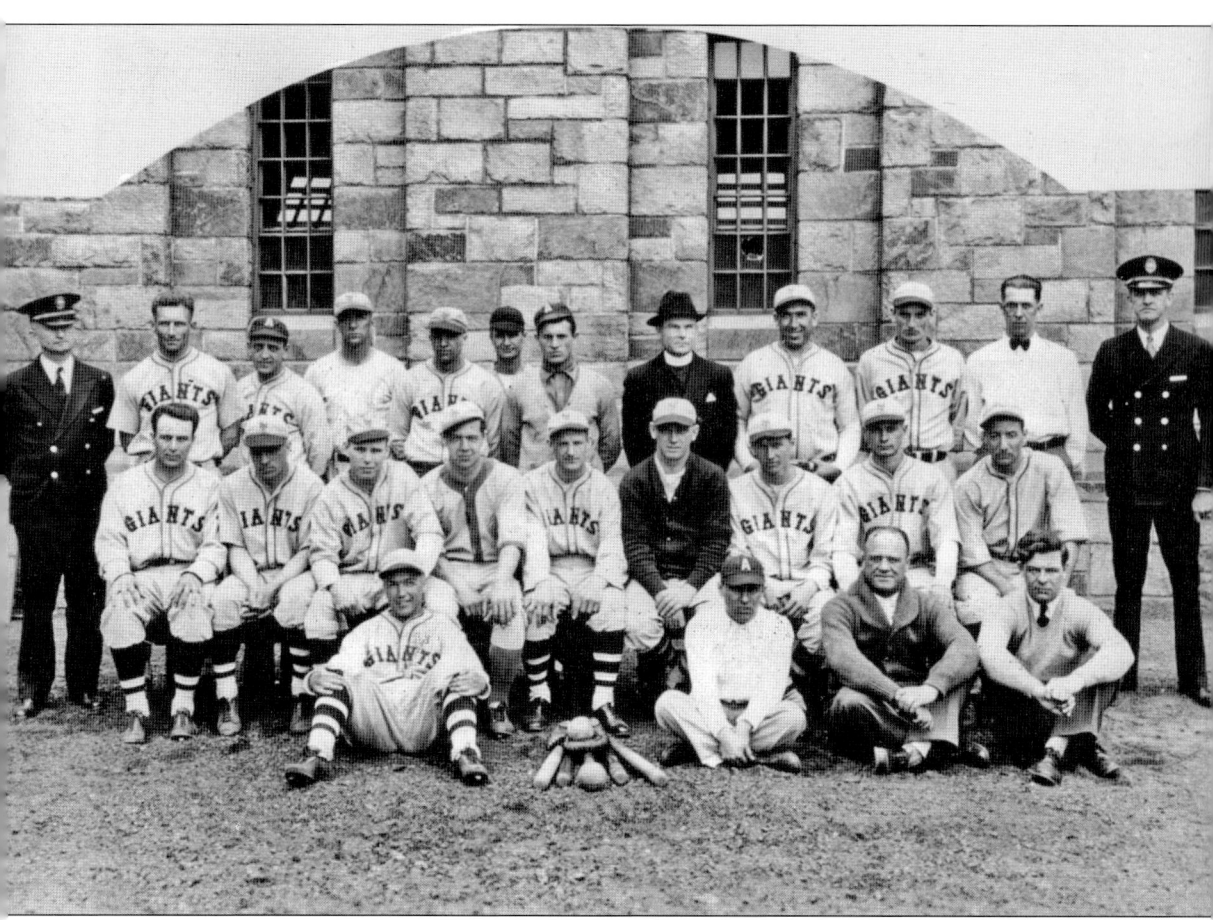

For years in the 1920s and 1930s, the Auburn Prison softball team played in the New York Giants uniforms. John McGraw, legendary manager of the New York Giants from 1902 to 1932, grew up in Truxton, New York. He had been boyhood friends with the Catholic chaplain of Auburn Prison, Fr. William F. Bergan. When the Giants received new uniforms, their old ones went to the prison team. (Courtesy of Michael Pettigrass.)

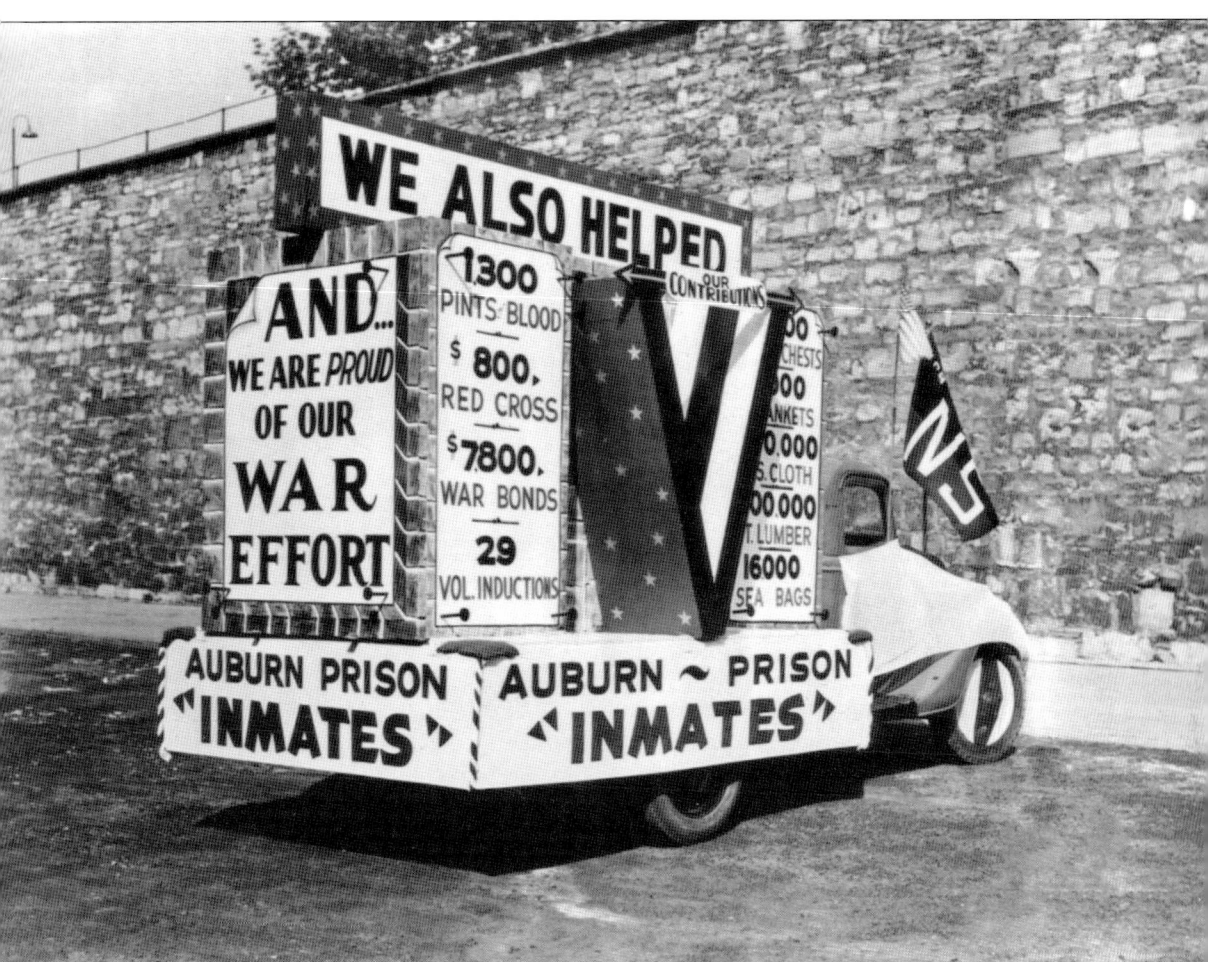

Construction on the prison was halted during World War II, but the inmates did what they could for the war effort. This is the inmates' float from the World War II victory parade in Auburn.

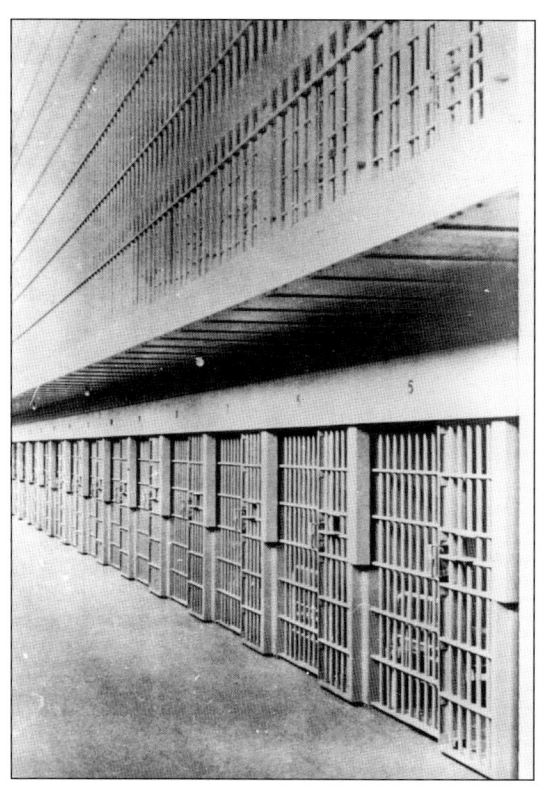

When the new cell blocks were built in the 1930s, the upper galleries in Auburn Prison were fitted with floor-to-ceiling rails. Too many inmates throughout the New York penal system had been killed by falls from the galleries.

This is cell block D around 1977. A pair of handcuff keys was found in the third ventilator on a frisk of the cell block.

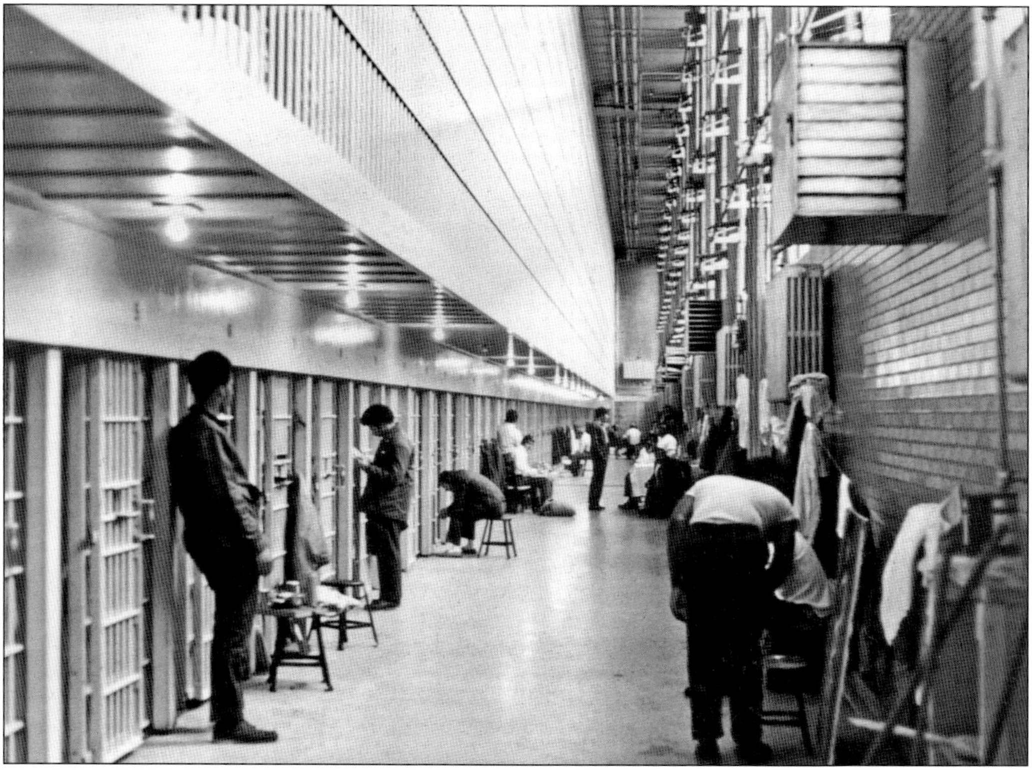

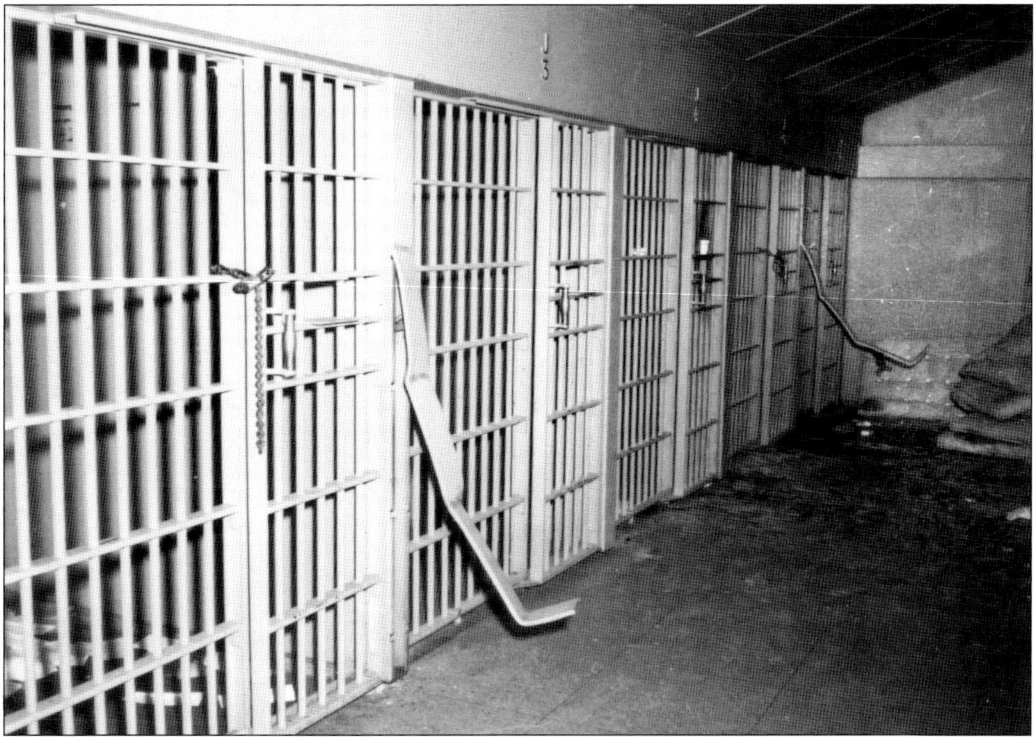

In 1970, responding in part to the civil rights movement taking place throughout the country, black inmates at Auburn Prison demanded a Black Solidarity Day observance. When their request was denied, a number of inmates refused to go to work or school on November 4. They took over the main yard and gained control of three cell blocks, the kitchen, and mess hall areas. There were 43 employees taken hostage. Inmates gave up when deputy commissioner Harold Butler told them that state troopers were ready to retake the facility using force. (Courtesy of Michael Pettigrass.)

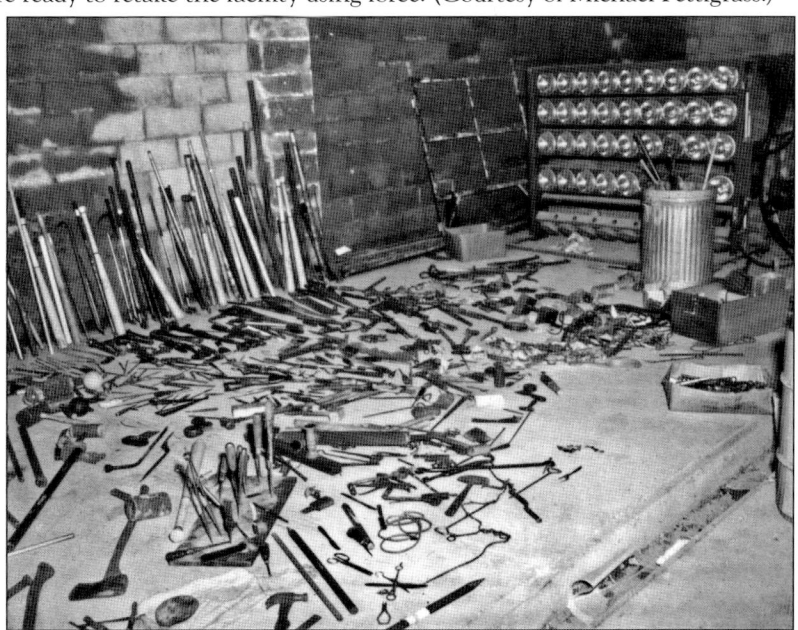

This is a display of the makeshift weapons found in the thorough search of the prison following the riot in Auburn Prison on November 4, 1970.

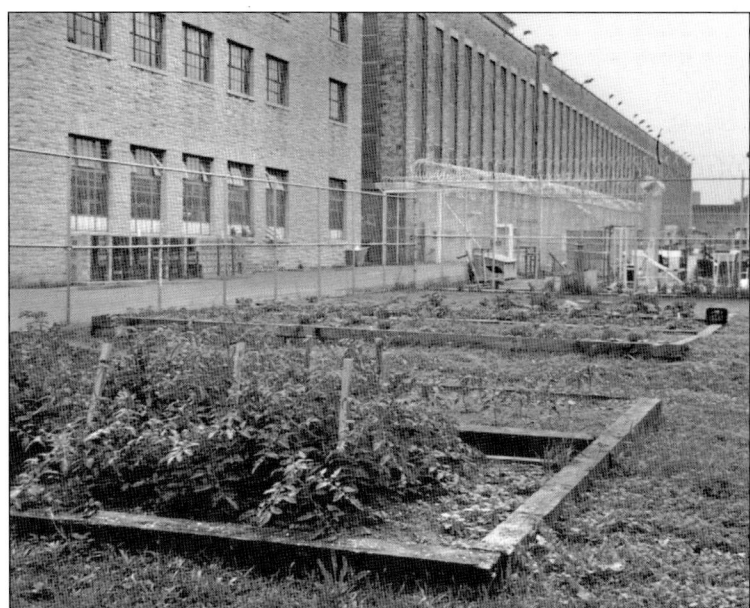

This prison garden, tended by inmates in the 1970s, provided the same benefits to them that earlier inmates received from working in the gardens of the asylum for the criminally insane or at the prison farm. This garden still exists in the same location and is maintained by inmates of Auburn's Intermediate Care Program. Tomatoes, cucumbers, and peppers are the favorite products.

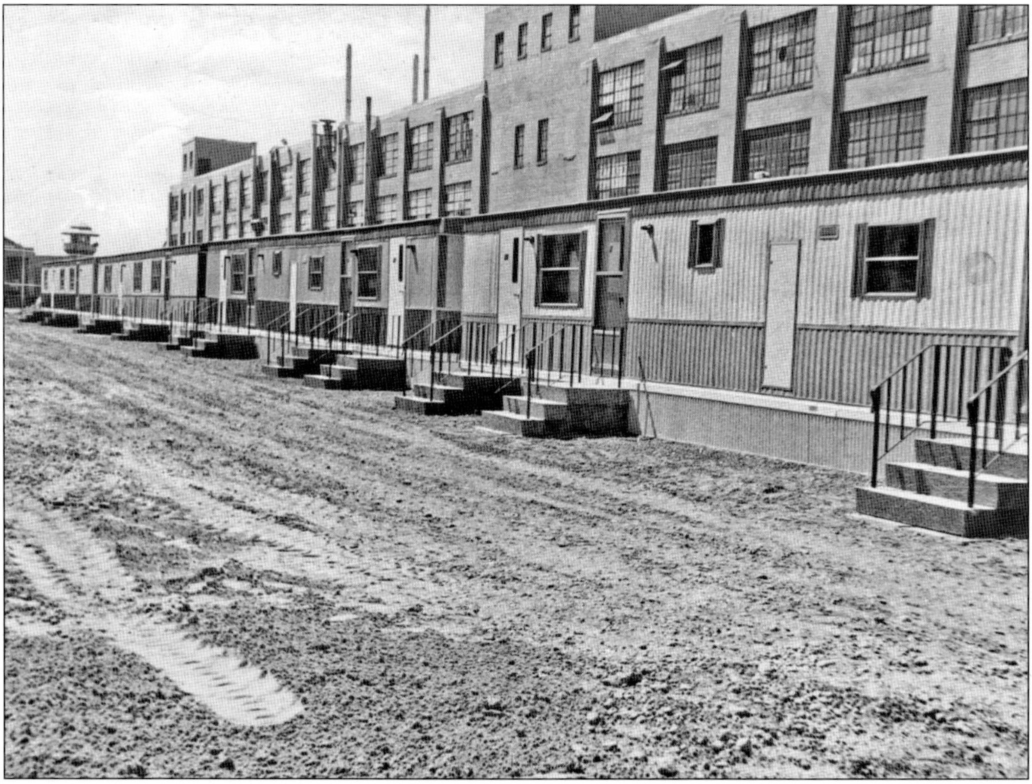

The Family Reunion Program is one prison reform program that remains controversial. Inmates can earn the right to visit privately with their loved ones in what are commonly referred to as "the trailers." When the visits first started at Auburn Correctional Facility in November 1980, they could be for as long as 72 hours. Today the program is still going strong, and the visits are 44 hours long.

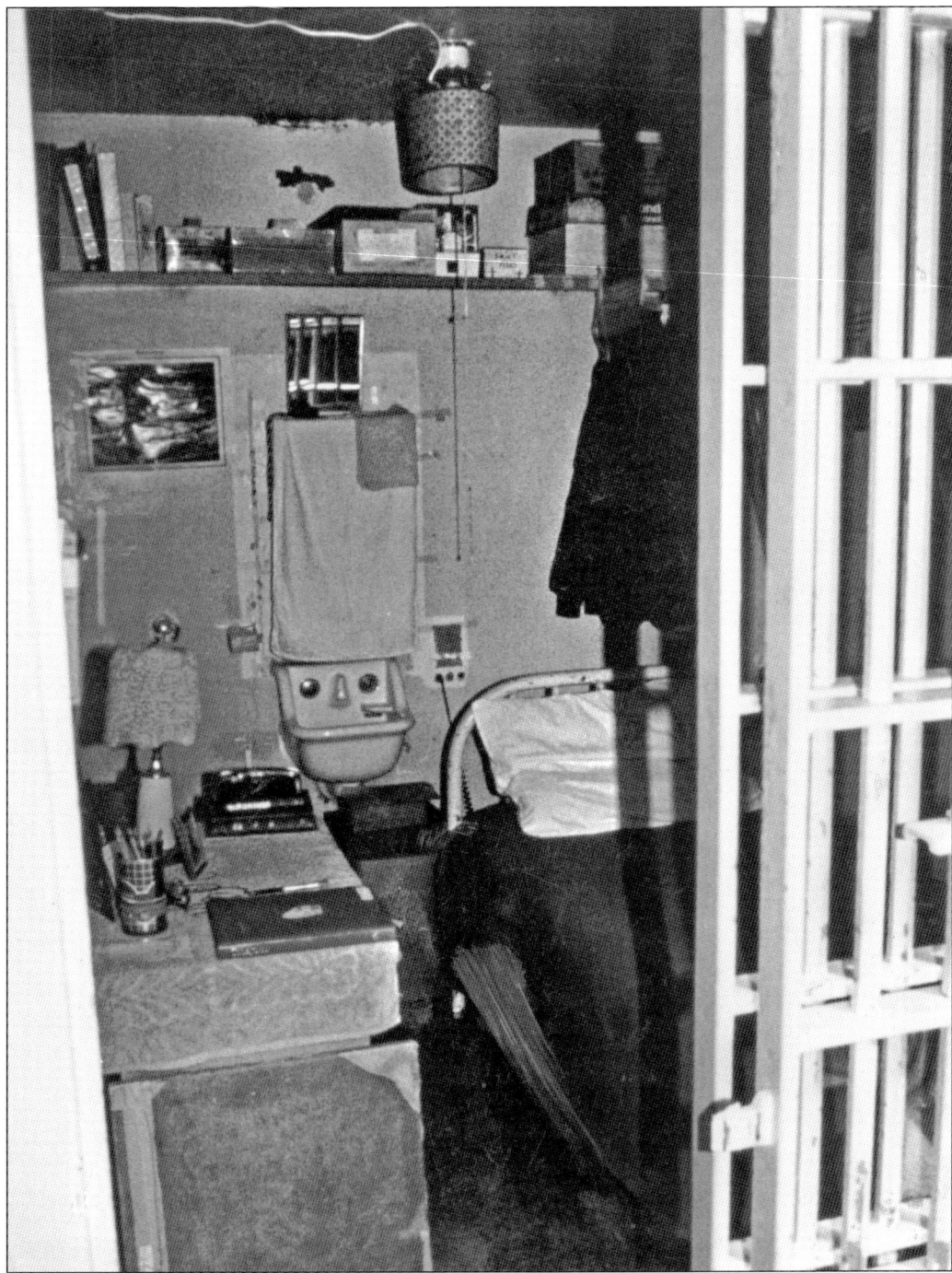

This is a cell in the Auburn Correctional Facility in the 1970s. Each man has a bed, a toilet, a sink, a light, and a locker. There is still no hot water in the cells.

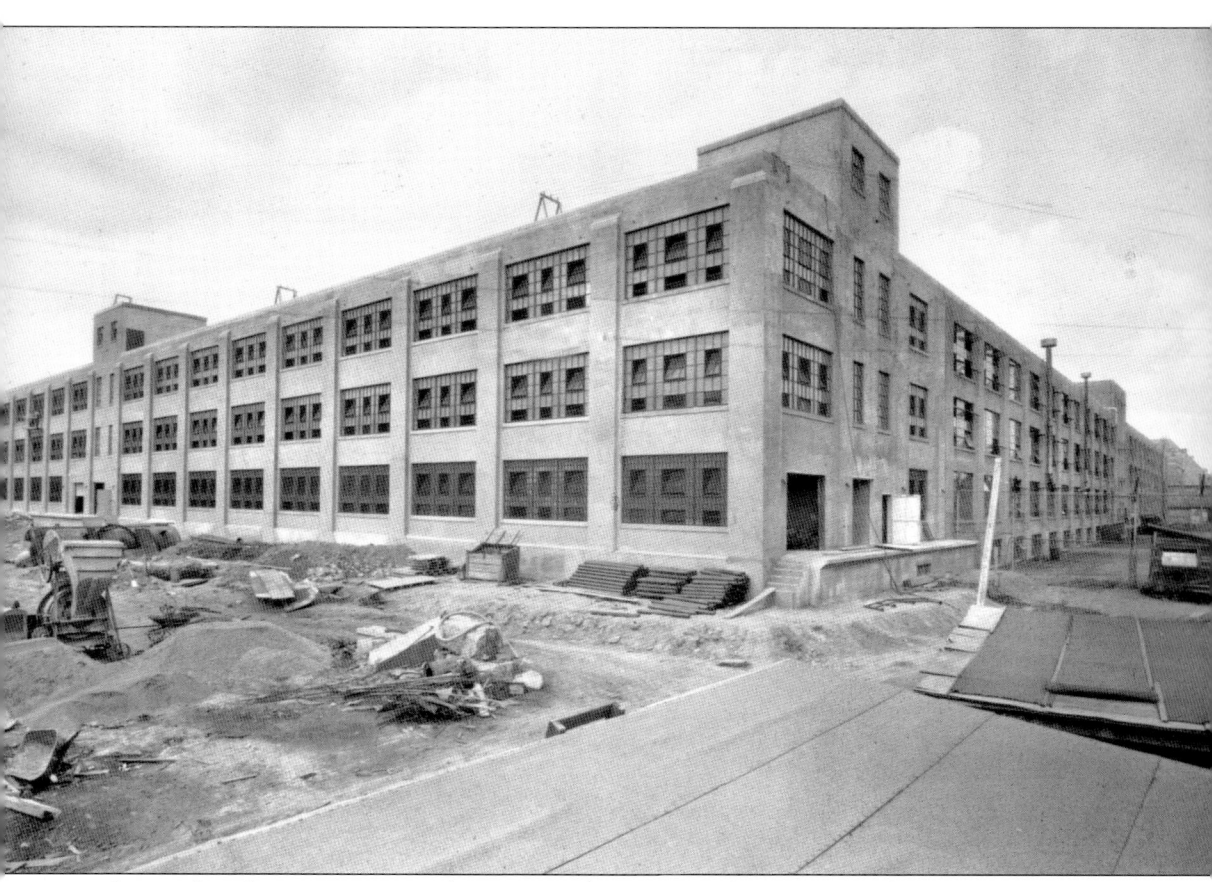

Corecraft is the name given to the prison industries at Auburn Prison. The Corecraft complex, at the time a state-of-the-art industrial facility, was built on the grounds of Auburn Prison in the 1930s.

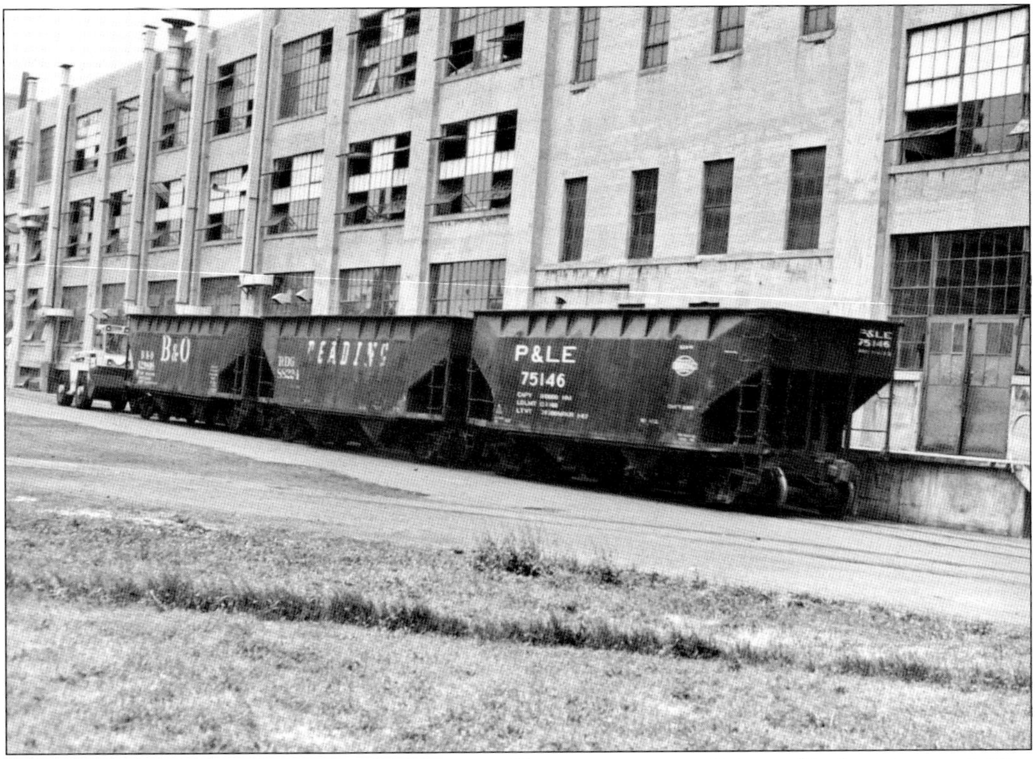

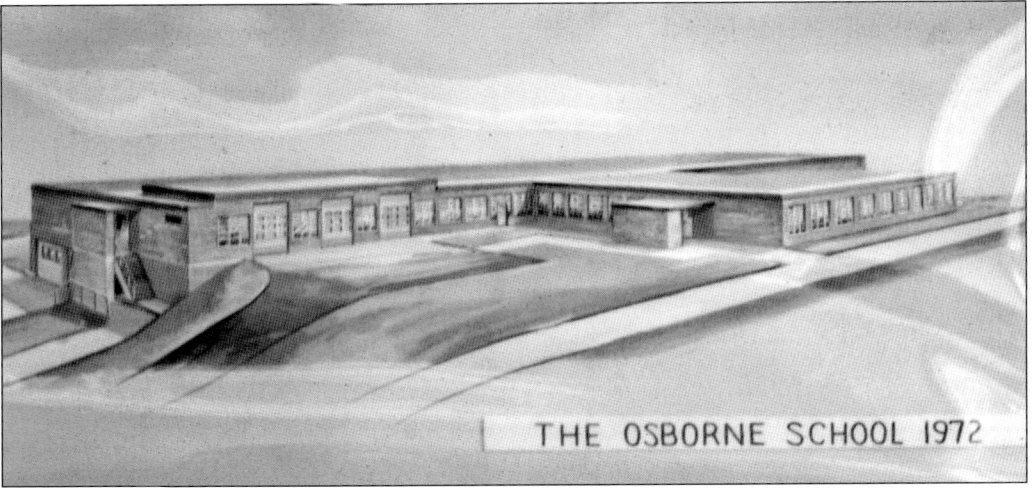

Up until around 1970, the prison's buildings and hot water were still heated by burning coal. The coal was brought in by rail cars, and the coal gang shoveled it. Today a work crew called the coal gang still exists; they maintain what used to be the coal yard and are responsible for recycling in the prison. The trestle, covered with a cage, still crosses the river to the prison, but the gate into the prison has been permanently closed.

Although it was already in the works, the educational program at Auburn Prison received a new emphasis from the reforms put into place following the disaster at Attica. When the women's prison building was razed, a school building was constructed in the rear of the prison complex in 1961. It was called the Osborne School in honor of Thomas Mott Osborne. In the 1970s, education programs expanded greatly.

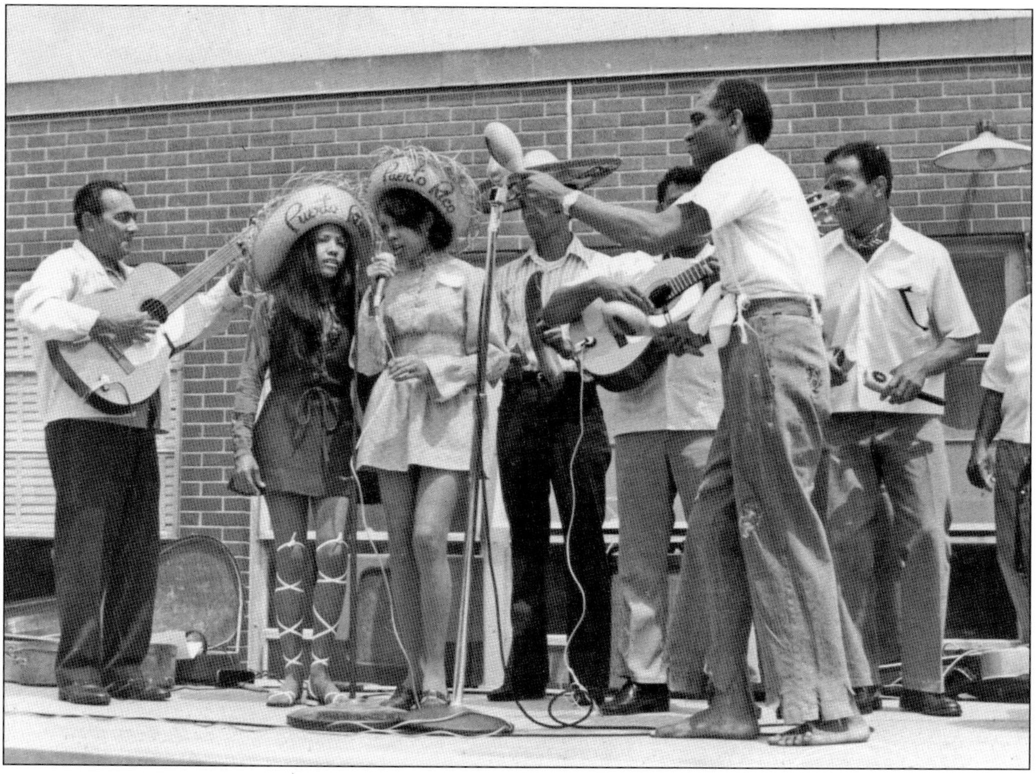

This photograph is from the first Puerto Rican Day celebration in the prison yard in 1973. A band was brought in to entertain, and there was special food and dancing.

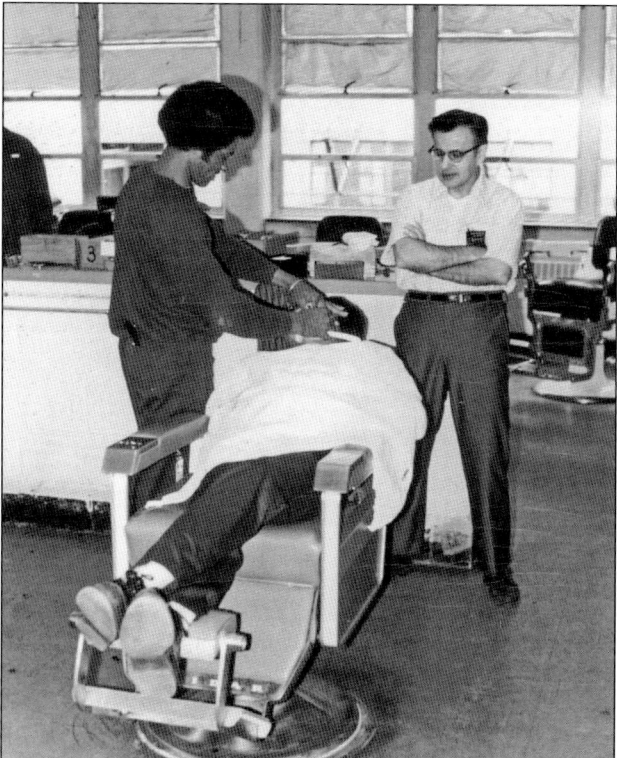

John Albanese was the instructor in the prison barbershop in 1978. The barbershops had a dual purpose, teaching men a trade while also serving the state's need. With a constant supply of men needing haircuts, there will always be a barbershop in the prison.

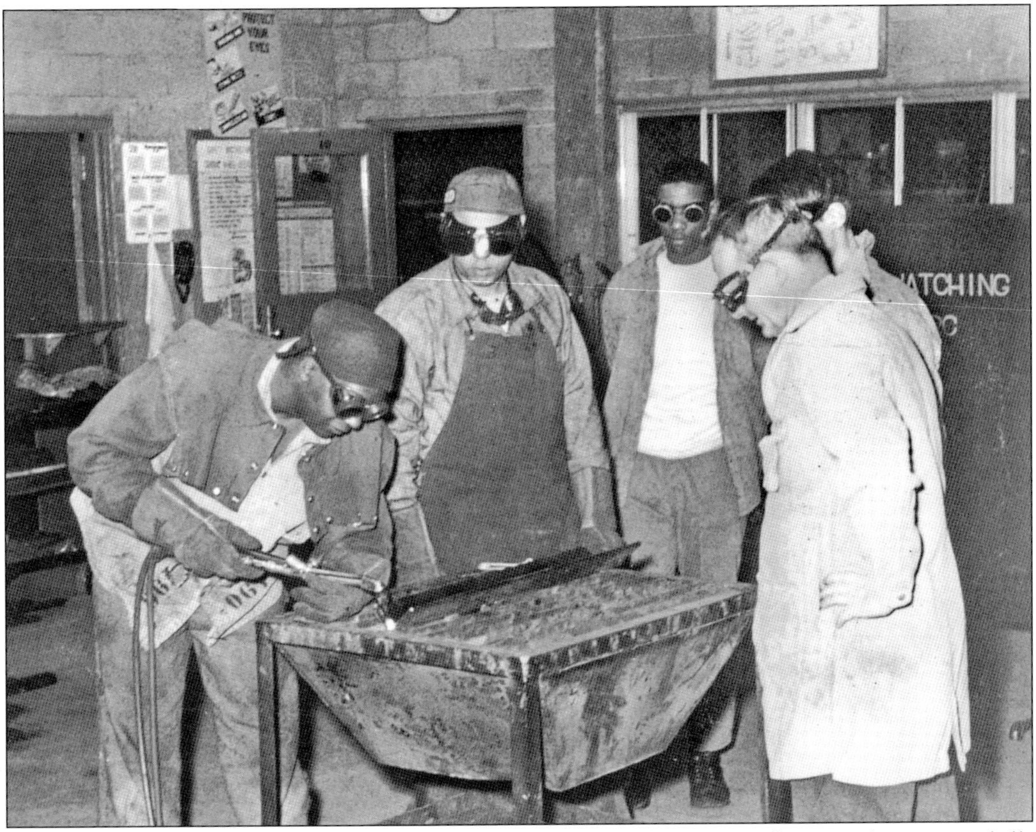

With the emphasis on rehabilitation in the late 1970s, an effort was made to teach inmates skills that could help support them after their release. Here is a lesson in the welding shop.

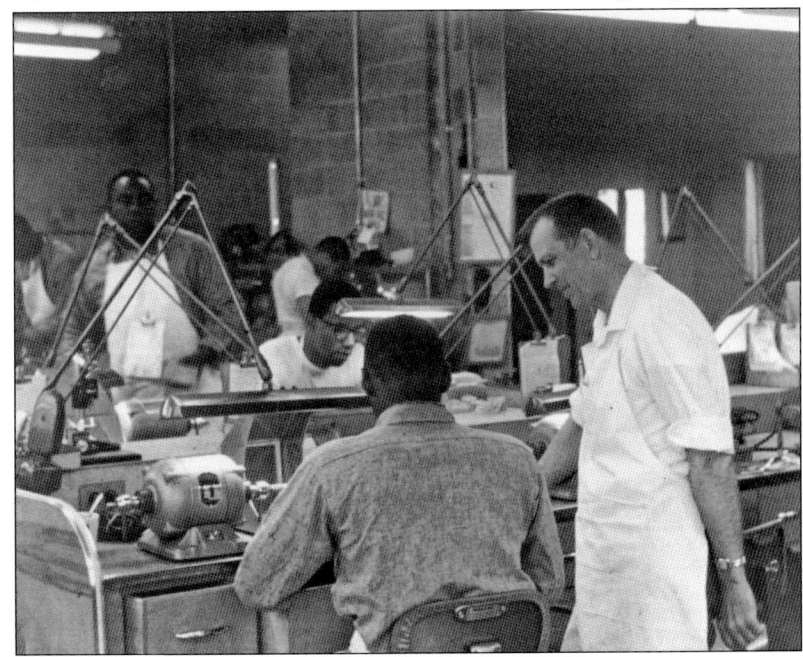

The dental lab served both vocational training and the state use system. Inmates learned the trade while producing false teeth for inmates in all the state institutions. This photograph was taken around 1978. Note the teeth molds on the back table.

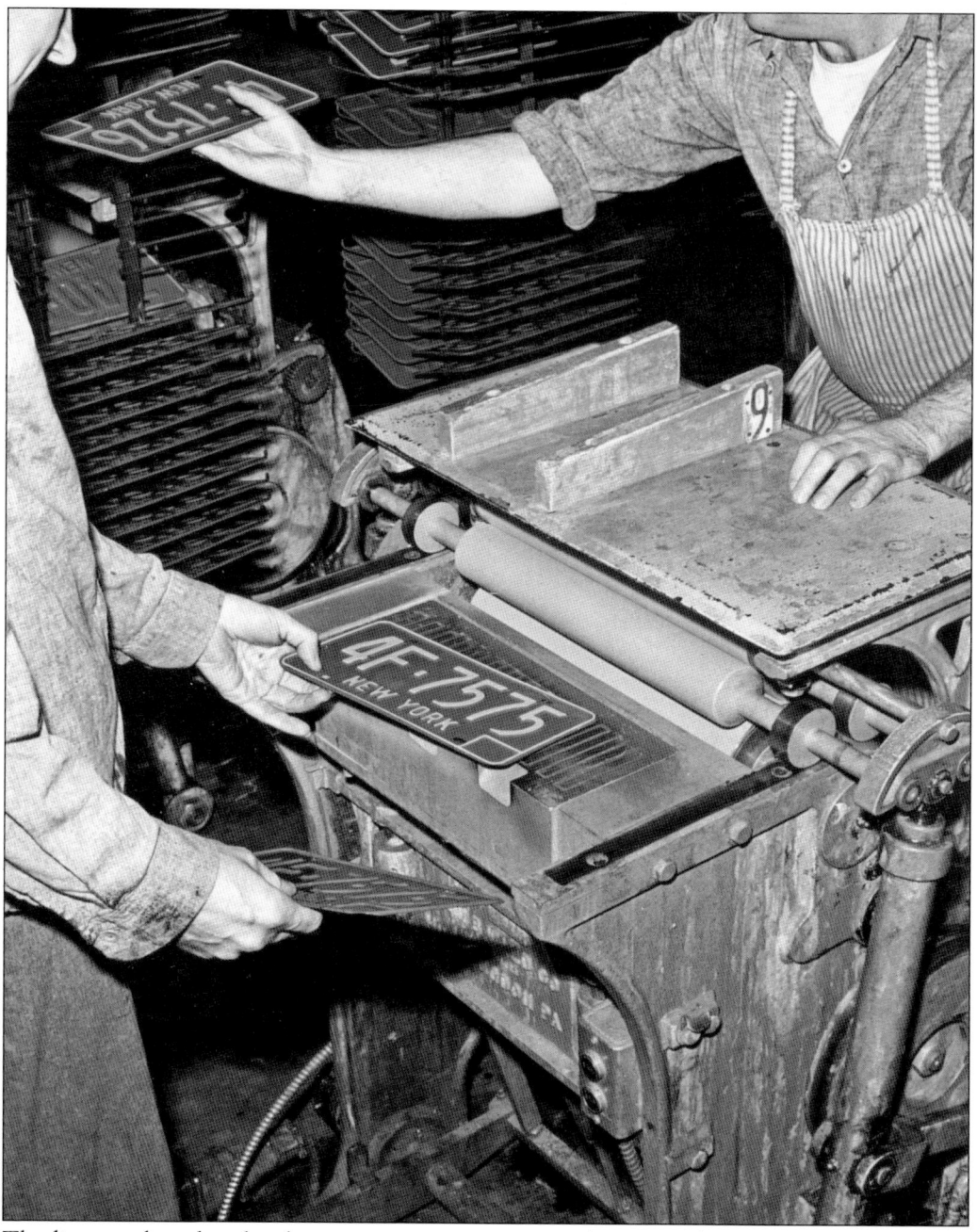

The license plate shop has become an important part of prison industry. This photograph is from the 1960s.

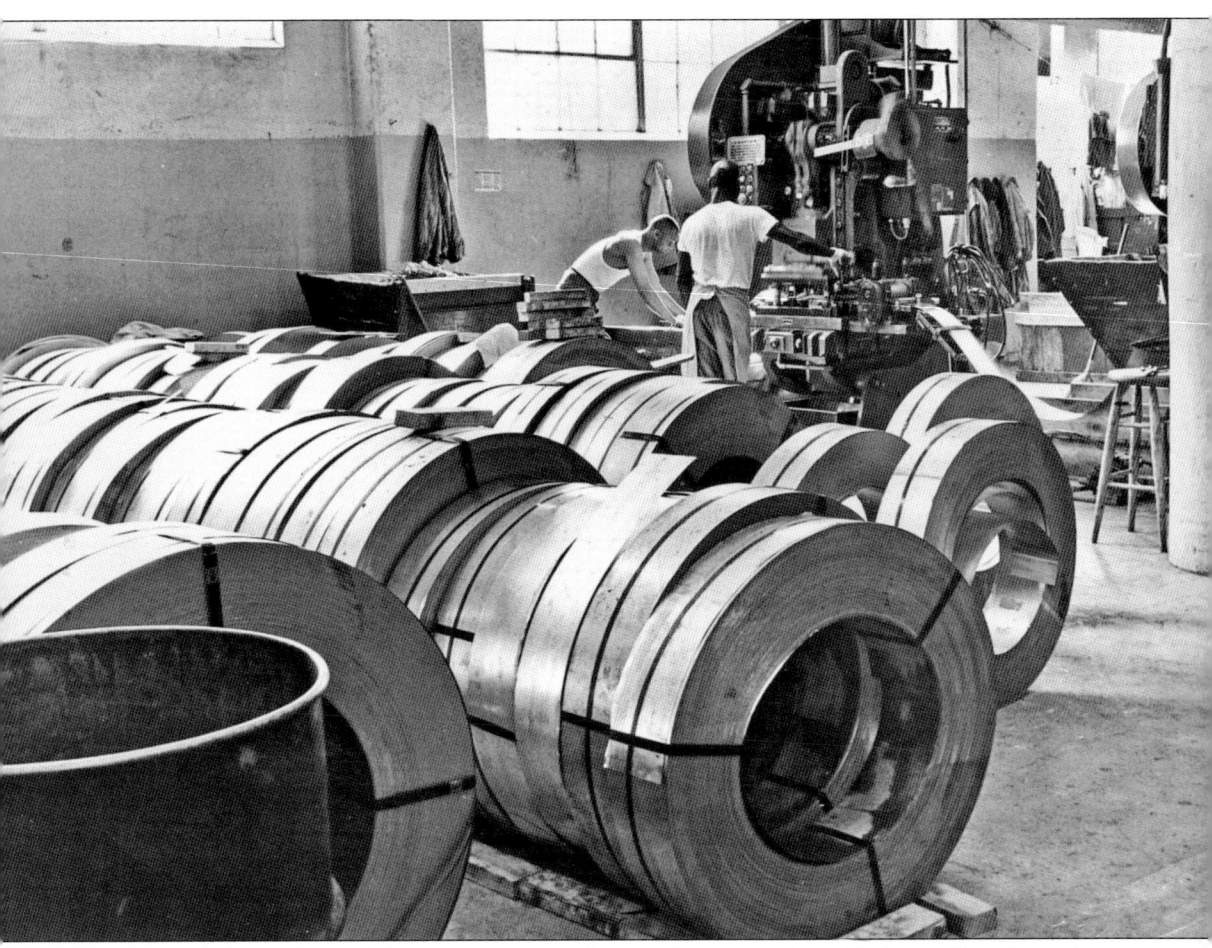
The materials have changed, but every license plate in the state of New York is still made at the Auburn Correctional Facility.

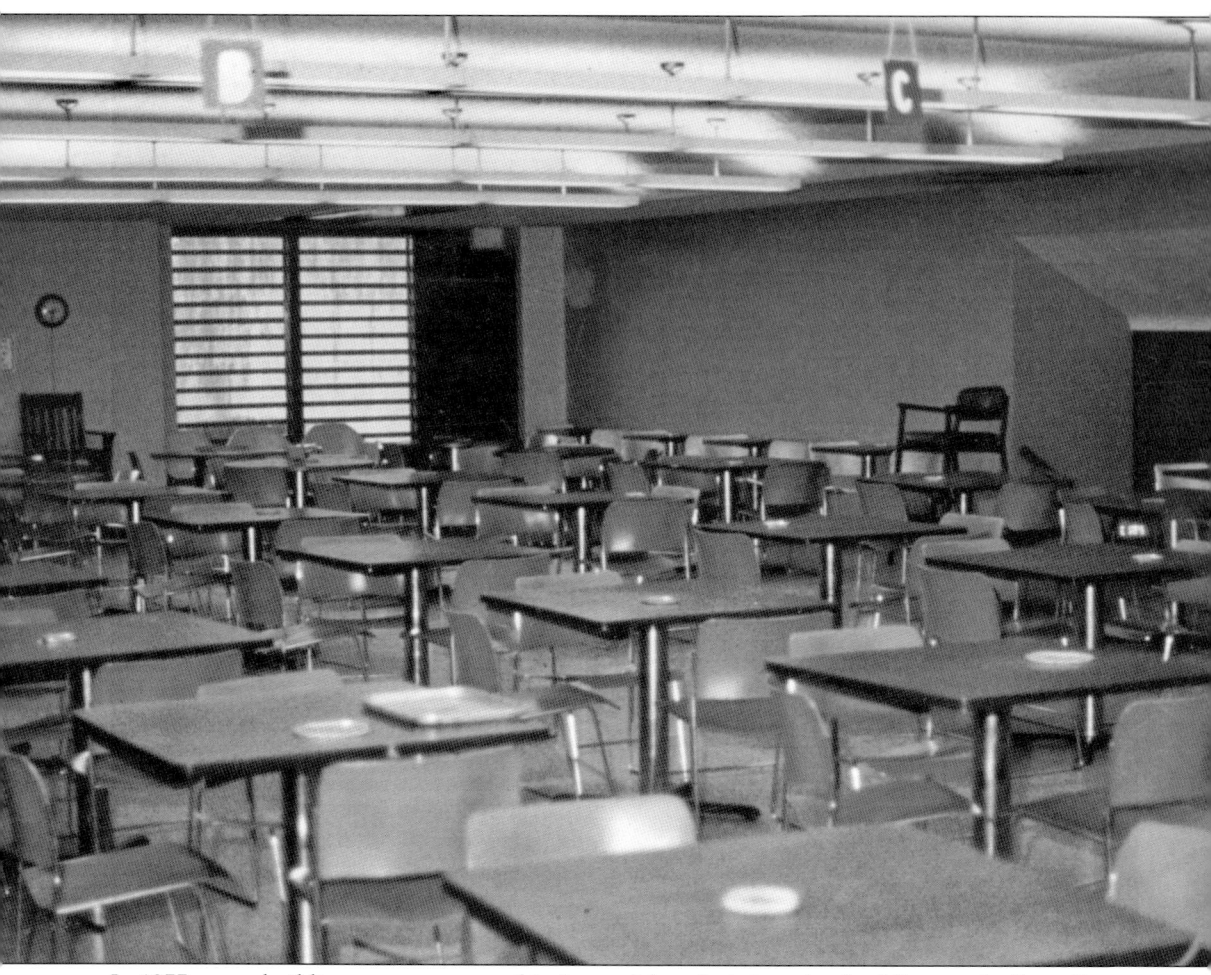

In 1977, a new building was constructed in front of the administration building, at the State Street entrance to the prison. Although the entire building is commonly referred to as the visiting room, this photograph shows the actual room in which prisoners can spend time with their visitors.

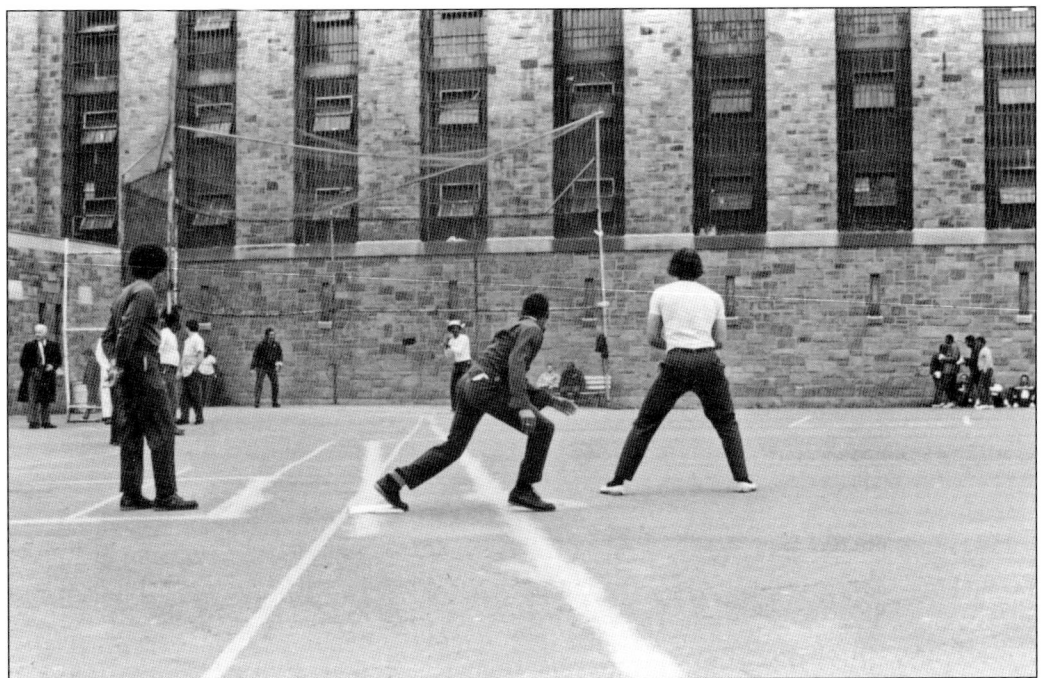

The baseball diamond was blacktop when this game was played in the prison yard in the 1970s. Lt. Charles Connors is wearing the blazer and trench coat that were the corrections officers' new uniforms in the late 1970s, another change that was made after Attica.

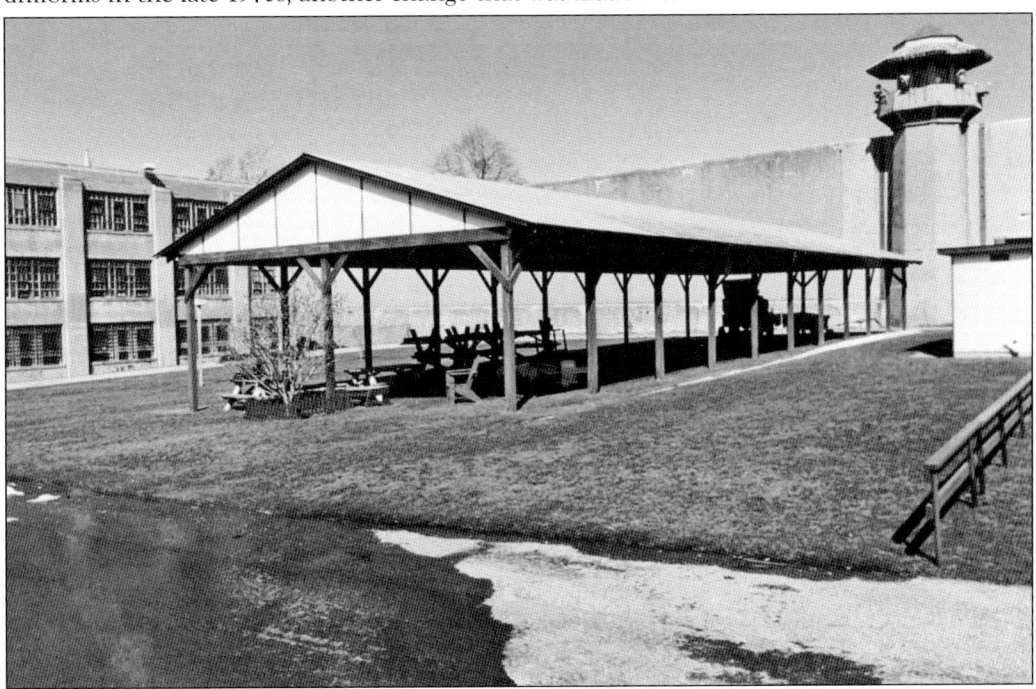

This covered picnic pavilion was in the prison yard in 1973. A rebuilt version of this pavilion, now with a concrete floor, is still used for special inmate events. The tree is gone; there are now no trees in the main yard.

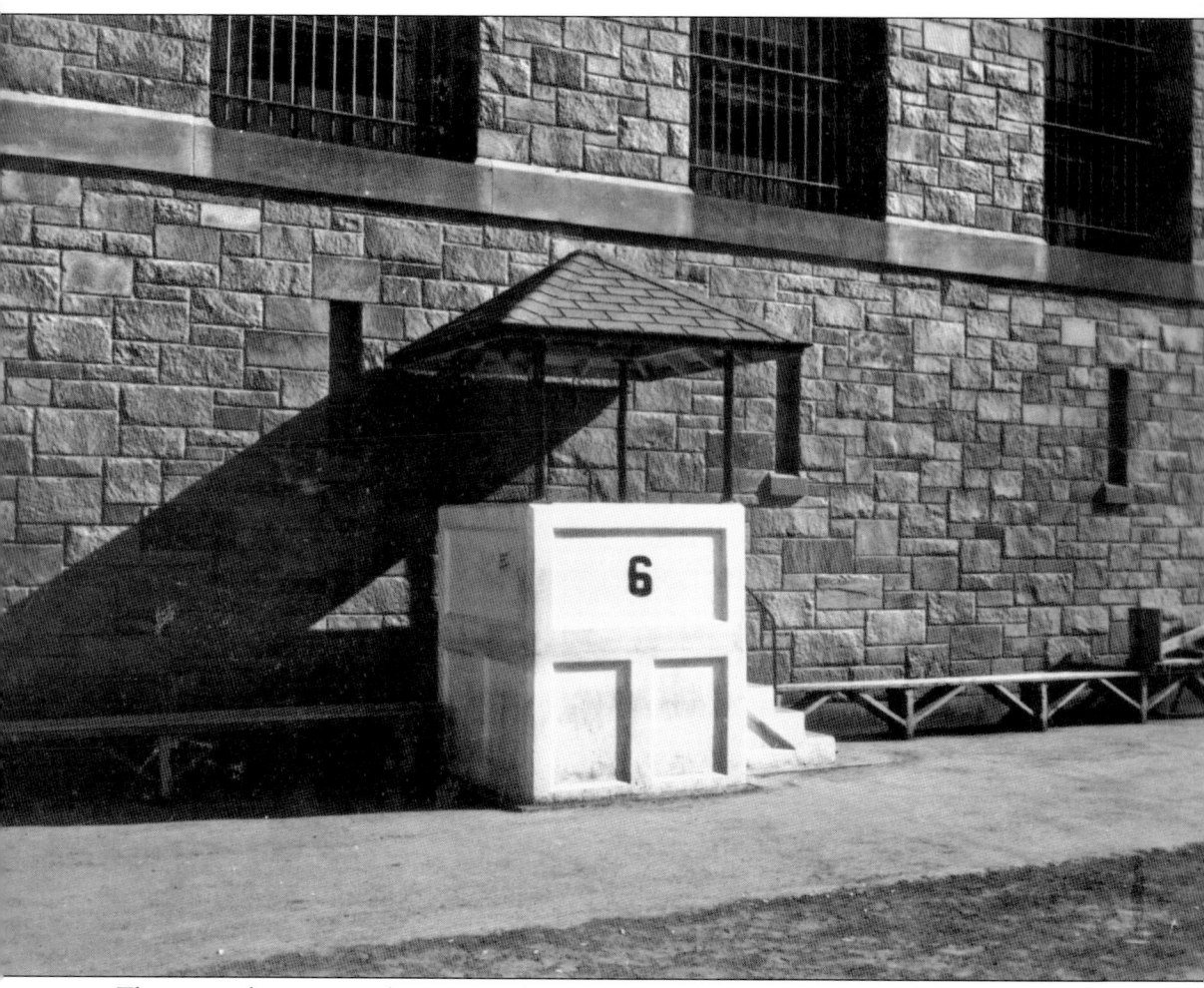

This is guard post six in the main yard, around 1980. A raised vantage point gives the officers a better view of what is happening in the yard. Made of precast concrete, the guard posts can be moved. (Courtesy of Michael Pettigrass.)

Ten
Auburn Correctional Facility Today

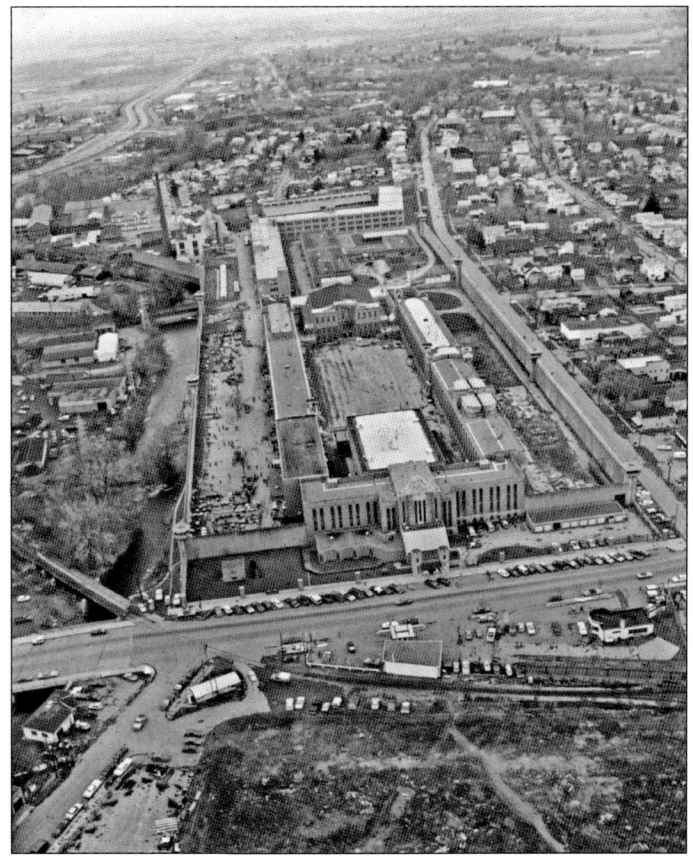

Today Auburn Correctional Facility continues to be a walled, maximum security prison for male convicts. With more than 800 full-time employees, the prison remains the largest employer in Cayuga County. Several men and women who work at the prison today represent the third, or even fourth, generation in their families to do so. It is the city's longest lasting business. (Courtesy of Michael Pettigrass.)

The prison walls today are 35 to 40 feet high (depending on topography) with towers on each corner and at intervals along the walls.

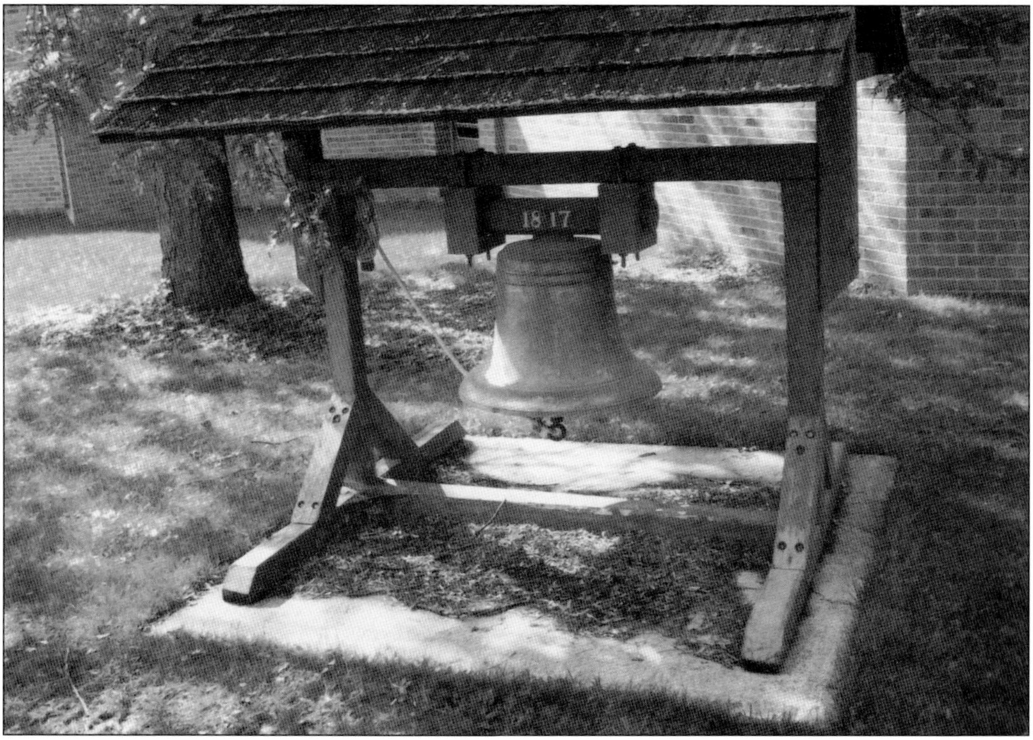

The giant bell, which used to hang just under Copper John on the pinnacle of the old administration building, now rests in a place of honor in the front yard of the Auburn Correctional Facility. (Courtesy of Michael Pettigrass.)

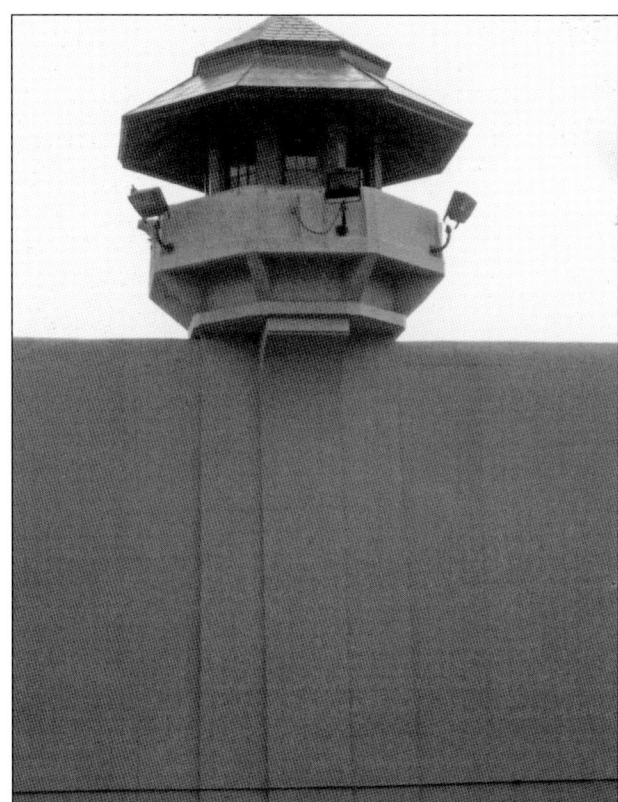

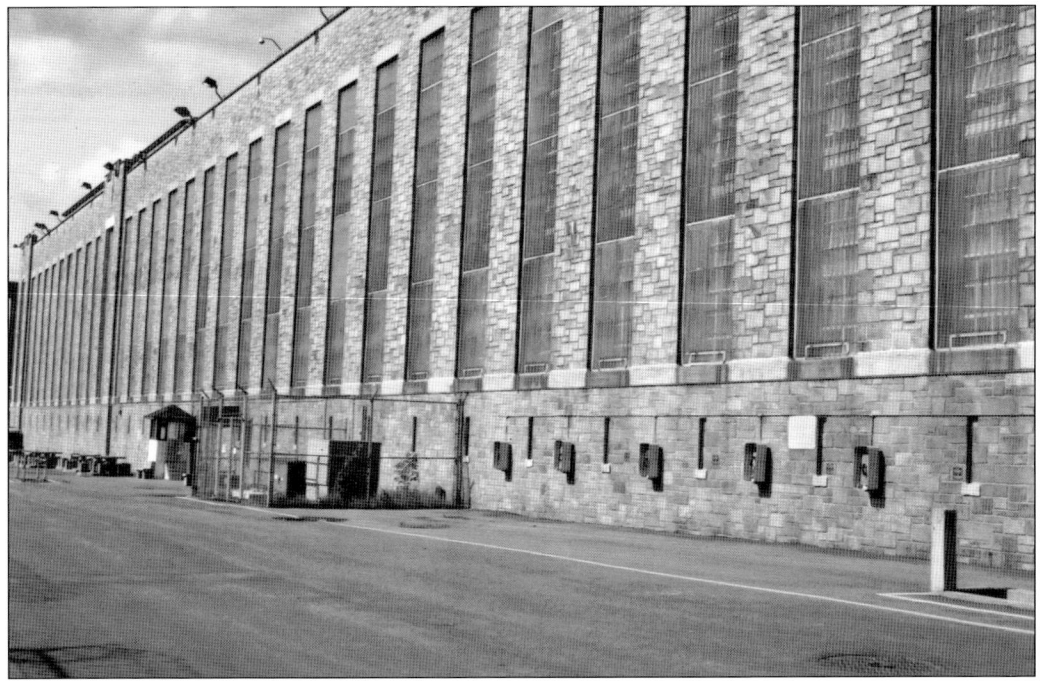

This photograph of the yard shows a row of telephones that the inmates have access to, as well as the raised station that a corrections officer can stand upon for a better view. (Courtesy of Michael Pettigrass.)

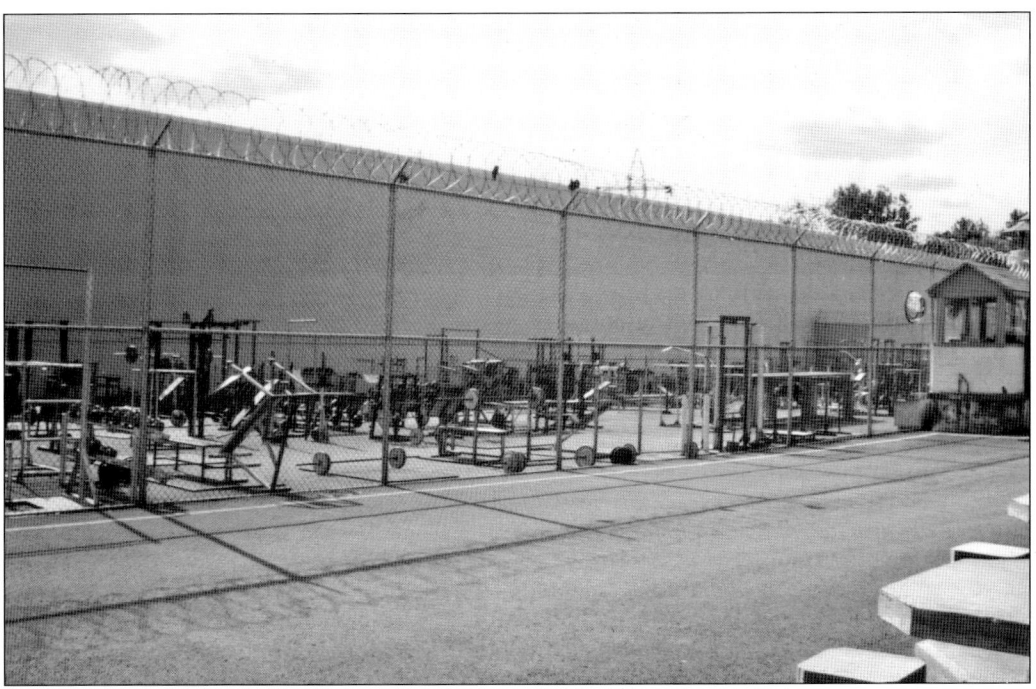

Weight training is one of the more popular recreational activities among inmates. Inmates are outside lifting weights 365 days a year, regardless of the weather. (Courtesy of Michael Pettigrass.)

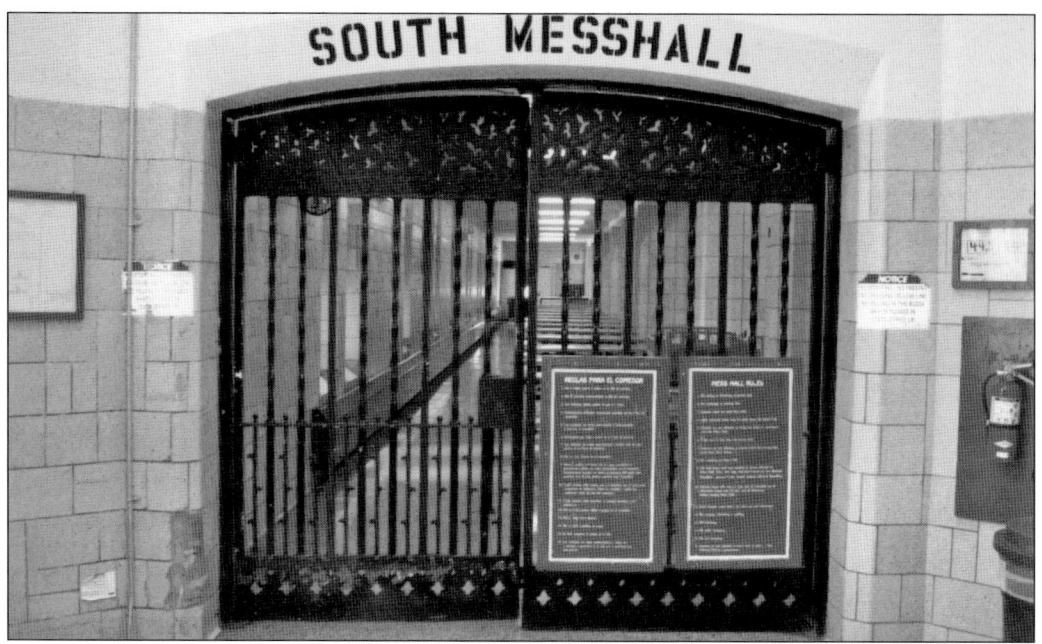

This gate to the south mess hall shows the decorative ironwork that still exists inside the prison, as well as the tiled walls that mark the hallways. (Courtesy of Michael Pettigrass.)

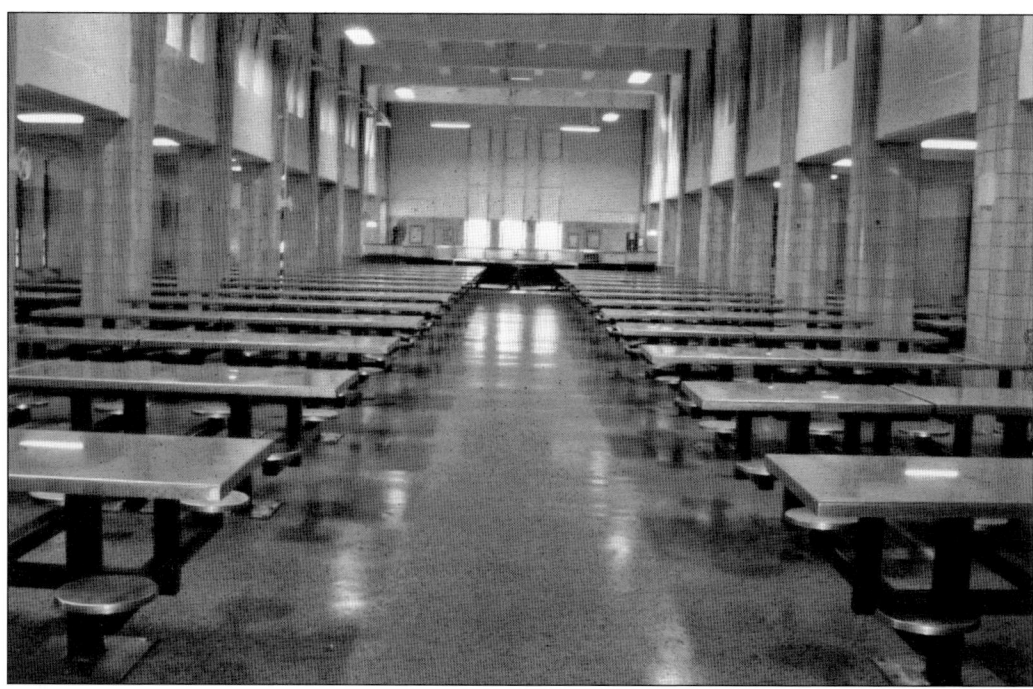

Today prisoners dine at stainless steel tables with attached stools, at which they can sit face-to-face. Almost all of the furniture in the rooms where the inmates congregate is fixed in place to prevent its use as weapons in case of a riot. (Courtesy of Michael Pettigrass.)

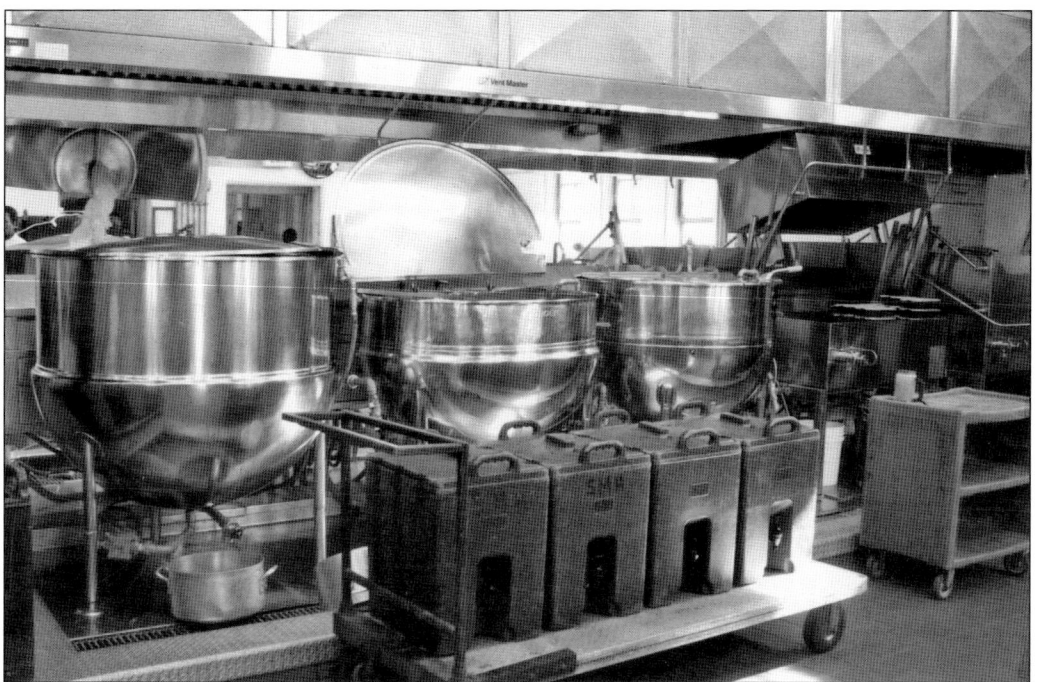

The giant cooking pots in today's prison kitchen do not look much different from those used in the 19th century. (Courtesy of Michael Pettigrass.)

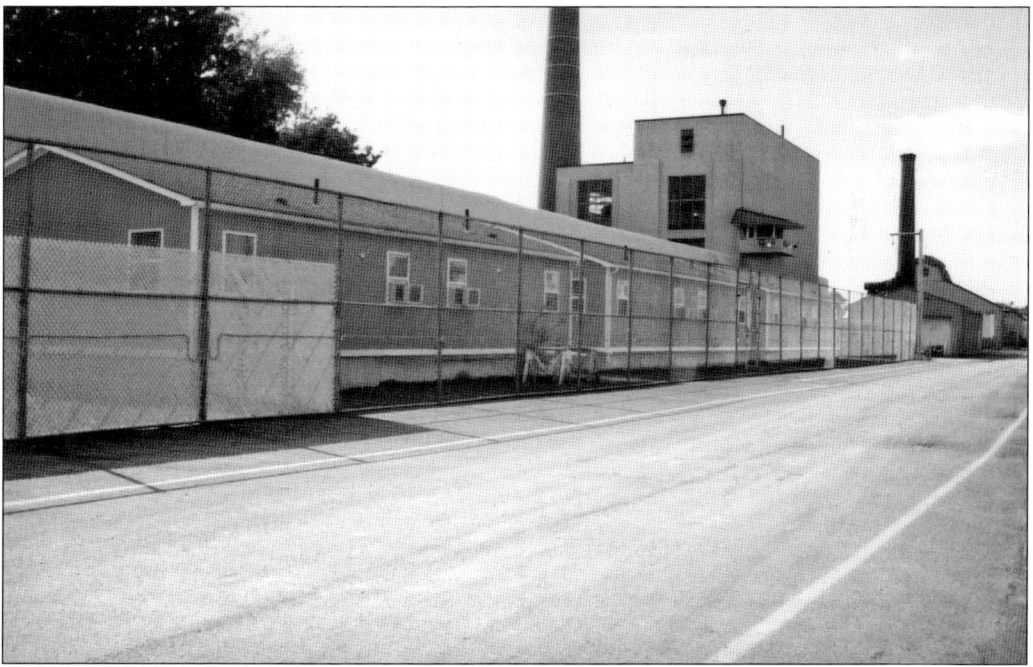

Called simply "the trailers," these modular units are used for the conjugal visits organized under the Family Reunion Program. Inmates and their approved family members enjoy two days together, living, sleeping, eating, and visiting within the modular apartments. The ones at Auburn were built in the Greene Correctional Facility.

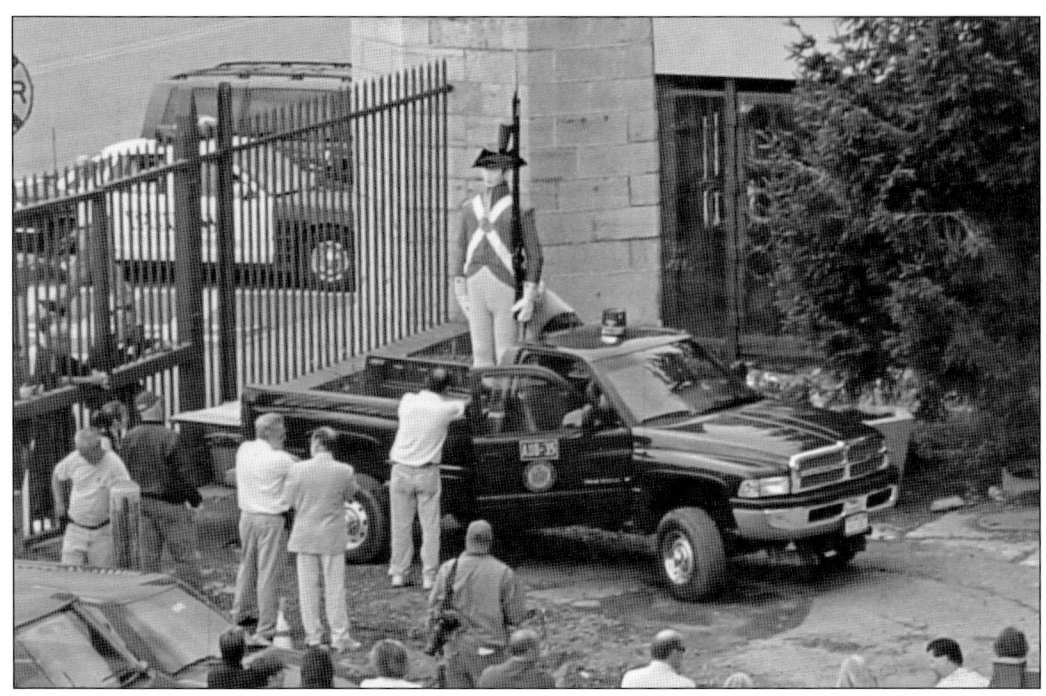

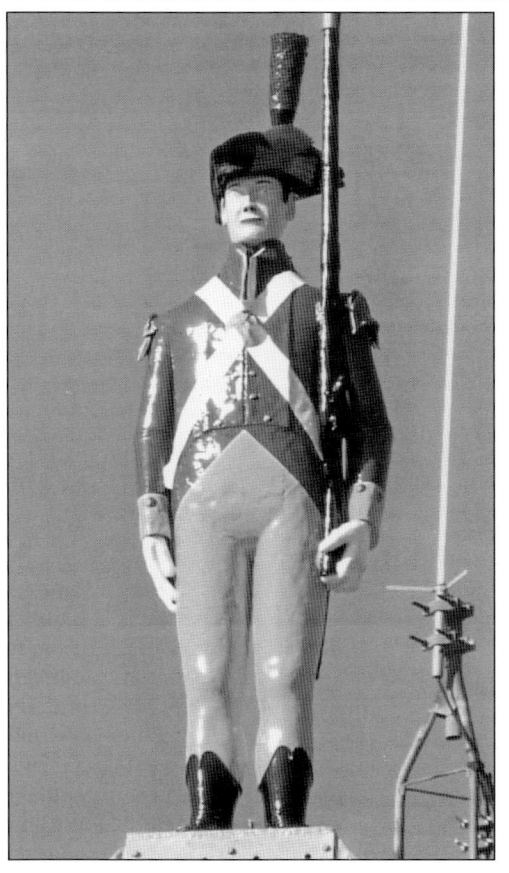

Copper John was taken down for maintenance in July 2004. For more than 100 years, rumor had it that Copper John was very well endowed. He was so high above street level that only corrections officers knew for sure. The Albany Department of Corrections decided to smooth him out when he was being refurbished. Corrections officers protested the change to this historic artifact. Prohibited by law from speaking while on the picket line, the corrections officers wore T-shirts that stated "Save Copper John's Johnson." Their protest was to no avail, and Copper John returned to his post in October 2004 as smooth as a Ken doll. (Both, courtesy of Michael Pettigrass.)

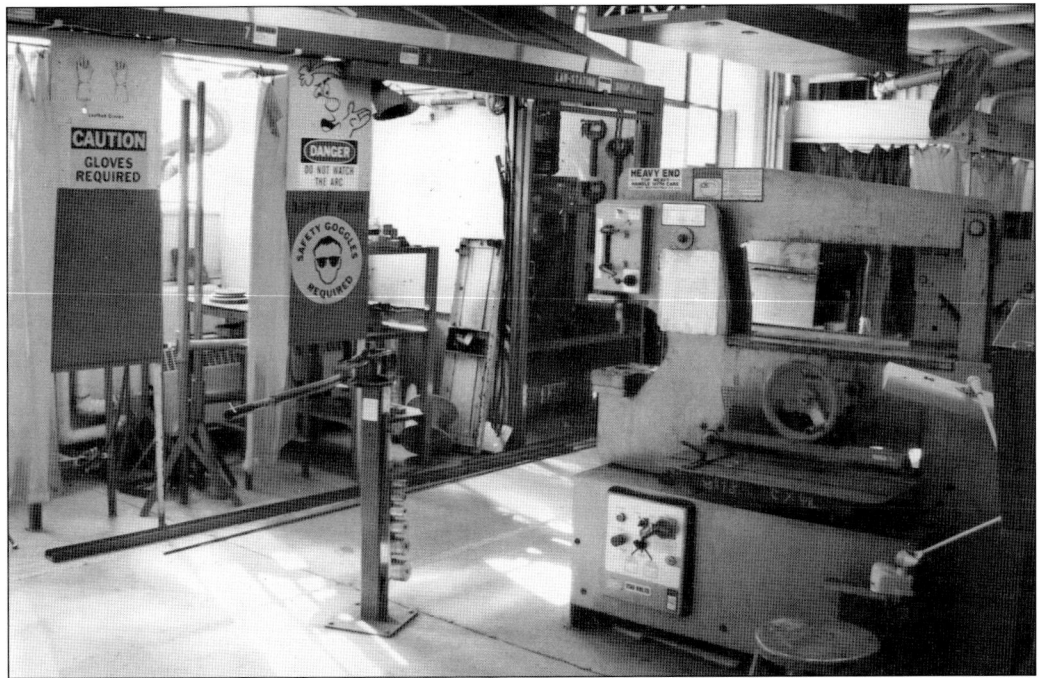

This is the vocational welding shop as it appears today. Welding is a marketable skill that can help a released inmate earn a living. (Courtesy of Michael Pettigrass.)

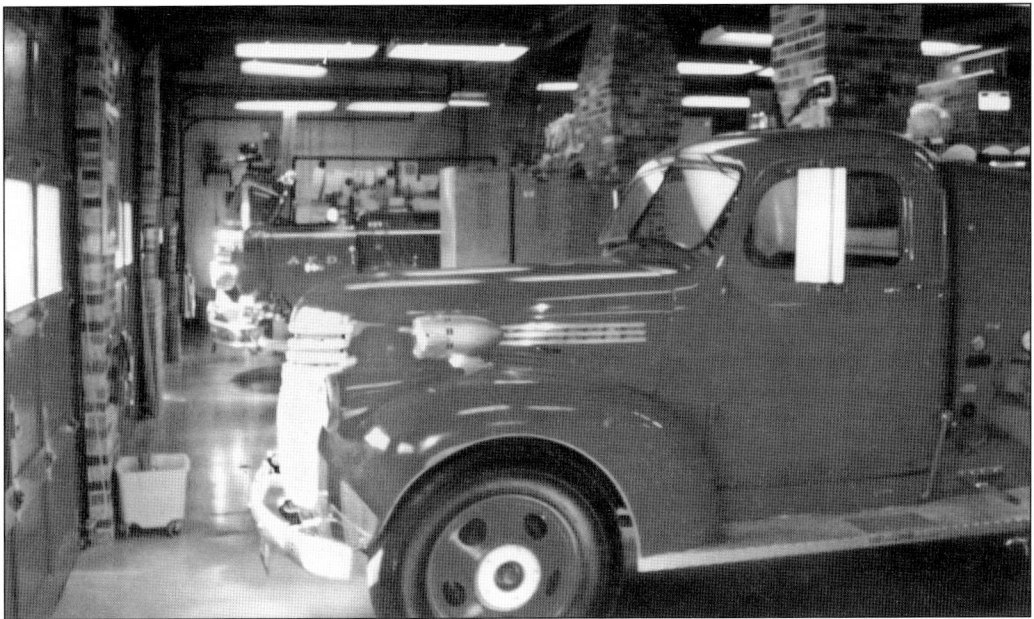

Auburn Correctional Facility has its own fire station, complete with truck and fire engine. Corrections officers have been trained to respond to fire incidents. There are also specially trained inmate firemen. Of course, if the fire warranted it, the Auburn Fire Department would also respond. The engine in the foreground is a war surplus Chevy fire engine; the one in the background is an American La France purchased from the City of Auburn for $1. (Courtesy of Michael Pettigrass.)

www.arcadiapublishing.com

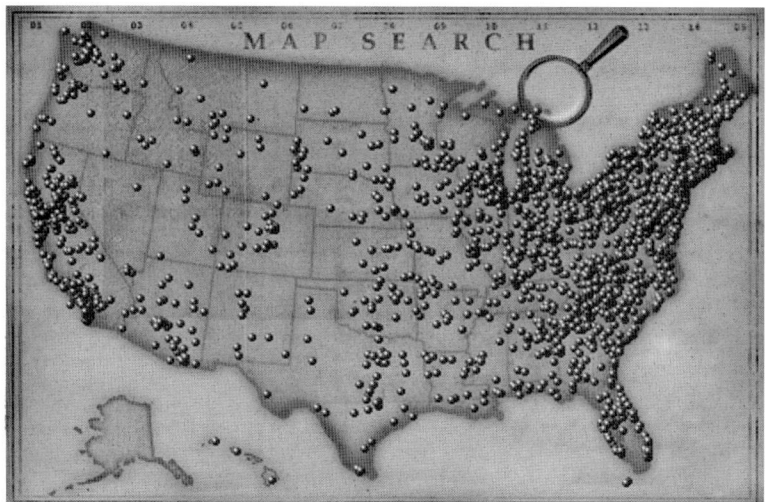

Discover books about the town where you grew up, the cities where your friends and families live, the town where your parents met, or even that retirement spot you've been dreaming about. Our Web site provides history lovers with exclusive deals, advanced notification about new titles, e-mail alerts of author events, and much more.

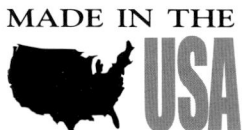

Arcadia Publishing, the leading local history publisher in the United States, is committed to making history accessible and meaningful through publishing books that celebrate and preserve the heritage of America's people and places. Consistent with our mission to preserve history on a local level, this book was printed in South Carolina on American-made paper and manufactured entirely in the United States.

This book carries the accredited Forest Stewardship Council (FSC) label and is printed on 100 percent FSC-certified paper. Products carrying the FSC label are independently certified to assure consumers that they come from forests that are managed to meet the social, economic, and ecological needs of present and future generations.

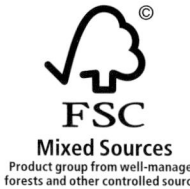

Mixed Sources
Product group from well-managed forests and other controlled sources
Cert no. SW-COC-001530
www.fsc.org
© 1996 Forest Stewardship Council

Find Your Place in History.